D1739864

Taking Back My Power

Miss Lena O 'Leary

ISBN: 1500860700
ISBN 13: 9781500860707
Library of Congress Control Number: 2014915141
CreateSpace Independent Publishing Platform
North Charleston, South Carolina

For Maisy the light of my life and my saviour

Acknowledgments

I would like to thank: all of my family for being completely support-ive as I took time to write this book. My co-orphans, especially Crumbs, Paddy, Sharon and the Newland family. The O'Leary family for their contributions and for accepting me and my brother, Michael, with open arms. Last but not least, I would like to thank Mel Dawson for her help and advice.

There is no greater agony than bearing an untold story inside of you - Maya Angelou.
Becky is my alter ego. She gave me power, to put this book together without deliberation.

Foreword

This is a true story about my life and my struggle for survival. Some scenes are graphic and I make no excuses for that. No doubt there will be arguments that I should have pulled my punches more, that I simply provide other 'wannabes' with vicarious thrills. To those people, I say, 'Get real! These monsters are probably the most organized of groups, photographing and videoing their acts and using the Internet and other sources for getting their filth to each other.'

I pulled no punches because when we sanitize these things, it becomes 'entertainment' for the readers ... the level of their shock is minimized and having put the book down, life goes on for them perhaps with a murmured, 'poor child'. If people are aware of exactly what some children are going through, even as I write these words, right now, they might be more vigilant.

We see today how fragmented our civilization has become. Why are people less caring about each other? Well, who knows what childhood horrors they survived? *The effects of abuse do not stop when the abuse itself has.* And we will never know unless we learn to recognize the pattern of behaviours abusers use ... how young children are groomed by strangers. We will never understand the pain of these children and adults unless we know what the abusers do. And we will never want to do anything about it unless the disgust for such evil people forces us to do something about it.

Despite these sentiments, I found myself somewhat constrained by particular needs:- namely those of fellow sufferers who want only to cope with their horrors in private;

of innocent persons who do not want the turmoil of attention when it is known what a relative of theirs might have done, or suffered;

of family members who knew nothing of the events that took place in my life until I, as an adult, found them and told them.

They do not deserve to be judged guilty when those who have guilt have always been protected.

Therefore although the places mentioned in this book are real, as of course, are the names of the few who were indeed accused or brought to justice ... a matter of public record, I have changed most individuals' names, except the first names of my immediate family, to offer them some degree of protection.

*[1]Taking back my power - Words and music © Sharon Murphy. Reproduced with the kind permission of Sharon Murphy.

Taking back my power
To live up to your point of view
No more will I lose my identity
Seeing life through you
So long you have held that belief
That I'm inferior to you
CHORUS
I'm taking back (taking back)
My power from you
I'm taking back (taking back)
My power from you
Someone once taught you
How you should perceive
But now you are older
Still you carry that belief
I'm wise enough to see
What you see is not me
CHORUS
A child will believe
What she is told even if untrue
From you, who should know
Can't face your own truth
And what is covered up
Is only hidden from your view
CHORUS

[1] From the album *Invisible walls*

One

Dreams and Shadows

The early morning was grey and cool, but I enjoyed the summer dew on my bare feet as I wandered across the lawn. I went to my favourite rose bush and with secateurs in hand, was about to cut some of the beautiful buds when I noticed the black, hooded figure of a woman hurriedly slip into the house.

Driven by fear, I ran through the door and looked around anxiously for her. A quick search showed that she was not downstairs. My *baby*! The words shrieked through my brain. I dashed up the stairs into her room, just in time to see the woman's hand rise and fall twice.

Screaming, I threw myself at that vile creature. I did not stop stabbing until she had fallen and stopped moving. Covered in blood, I dropped the secateurs and rose to check my baby in her cot. She was staring at me and it seemed to me that she had such horror in her eyes that I screamed and screamed!

"Lena! Lena! Wake up! It's just a dream." Scott's voice was urgent.

The bedside light was on, the sheets were tangled round me. Scott was leaning over me looking resigned. I leapt out of bed and hurried to Maisy's room. She was fast asleep. I squatted beside her cot aching to pick her up and hug her, but I'd recovered enough from my nightmare to realize that this was the middle of the night, and that she needed her sleep without being disturbed by my problems.

When I felt Scott squat beside me and put his arms round me, I realized I was trembling. He persuaded me to go back to our room and I huddled beside him, knowing I would not sleep again this night. He didn't ask any questions. He knew well enough why I had these dreams, and we had reached the point in our relationship where he also knew it was enough to just be there for me ... to be my rock. With his arms holding me close to him, my rock fell asleep, and I was sufficiently calm to think.

This was the first time my nightmares involved my child, and although in reality, I have often wished one or other Sister of Mercy dead, it was the first time I had attacked one, even asleep.

I considered the shape of the nun in my dream. She was in one of the habits I remembered. She wore a black veil and dress ... her forehead and neck were covered by a white coif and headband. A stiff, white guimpe hid her chest. At her side, large rosary beads clicked as she moved towards me.

In her hand was a thick strap. She raised her hand and as she did so, she seemed to grow bigger and bigger until she was enormous. Her face was stern, her lips a thin line and I was again the underfed, underweight four-year-old in her care. She was the Reverend Mother, the Reverend *Demon* and as her hand fell, the strap sliced through my arm drawing blood but no screams. I had learned well, even at that young age, that screams could unleash an avalanche of blows. Even so, tears filled my eyes and my mouth began to tremble.

I sniffed, wiping my nose as the tears fell onto my pillow. Scott stirred but did not waken, and I fell once more deeply into time. Time long past but not forgotten ... never forgotten ... It's funny how the ordinary things, small 'sadnesses' and 'happinesses', one forgets. Better to remember those and forget what one remembers - the great highs and the massive lows. There have been few great highs in my life - two of them are right here in the house with me. They give me the strength to do what I must to survive. One lies beside me and the other sleeps peacefully in her cot. Then there have been so many massive lows, unnecessary and unasked for. They too define who I am and I struggle to find and take the positive from them and, why did it happen? Why did it happen?

September, 12th, 1963

"Whereas Lena Christina O'Leary appears to the Court to be a child under fifteen years of age ..."

"She's four months old M'Lud."

"... It is hereby ordered that the said child be sent to the Certified Industrial School at St Joseph's Clifden, being a school conducted in accordance with the doctrines of the Catholic Church ... to be there detained until the 16th day of May, 1979 ..."

The judge crossed out some lines about parents paying the Inspector of Reformatory and Industrial Schools, on the Detention Order he was reading from and signed the document dated September 12th, 1963. Lena Christina O'Leary was in effect sentenced to 16 years confinement in an institution that was part school, part orphanage and was inspected by the Inspector of the Reform Schools system. With a stroke, she and her eighteen-month-old brother, who was also sentenced, had been criminalized - a stigma that was to be the least of their worries. She was five days short of four months old, 25" long, weighed 10 lbs 8 oz, appeared to be able to hear and see and had no distinguishing marks - not even teeth! The charge? Not having a home!

Homelessness was just one of the 'crimes' for which this type of sentence could be handed down according to the Children's Act 1908-1941. The others were 'wandering, destitution, begging, lack of proper guardianship and non- attendance at school'.

Trying to deal with the issue of what to do with 'problem' children and in this case, two homeless babies, was a thorny conundrum, but the Children's Act was designated '1908-1941'. Why was it in 1963 that nothing better was in place? Truthfully in these days, there were not many in Ireland who wished to adopt and throwing 'unattached' children into the sewers was not an option any civilized society would sanction. Finding them protective refuge was therefore at the heart of the problem and orphanages have long struggled, with varying degrees of success, to provide that refuge.

What this judge may not have known was that he'd sentenced them to an institution run by the Mercy nuns; that would be part servitude, part school, part orphanage and all hell. The sewers might have proved to be more friendly. Murderers have been treated more kindly and they deserved to be punished ... and these two babies, just like any other prisoner in the system, were given the numbers, which were to be their identity during their formative years.

So who are Lena and her brother *Michael*? Where did they come from? And what happened to bring them so low at this young an age? Lena and *Michael* had scarce time enough to have history so we draw on that of their immediate ancestors, for their problems began there.

July, 1959

Teenager Frances O'Leary seemed very happy to be pushing her two young charges in their buggy round the streets of *Donnycarny*, near her *Dublin* home. The children, her younger sister and brother, had provided her with a good excuse for getting out of the house and her father's shouts were beginning to recede from her head on this clear, sunny day. She was a pretty young woman, probably just creeping into her late teens, with dark hair framing a pale, elfin face. The brown eyes that peeped out of that face radiated pure joy at being free.

"Why was *Dada* shouting?"

The question from one of the children caused Frances to pause momentarily before she moved towards a nearby bench. She applied the brakes to the buggy, and sat down so the children could see her.

"Now don't you be worrying about all that! That is grown- up stuff."

"But *Dada* is always shouting." The child persisted. "He shouts at Mammy and you and me and ..." Here he paused and Frances smiled probably wondering if he had forgotten a name, for her parents had provided her with the grand total of 21 brothers and sisters. Even her exhausted mother, the mother who had produced her second babby just after her twenty-first birthday, perhaps especially her mother, was always getting their names wrong.

"Never mind lovey. Let's just enjoy the day before we have to go back."

"Can we get taffy?" The other child, a girl, asked eagerly. Both children were as fair as Frances was dark, but it was easy to see the family relationship etched on their faces.

Frances sighed. "We don't have money." She responded briefly after a pause. She would have liked a bit of taffy too, as treats were rare. Indeed the only thing that was common in their home was her father's loud voice and aggressive manner, especially if he thought one of them had stepped out of line.

"He's a hard man." She thought. "When I find me a man, he'll have to be one that gives me a rest between babbies. No way am I going to end up with twenty-two. And he won't cuff me around. He's got to be nice to me. I won't have a man who is always shouting at me and the children, bashing us when we don't please him."

"Oh look! Maggie!"

Frances looked and saw her friend Maggie crossing the road up ahead. She jumped up, released the brakes of the buggy and ran pushing it before her, as the children screamed, "Maggie! Maggie!"

Maggie looked around and stopped at the kerb to wait for them. The pedestrian traffic lights at the crossroads were still on green and Frances hurried across the road. On the other side and breathless from her run she simply said "Hi!"

The two friends had just begun to speak when Frances, who had been standing right on the edge of the kerb slipped off it, pulling the buggy backward with her.

"Look out!" Maggie screamed as she lunged forward to grab the buggy.

Horrified, Frances saw the bus bearing down on her and she pushed the buggy hard towards Maggie as she tried to get back onto the kerb.

As Maggie grabbed the buggy, she heard the thud and watched helplessly, her mouth opened in a silent scream as the bus hit Frances with a glancing blow. One of the wheels ran over her foot as she fell, and her head hit the kerb with a sickening crack. Then the scream became vocal, harsh and guttural.

January, 1960

Frances O'Leary opened her eyes and frowned. This was not the crowded bedroom at home. Where was she? She tried to turn her head but everything seemed stiff. From what she could see all the walls were painted white and the glare hurt her eyes, making it all seem a little fuzzy. Squinting, she slowly turned her head, ignoring the sharp stab of pain, and peered around. She was in a hospital! But why? The last thing she remembered was getting the two little ones ready for their walk.

"Yes! She's awake." Her eyes flashed to the door in time to see the nurse walking into the room. "Hallo Frances. How do you feel today?" The nurse asked like they had known each other for months, but she didn't know her from Adam!

"Who are you?" She asked. "Why am I in hospital? Why does my head hurt?" And then with a flash of anger, "and why am I talking funny?" She thought she sounded drunk.

"*Don't you remember?*" The nurse asked kindly.

The anger burst through Frances like water released from a dam. "If I bloody remembered, I wouldn't be having to ask a stupid scalpeen like you now, would I?"

As suddenly as the anger came, it rushed away and Frances was appalled at her bad manners. Just as she was about to apologise, a man she recognised to be clearly a doctor from his stethoscope, his white coat and his air of knowing it all, walked into the room. The anger began to simmer quietly.

"Good afternoon Frances. How are we feeling today?" He spoke loudly, like she was deaf, or an eejit. She glared at him and breathed hard out her nose.

The doctor moved over to the nurse and said. "Underlying aggression. Only to be expected at this stage. How do her signs look?"

"I don't have any bloody signs and as for how we're feeling today, you'll have to speak for yourself. As for me, I'm bloody hungry."

"Good! Good!" The doctor replied cheerfully, as though her rudeness meant nothing to him. "We'll try you with some solids in a day or two perhaps, but for now, the nurse will bring you something to drink, to see how well you tolerate it."

"Yes Doctor. Thank you doctor." She replied meekly. She suddenly felt exhausted and somehow ashamed at her outburst. Wherever did that come from?

By the time of this awakening, Frances had lain in a coma, in her hospital bed for the best part of six months. She had suffered a fractured skull with some brain damage in the accident and her crushed foot. She would now walk with a permanent limp. Her friends and family said that she was never again the sweet- natured girl she used to be, with periods of apparent normalcy interspersed with aggressive outbursts. It would be pitiful to see this once vibrant young woman, limp her way, literally and figuratively, through the rest of her life.

On leaving the hospital, she learned that she was due some compensation from the bus company, something that greatly pleased her father. Anger surged through her.

"Why does he think he has a right to this money?" She thought, "It's my foot that's gone and my brain that's addled. Well I'll just fix that idea!"

She met with her friend Maggie who she knew was always daydreaming about having amazing adventures in the great, wide world. Maggie got into the spirit of the plan immediately.

"We could go to England for starters! Then Europe, maybe Asia, even Africa or Australia! Maybe there's a chance we could get to the States. I have family there." She said excitement oozing from her every pore. "But what about your compensation?"

"They can send it to me wherever I am." Frances replied, "but I'm not staying here for him to take it all from me and spend it down the pub. If he'd spend it on Mammy it wouldn't be so bad, but I know him. Anyway, it's my body that paid for that compensation and I want it."

"We have no money. How are we to travel to England?" Maggie asked as the facts of life hit her in the face.

The two girl-women, now aged around eighteen and nineteen years old, put their heads together, one buzzing of travels to far away places, the other trying to hold down the anger that always seemed to be simmering just under the surface.

Two weeks later, they sauntered around the ferry going from Dublin to Liverpool like they belonged there, after having slipped past a ticket collector who was being besieged by a family wanting something or other. After the stress of getting on-board Frances, the younger of the two, relaxed on the deck not minding the coolness of the night air. Earlier that week, and with her father looking over her shoulder, she had filled in the forms for her compensation from Bus Eireann and before she boarded the ferry she had posted them another letter saying that she would be abroad for a few months and would send them a new address shortly.

"That should fix the old devil." She thought.

A few days later, she arrived in Birmingham having had a blazing row with Maggie. The two had apparently parted company in Liverpool. In Birmingham she met Sheila Simmons and her family and for a brief time, had a relationship with Bobby Simmons, Sheila's brother. Despite her frequent moods and unpredictable behaviour, Bobby was besotted with her, but the demons now drove Frances and soon she broke it off. By this time, she had met a handsome young Pakistani, simply known as Nazir Ali, and embarked on a passionate affair with him. She quickly became pregnant and bore him a son. Baby Daniel was just five months old, when she became pregnant with Lena.

So here she was - unmarried, pregnant with her second child who would arrive before she was twenty, and she began to understand something of her mother's position. She'd once heard someone say that her mother 'popped them out like peas' and it seemed that she too, might be destined for that same future. The difference between them was that her mother was married!

It is not clear whether her by now famous temper precipitated what happened next, but Nazir Ali deserted her. Bobby saw this as his chance to be re-united with her and even offered marriage, but she refused him. The baby girl was born on Friday, May 17th, 1963 and Bobby hopeful of the joys of fatherhood with these two beautifully, exotic looking children and no doubt some of his own, asked her once more to marry him. It isn't clear what happened but harsh words were exchanged and both furious and hurt, Bobby got on his motorcycle and raced off. It is also not clear if what happened next was an accident, or whether in his despair he wanted to end it all, but there was a crash, and Bobby died. That brought to an end her friendship with the Simmons, who blamed her thereafter for the death of this beloved son and brother.

She was now without a man, friends, or a job. She did have two small, demanding babies, rooms that needed paying for, and not enough Social Security to see them comfortably off. The bedsit was a tiny one person room, painted a depressing brown. The double bed in the centre took up almost all of the space in the room and her child slept beside her. When her man was with her, the baby boy slept in a basket.

A greedy slot for the electricity took whatever coins she managed to have and the place was always cold. It wasn't good enough and her new born baby girl needed things. So she wrote to Bus Eireann asking about her money. Somehow, her father found out where she was staying, and scant months after the birth of her daughter, still intent on getting hold of her as yet unpaid compensation for himself, he came to England, turning up on her doorstep and barging his way in.

When he saw the two children his mouth fell open.

"Two of them! Two! And for a black! You're nothing but a whore!" He roared as she crumbled before his onslaught. "I should wash my hands of you, you little slut!"

"But you won't, not with the compensation keeping you tied to me." Some fight returned to her as her head began to pound.

He slapped her into submission, amazed at her temerity, then, bundling the children into the old pram she used, he took them off to the local priest who sent them to Barnardo's.

Somehow, Frances managed to retrieve the children, and she, her father and the two babies turned up in Dublin a few days later. She stayed at a mother and baby home with the children overnight, then she dressed them, and took them to Dublin Castle where she abandoned them and escaped back to England with her compensation paid. Shortly after that the babies were picked up by the police - arrested and charged with being without a home.

Two

The Horrors Begin

Maisy began to fret as I pushed her in her stroller along the sidewalk. I had picked her up from the nursery where she stayed while I worked at a part-time job. We had then gone to the shops for a few items and she was probably as tired as I was beginning to feel. As she struggled to turn round to look at me, I spoke, "What is it lovey? Are you tired?" The sound of my voice made her struggle more and as she began to protest loudly, I went round where she could see me and stooped before her.

"Mumumu ..." She reached out for me and I gave her a hug, which was a mistake as she grabbed me fiercely and tried to climb out of the stroller. I disentangled her gently, soothing her and trying a bribe.

"Shall we go and get a little drinkie? Would you like some juice?"

She nodded and then once more when I asked her to be a good girl and stay still while we went to a cafe we liked, which was just down the block.

In the cafe, still fairly full with people having a late lunch, we found a table near the big window. It was a favourite spot for both of us as we generally ate and drank and watched the people go by whenever we came in. The cafe also catered for the many mothers who lived locally and had a menu which provided for children's tastes in kiddy sized portions. I got Maisy one of the high chairs available and, after putting her in it, sat down gratefully. I ordered our drinks, and when they arrived, poured Maisy's juice in her trainer cup for her, before wrapping my hands round my mug of tea.

"Ahhh!" I said after my first sip and was amused to hear Maisy say "Ahhh" as she mimicked me. We played "Ahhh" for a while and I marvelled at the vision of the beautiful little girl that sat before me. My Maisy. My little girl . the light of my life. Even as I thought that, another vision rose in my eyes, and I turned away to stare out the window, seeing not what was out there, but what lurked behind my eyelids. A little girl, lost, alone, and afraid, very afraid.

"Ahhh." Maisy, still playing the game, drew me back from that dark place and the rush of love I felt for her caused tears to come into my eyes.

"May I join you?" The voice asked. "There are no free tables left."

I looked up into dark, brown eyes that seemed to peer deep into my soul. They gazed with such intensity that I felt a shiver of fear. The eyes flicked over to Maisy briefly and a tiny, enigmatic smile crept onto the woman's face.

"Yayaya." Maisy yelled.

"What a beautiful child!" The woman said. Her voice was quiet, young, yet for a brief second I thought of my mother. I tried to guess her age but couldn't. She seemed ageless. As she turned to look back at me, for I had as yet not answered her, I whispered, "Please do."

She must have heard me because she drew the extra chair back and sat down, placing a capacious, black leather bag on the floor beside her. The waiter brought her a mug of black coffee and she took a sip, briefly closing her eyes. My mother, I thought. Why couldn't she keep us? I stared at the table.

"My name is Becky."

"I'm Lena." She didn't stick out a hand for me to shake so I kept mine where they were, round my cup, which I suddenly found quite fascinating. "I saw you in the window."

I looked up quickly to see the eyes again, the hint of a smile. It seemed a sad smile. Her hair was cut short, her face wrinkle free. She could have been thirty ... or sixty.

"Pardon?" I responded.

"The eyes are the windows of the soul. At least that's what they say and I believe it. I saw your windows as you looked out the window. They drew me in here."

I didn't know what to say. I felt weird. I felt like she knew everything. I wanted to ask what she had seen. I wanted to know what she knew and I didn't.

"The eyes that stared out of the window have a dark history that is deep, deep, deep. You were in the abyss. I know."

With those words uncertainty left me. This woman was strange, different, yet I felt no fear, and Maisy, chattering away, clearly was comfortable too.

"I ... um ... you know? What ... what do you know?"

"I know the abyss. It's a dark, dank place where the rays of the sun never reach. It's a place that can only be escaped by a long, hard climb. But it's tricky. Often what looks and feels secure dissolves to sand and you slide back to a point that took weeks, months, even years to climb out of. You have the look of someone who knows the abyss."

I looked away from her. The shadows fell into place and I saw the spot she spoke of. I do not know how long I was there. Probably minutes, seconds, but it felt like a long time before her voice called me back.

"Have you talked to a counsellor? Or do you always depend on your baby to ease the pain?"

"I have talked to many. Sometimes it helps, sometimes not."

"It is good to talk. It lets the poison out. Once the air is polluted with the pain, everyone has to help to clear it away and everyone learns it is better not to cause this type of pollution. The people who wish to continue to cause such pain will find that those who don't wish it will fight to either change them, or put them away."

We sat in silence for several minutes, drinking our beverages and I thought of what Becky had said. Why weren't there people who thought this way in my life when I was Maisy's age? Why weren't they there? How could they allow what happened to me and countless other children all over the world, to happen? How were these people followers of the Church? After all, the Church tells us that Christ died to cleanse us of our sins. Why did they let him die in vain? Why didn't He cleanse them while He was at it? I became aware that Becky and Maisy were playing a game of 'poke your tongue out' and I smiled. Appearing to hear the release of air as I smiled, the woman turned to face me once more.

"Please ... Maisy and I have to go now, but we're on our way home. Will you come back with us for a cup of coffee?"

"Will you talk?" She countered, the look and the ghost of a smile still in place.

"Yes." I didn't know why, but I felt drawn to her.

Her right eyebrow rose slightly and she inclined her head. With that, we got up, gathered our things together, got Maisy into her stroller and walked the couple of blocks where my car was parked.

In my house, she watched as I made Maisy comfortable on the couch where my wee colleen soon fell asleep grasping her favourite terrycloth teddy, and she followed me into my sunny lime green kitchen and helped by getting out the cups as I prepared the coffee. When we were seated at the kitchen table, with cups of coffee and a plate of scones between us, the eyes, smile and eyebrow fixed themselves on me. All anxieties had gone and I began to talk. It was like a dam had burst. I had of course spoken with others, mostly my fellow orphans and over the years many of us held fast to each other with visits to each other even between the two countries of Eire, where I was brought up, and England where I now live with my much loved Scott and our Maisy. I'd also spoken to Scott and others who had been close to me, but I sensed that with the telling to this woman, I'd be telling the world, "Enough! No more!" And so the dam burst.

"My earliest memories are of Sister Philip, the Reverend Mother. She was a large, round barrel of a woman with a face that was bright red, probably from her exertions hitting out at us, but which she could make look quite jolly when there were visitors about. Yet most of the time her face was simply frightening to us kids. She was a spiteful woman who believed that children should be seen, not heard. She also thought that hard work made a good servant of the Lord and as soon as you were old enough to walk, you were old enough to work. I was always a quiet child, and I think it was because I learned early from this vile creature that I would deeply regret crying or making any other kind of sound. She was the one who started a refrain that I would hear often in my life. It was one all the nuns used for most of us. They thought we were 'wee divils, who'd burn in hell'. I literally had to learn to be spontaneous later in my life. Other than her cruelty, I remember little about her.

I can't tell you an exact number, but there were many of us living at St. Joseph's during this time, perhaps around a hundred. We slept in huge dormitories, separate ones for the girls and for the boys. The older children also slept separately from the younger ones and some had their own cubicles. They also had unrestricted access to us. The beds in our dormitory were shoved close together, so you could literally run along their entire length without getting out of them. I remember when something special was happening, the beds were separated and little bedside tables would appear between them. Then when the 'event' was over, things went back to normal. We little ones never had beds of our own, no single, special place that we could call our own, where we would sleep each night. We simply slept wherever we could find a spot."

"How did you feel about this?"

"As a little one, sometimes it was frightening because a slightly bigger child might accidentally roll over on you and it would often be a struggle to get out from under them before they crushed you. In the winter months, it was welcome warmth and in the summer months it was too hot. But I guess I didn't really mind it. It wasn't until a bit later as I grew older I longed to have a spot that was my very own ... a spot I didn't get until I was around thirteen years old. I was like a wanderer never seemingly able to settle in one place, yet

I'd never travelled outside of the places where the nuns sent me. We had designated places at the table at mealtimes. Why not at bed-times? As I grew older, it bothered me and I missed that. I suppose, all in all it was better than nothing. Some kids in other countries didn't even have that."

"Did you know that then?"

"Oh yes! The nuns made sure of that. We had to be properly grateful for the blessings we had, which were provided by them. We had to be thankful for God's mercy ... for their mercy ... and they made us pray for all the world's unfortunates. We prayed for the homeless somewhere out there in the wide world ... everyone but ourselves, for didn't we have a place to live . and their good charity? We prayed for sinners of all types and stripes . I generally included them for as far as I was concerned, they were the great-est sinners of all. I prayed that they would all go to their home in hell pretty damned quick. We prayed for prisoners - people who presumably included rapists and murderers and who deserved to be incarcerated for their crimes. We prayed for the sick and dying, for the starving, black babies in Africa and elsewhere in the world ... oh the list was endless. What was funny at the time was I had no idea about what this 'world' was, as I really only knew of our little corner, and as for black babies ... I couldn't really picture them, even though there were two of us that were mixed race. I never looked at myself and even if I could, I would only see an Irish child with a vague tan and brown eyes. My friend, Ann, had rather curly hair but it never seemed strange to us and like me, she was not particularly dark-skinned, so it was a big stretch for any of us to imagine these 'black babies'. I used to imagine that they must look like the blackboard. Anyway, pray for them we did. We even prayed for the Bishops and the Holy Father in Rome! All of it reinforced in us, what lucky children we were to be having such a wonderful life."

"We'll talk some more about your feelings for the religious com-munities and the Church later, but I'm curious about what your daily life was like as a small child."

"Well, we would be roused early in the morning to go to Mass. Sometimes one of the nuns would walk along the bottom of the beds - the kinder ones would rattle a stick along the metal frames while the crueller ones would use their sticks or straps or whatever to hit out at anyone still asleep or not scrambling out of bed fast enough. As they were all pushed together, it was usually only those kids sleeping in the end beds who were out fast enough. As I grew older, I used to listen for their footsteps and get the hell out of there when I heard them. Once up, we would go to Mass, come back for breakfast and then it was 'school-time'. There were a couple of classrooms just off the recreation room and the smaller children attended school there. The older ones attended school in another building in the grounds. I remember when I was older it was like freedom, just running from the 'orphanage' to the 'school' even though they were so near to each other. My first language was Gaelic, which we learned at nursery school and it wasn't until I reached the age of four, that I attended the 'big children's' school where I then had to learn to speak English.

After school, we would all be locked in the recreation room, unsupervised. We had no toys or books or anything to occupy us and often there would be fights. The older children would beat us or force us to do things they had no right forcing us to do."

"What sort of things?"

"It was mostly sexual ... you know, showing what we've got or touching ... that kind of thing. As I grew older, I began to understand why these things happened. It was all they knew ... all I would know."

I hurried on before she could ask any more questions. I was not ready to talk about sexual abuses. "In the evening, after dinner, we had religious lessons in the orphanage and after a brief break we would have to say the rosary. You knelt where you were and there was usually no time to try to find a soft bit of anything to kneel on. Normally the nuns would pick one of us at random to say the Mysteries. We had to say different ones on different days, and there were five of them. If your name was called out and you did not know the prayer for that day, they would beat you from behind and without warning. We got hit with whatever they had in their hands, and they didn't mind where they hit us. I've been walloped on my head, across my back, legs and arms - any place they could reach. The leather strap was generally their weapon of choice and I had my fair share of beatings. One particular nun liked to rap us hard on the forehead with her knuckles, like she thought it was a door and wanted it opened immediately. It's a wonder she didn't addle our brains. Anyway, with each decade of the rosary, a child would say the appropriate Mystery and the rest of us would give the responses, praying quietly that we would get it right. Soon after that it would be bedtime. After lights were out, a nun would come in and this time, she would say the Mystery and we would give the response. Then we could sleep."

I looked up to see Becky sitting quietly, waiting. She smiled slightly and encouraged by her still attentiveness, I allowed my thoughts to wander. I knew somehow that she would wait for me to tell her whatever I needed to, in my own time.

"There was another time when we were locked up in the recreation room. I was desperate to go to the toilet. I got under the piano and soiled my knickers. I sat there for the whole period of 'lock-up', for fear I would be beaten up either by the other children, who thought the whole episode was hilarious, or eventually by the nuns when they returned.

Another time, two of us, myself and another girl I'll call Sinead, became ill. We had the measles and were taken to bed. The nun who cared for us was a small witch-like, mean, really evil person. She was called Sister Bridgette. She liked to pinch us and she had really sharp fingers. She also liked to twist our fingers, even when we hadn't done anything wrong. Our knuckles were constantly swollen, just like old people's. Anyway, Sinead and I were both so sick that we couldn't face food, even if it had been good, which our meals were not, but that old witch force-fed us. It didn't help that our meal was the normal fare of potatoes and peas, and as always, the potatoes were too salty and the peas too sugary. Just having to eat it made us feel even more sick and when we threw up, she tried to make us eat that too. Of course that just made us worse and after a while she gave up."

When I was about three years old, I was taken for my first walks. Before the walking excursions, I had never been outside of the grounds of the school. I had no idea that there was anything outside in a bigger world. I had no idea of family life and I only saw the outside of the orphanage when we were in the grounds. Later, when I understood that children had mothers, I used to look at the women I saw outside and wonder whether this one or that one was my mother. I thought she must live somewhere in the town so she could be near the school."

"I'm a little confused. Sometimes you say 'school' and sometimes 'orphanage'. Where exactly were you?"

"I have to explain a little of Irish laws of the time, so it becomes clear." At Becky's nod, I continued, "There was a law enacted in Ireland sometime in the1800s, which allowed the religious organisations to care for children who had committed criminal acts and who were incarcerated in Reform Schools. This was followed by the Industrial Schools Act 1868, which allowed the same organisations to care for children who were orphaned, abandoned or neglected, and who lived on the premises. These schools were funded by the Government, through taxation, and were all were run by various religious orders of priests and nuns. Then in 1908, the Children's Act bound the two types of 'schools' even further together by having them both visited for annual inspection, by an inspector of Reformatory and Industrial Schools."

"But surely all this would cause the children in the Industrial Schools to be seen as criminal!" Becky exclaimed. "That's how we all feel about it, but the children of the day had no say and that's what the Government did. Anyway, the Children's Act allowed destitute children to be sent to Industrial Schools, even if they hadn't committed a crime. It became so prevalent to take children from their families if there appeared to be even the slightest problem (usually in the eyes of the local powers - often the priest), that in 1933 when a Commission looking into pensions for 'widows and orphans' checked the numbers, they found that only five percent of the children in Industrial Schools were actually orphans."

"What do you mean about the 'slightest problems' in the family?"

"I don't know for sure what these were but I've heard, and read, that in poor families, if a child played truant or was too cheeky or maybe the family didn't attend Mass too often, they could break that family up. Just anything ... maybe the father or mother or both drank ... it could be just anything." "So the children were taken away and sent to one of these schools?"

"They were indeed."

"Perhaps they assumed that they were taking children out of a home that was bad for them and sending them to a place full of God's love."

"They knew that this was not the case. There were various reports over the years of problems in the management of these schools, of cruelty, even of unexplained deaths, but none were ever adequately investigated. They were taking the children, often because the priest suggested it. The schools were being paid for each child, so the more children the religious orders could acquire, the more money they got! They then used us as slave labour, starved us, beat us, vented their perverted spleens on us ..."

The hand that reached out to briefly touch mine was cool, and I stopped abruptly realising that I had begun to shout. Maisy, cried out and I sprang up but when I looked at her she was asleep again. I returned to the kitchen table feeling more composed and without preamble, continued.

"Anyway, to continue with my explanation of the 'school/orphanage' system, where I was in Clifden, the Industrial School occupied a large area which had several buildings. The convent, the nuns' living quarters, was closest to the Church where we went to Mass, just across the road. To the side of the convent was the school were the older ones went, and behind it was the building where we children lived and the younger ones went to nursery school. Beyond our house were other buildings including a mortuary, an 'infirmary' which just served the school complex, the laundry where many of us were forced to work as we grew older and other out-buildings like boiler rooms, and so on. So it was orphanage, school, convent - everything was to hand."

"And for your first couple of years you were literally locked away in this place?"

"Yes. That's right. I remember one day, I couldn't have been more than perhaps three, for it was one of the first times, I had been taken for a walk. Sr. Clare and some other nuns were leading a group of us along Beach Road, when a huge dog ... actually it was what we used to call a 'spotty dog' - a Dalmatian ... came flying out after us. He got hold of me and bit me on the eye and his tooth almost entered the eye socket. There was blood everywhere." I raised my hand to push my hair away from my right eye, but Becky smiled saying.

"I had already seen the scar and wondered about its origin. Go on."

"I was scared out of my wits. I'd never seen a dog before. They took me to the hospital for the wound to be stitched up and after that I was sent to the infirmary at the convent where I remember being placed in a cot. They locked me in that huge room . just locked me in. I was just a child for heaven's sake! And I was literally starved!" I paused in anguish, remembering, and Becky's quiet voice brought me back.

"What you mean by 'you were literally starved'? How long were you there for?"

"I'm not sure. It felt like many weeks but was probably just a week or so. I remember being very, very hungry. They didn't bring me many meals and no-one came to see how I was. No-one came for ages. I was alone and terrified. Every sound I heard frightened me and one time I could hear the others outside. I wanted to join them but couldn't. I felt totally lost and neglected. It was a really scary time for me."

Becky looked at me sympathetically, then she said, "Tell me more about the nuns who were responsible for your upbringing. You mentioned the Reverend Mother, another nun who took you for walks and the Reverend Witch. Were there no others? Perhaps some who were more humane?"

"Yes we did have a couple of nuns who were okay, but most weren't and those who were, generally had to be nice when the other nuns were not around. Unfortunately, as these things go, I tend to remember the many horrors that called themselves 'Sisters of Mercy' more often than the couple of nuns who clearly wished to, but couldn't always be merciful.

While Sister Philomena was there, times were very hard. I remember beatings with rods, sticks, canes, leather straps and of course their hands. Sometimes they slapped us, punched us, pinched us, shoved us ... it was horrible. We were forced to watch the other children being beaten and psychologically abused as a warning to keep our noses clean.

Needless-to-say, fear was probably the first emotion I knew during this time with Sister Philomena. I never left the orphanage except to go to church next door. I have virtually no memory of happiness or of any good times. All I knew was I had to be quiet and hope no harm would come to me. As a mother, when I think of my child, I truly understand what I was denied ... the care, love and time babies really need.

I do not remember laughing or playing. It seems to me in retrospect that I had or showed virtually no emotions whatsoever. Every day was the same. We were like outcasts from society. This was no home. For a long time, I choose to ignore what had happened to me, to try to forget. I felt like I was a 'nobody'. Nobody wanted me. I realise now that deep down inside me at that time, I felt like I never deserved love, attention or even recognition as a human being. I was a child amongst children who were also unknown, bless them! And we were completely forgotten about by the State. How often have I wished that the State had remembered us and the Church had forgotten us!"

Becky got up and filled my empty cup as my voice broke and tears threatened. Then she filled her own cup and briefly touching my shoulder before sitting down again, she waited for me to compose myself.

"I remember clearly the day Sr. Clare came. For some reason she was there in front of me. She picked me up and I am not sure why as I do not recall any great fear, but I involuntarily slapped her! It was just a small slap, and that act was more fearful to me than her picking me up. She simply looked at me, and put me down again.

With her arrival, came some changes and it looked as though life was going to be better. Up till then we'd had no toys or anything that would help us to develop like normal children. She changed that. Books and toys appeared. She got us some swings, a merry-go-round and an area at the back of the orphanage was designated the playground. In time, we also got tennis and football courts, though there would be little time to use them after we had done all our chores. Before her arrival, we all wore uniforms, the girls wearing what should have been a white shirt with a grey pinafore dress over it. This meant that half the time, the nuns could not tell one of us from the other, which probably explained why so many of us who had done nothing wrong would be punished for something or other. It seemed to benefit only the outsiders who would immediately recognise us as one of the 'wee brats' from the Industrial School. Sr. Clare replaced our uniforms with two sets of clothing – one set for during the week and of course, Sunday best for Mass."

"So she was one of the good guys, was she?"

"Not really. She wasn't as cruel as some of them, but she was no angel either. She didn't always assault us herself. She got the others to do it, and if she thought we were being dealt with too harshly, we never knew it. Her special skill was more mental cruelty. She was very hot on telling us how worthless we were and how we would burn in hell. Even so, often I get the feeling looking back on it all, that she perhaps wanted to do the right thing by us, but simply had no idea and so ballsed everything up. She was indirectly responsible for many of us being sexually abused, and when she found out, she acted in a way that only someone like her could. She tried to stop the abuse by not sending us back to a particular house, but she never reported the abuser, and if any of us spoke of it, she either beat us herself or had someone else do it."

"How was she indirectly responsible?"

"I suppose she thought she was doing something to allow us kids to have a chance of family life, but she never thought things through properly. At Mass one Sunday, she asked the congregation if they would be kind enough to accept children into their house at weekends and holidays. We were sent to whoever said they would take us. Just like that! There were no checks or anything made on these families, whether they would provide us a good home for the time we would spend with them, or not. That is why she was responsible for what happened to so many of us. I know she was a nun, but I can't believe that they lived so far in cloud cuckoo land, that they never imagined that we might be beaten or worse. Of course they beat us themselves, so she probably didn't care or thought that for us to be beaten or overworked would be good for our souls. She used to say that sometimes. 'Work is good for the soul.'

Occasionally visits to strange families worked out just fine. Some of my few happy memories are about Bryan and Gaby and the trips I took with them. Bryan was a young policeman and Gaby was his wife. They were the best people I knew in those days. Both of them were tall. Bryan was about six feet tall and he would swing me up onto his shoulder. It was wonderful and I could see the whole world from up there. I used to pretend that they were my parents and I saw them often as their police quarters were just across the road from the orphanage. They were really lovely." I paused, briefly remembering before continuing.

"In all, I was sent to maybe about twenty different families. They were all complete strangers to me and I'm sure to Sr. Clare. A few, like Bryan and Gaby were fine people, and some were strange but not evil. One time I was sent to Cashel, about twelve miles from Clifden, to a woman called Mrs O'Toole. She was sixty years old and her husband was bedridden. She was a lovely person and very good to me. Her house was on a very remote piece of land on the west coast of Ireland. There were no other children to play with for miles around and Sister Clare never sent my brother *Daniel* with me. He and I were seldom together. I was perhaps between six and eight years old and I was very lonely. Still I preferred to be there than some other places I had by then experienced. I used to spend hours in the fields playing alone for the whole summer. Sometimes ..."

I hesitated, feeling a little awkward. I took a quick sip of my coffee and peeped over at Becky, who was sitting as still as a statue, her attention completely on me. I cleared my throat.

"Sometimes I would act out some of the scenes from other homes that I was sent to ..."

I paused again, but still Becky said nothing. "I guess you would call it masturbation, but I shouldn't have known about these things ... I was not only very young, I was also small for my age ..."

Still Becky said nothing and I sighed with relief, for in truth, I didn't want to remember those things - not today. I continued with my memory of the O'Tooles.

"Mrs O'Toole's husband died in the house whilst I was there and the smell of his death remains very much in my memory, as does the smell of his urine. I used to have to give him the bottle he urinated in. This is something I do not like telling anybody because it was just so horrible. It was all wrong and it was happening to me. I used to wonder if it would ever stop.

Whenever I returned to the school from the O'Tooles, I always wanted a nice bath. Back in the 60's hot water was a little bit of a luxury, so it was seldom that us kids had a bath. Usually we were allocated a certain amount of time by a sink. If we had a bath it would be three of us at a time. The nuns in charge of bathing never checked the water temperature, and sometimes in the case of the Reverend Witch, as you called her, she would check the temperature, and as far as she was concerned, the hotter the better. Most of us wanted to squeal with the agony of being in such hot water. We would be skipping about, wanting to get out but knowing that if we tried that we would be given a battering or be pushed completely into the hot water. I was terrified I would cry out, and of course occasionally I did, but I soon learned that cherry red legs was preferable to being submersed in that water. I remember one day wondering if my eyes cooked, would I be able to see again? Fortunately, they never kept my head under long enough for that to happen.

Now I enjoy bathing and I can even put my head under water briefly without too much angst. This only came after years of trying.

I was determined that I should have no fears left over from those days. It hasn't always worked, but that was one of my successes. There were times in my childhood that should have been pleasurable, simply by virtue of the activities we were doing, but they were deliberately made as unpleasant as possible. For example, I remember learning the accordion. Sr. Concepta was the music teacher. She too was a cruel woman. She would beat hard on your fingers with a narrow chunk of wood or a belt-buckle if you got your notes wrong. On her better days, better for us that is, she would make you stand in the corner of the room facing the wall, learning your notes."

Becky grunted sympathetically and shook her head as though unbelieving, but as I looked at her eyes, I could see that she was right there with me ... in the abyss. Comprehension hit me, and I found myself wanting to take her away from that scene.

"I was six when I started working 'outside' the convent." "What do you mean?" Becky asked.

"As long as I could remember, I had to work. Even though there were a couple of women who came in to the convent, mainly to help out with the cooking and when extra needed to be done, we did most of the work. We knew them as Mrs. Scully and Mrs. 'F' whose name was really Fahey, but even the nuns called her Mrs. 'F'. Anyway, everywhere had to be cleaned including the orphanage. I did jobs like cleaning up rooms, scrubbing some floors, including in the nun's residence. They made us wear dusters on our feet so we could shine all the floors. We walked up and down for hours often supervised by Scully and 'F', both of whom were snitches for the nuns. At the nuns' mealtimes, although I wasn't allowed to take their food to them in case I dropped it, I ferried dirty dishes from their table to be washed up by the older girls in the kitchen. Outside in the yard, I would also sweep up and so on. That was all considered to be 'inside' work, but when I was six, I was considered old enough to work in the laundry, where we not only washed and ironed all of our clothes, but also the nuns' and those of the townspeople who sent their clothes to be laundered. This was a service they paid the nuns for, but of course we weren't paid anything.

"Mamu!"

Maisy's cry startled me and I jumped up to go to her. Becky followed me as I picked up my baby and cuddled her, talking to her in our special 'language'.

"Maisy needs you now, and it's getting late. I must go." "Will you come back? I mean ... you're welcome to."

She reached into the black bag, which she had picked up, and pulled out a card. I looked at it. The card, on which a paintbrush with a rainbow coloured painted strip was flowing from it, simply gave her name and a telephone number. I looked at her. She smiled.

"I paint. That's how I get release. Often I have a canvas that is dark and painful. When I am able to release that pain, I paint over it, something cheerful and uplifting. It helps, though there are times when I remember what lies beneath. We do what we can to carry on, lead normal lives, but it is always there, underneath."

She reached over and touched Maisy's cheek. "You take care of Mommy." She said before turning back to me. "We will speak again. Just as soon as you call that number."

Three

Fire, Fire, Burning Hell

Clifden, 1968

The Recreation Room was large by normal standards, perhaps about 40' long by 20' wide. However it was too small for the group of children crowded into it. Along one wall was a piano, which a small boy, after looking around nervously, opened. He peered longingly at the keys and ventured to touch them after another quick look round, but he refrained from pressing any of them. Hearing footsteps approaching the room, he quickly shut the piano and sat down on the floor to one side of it. He pulled his legs up to his chin and watched the nun who was looking into the room with a curious sideways look. It was clear that she worried him.

His gaze shifted to a tiny girl sitting under the window on the opposite wall. From where she was, the nun was unlikely to see her and he was happy for that, for she was his little sister, Lena. He wasn't sure why, she was just another of the throng of little girls here at the school, but even now at the grand old age of six-years-old, he felt some kind of responsibility, some kind of connection with her. Maybe it was because she was his sister, but the word meant little to him. They were all his sisters, even the demon he could now hear walking away from the door. She was even called 'Sister' and now she had closed and locked the door.

As he watched little Lena, he noticed *Dermott Magee* slide nearer to her and say something to her, his face inches from hers. Lena immediately lifted her dress and pulled her knickers down. *Dermott's* hand slipped quickly between her legs. *Daniel*, for that was the boy's name, simply shrugged. His sister and *Dermott* were just playing the game. It was a game they all played ... a game he would soon be playing himself when he got off his arse and went over to Marie O'Dwyer.

He'd rather be playing with what she had than with what the bigger boys had. He didn't mind the girls. What they had you played with your hands, not what some of the older boys wanted. He'd seen them shove their things in other boys' mouths. One had tried with him but he showed him what fine, sharp teeth he had as he made scissor-like biting motions, and the other backed off. He knew though that unless he was quick on his feet, they would probably gang up on him. At least that's what he would have done if he liked boys. But he didn't and he liked it better when the girls wanted to play too. He couldn't abide those that started crying if you did anything. Anyway, if they didn't want to play, it wasn't right to make them, just like when he didn't want to play with the older boys, he'd fight like a wildcat.

Girls were fascinating. You looked and checked out their 'gee' against what you had. Sometimes you tried to make a connection between what you had and what the girls had. He'd seen some of the bigger boys and girls doing it, but it seemed to him that they had more fun connecting than he did. He preferred to examine, to take a good look, like when they played 'doctors and nurses' or even 'priests and nuns'. Boys weren't interesting. They all had the same 'long thing', but the girls had 'gees', which were like flowers and sometimes you found a rose, sometimes a daisy or whatever. Yeah! Girls were definitely more fun.

He looked over at Marie O'Dwyer and saw Liam O'Shaunessy walking towards her. Quick as a flash, he was up and over by Marie's side. He gave her a quick smile, said 'please' and 'thank you in advance' like he'd heard one of the older boys say, and he and Marie were soon playing the game. Liam changed direction and began to check out Ann Flaherty. *Daniel* smiled. He planned to check her out one day soon too - see what kind of flower her 'gee' was like.

An hour later, Lena was outside watching the others play. There were two girls on the swings. Another four were standing by the merry-go-round watching some of the bigger girls go round on it. She didn't notice Mary Noonan nearby. If she had she would have run a mile, for Mary liked to see her 'gee' and she didn't like showing it, because Mary hurt. Whatever it was she did down there, she hurt.

"Hi youse. Come here." Mary's voice startled her. Lena's eyes grew wide with fear. She felt like peeing herself. She stood still as though hoping that standing still would somehow make her invisible. She didn't look around, but she caught a whiff that told her Mary Noonan was approaching. Still rooted to the ground, Lena began a silent prayer. Where was a stupid nun when you needed her? She thought as she prayed.

"Our Father, who art in heaven, please get off your throne, and come down here. Sort Smelly Noonan out and stop her hurting me ..."

"Open yer eyes, you stupid little git. When I tell you 'come here', I bloody mean 'come here', you understand? Youse to come here!"

Lena opened her eyes, but tried to close her nose. The one thing you could depend on Mary Noonan, other than her messing around in your pants, was for her to stink the air up. Good and proper. Lena never voiced her thoughts and she tried to speak without breathing.

"I'b soddy. I dibn't dink you war dalking do be."

"What? Youse talking gibberish. Talk proper, or I'll clatter your brains out."

Knowing she would do exactly that, Lena took a quick breath and apologised explaining to the stupid mutt that she hadn't thought she was speaking to her.

"Well I was, so march! Quick smart!"

"Where are we going?" Lena asked, her heart sinking. "You'll find out soon enough."

"Mary Noonan! Mary Noonan! Now where is that devil of a child?" Sr. Clare appeared in front of them, holding a pair of black shoes in her hand. "There you are you young scallywag. Why didn't you answer me? I call, you answer. *Do you understand?*"

"Yes Sister. I was going to answer Sister but I didn't get a chance." Mary responded quickly and with the requisite amount of respect.

Sr. Clare grabbed Mary by the ear and from the look on Mary's face she wasn't enjoying it. Mary was a thin, lanky, sixteen year old with long fair hair and a pasty complexion. 'If she wasn't so mean,' Lena thought, 'she could be pretty'. Mary also had long, sharp fingers that poked at Lena every time she saw the child ... almost as long as those gripping her ear now.

"Look at these shoes, Miss Noonan!" The nun twisted Mary's ear some more and Mary looked. So too did Lena for she had not yet found the power to fuel her running muscles. Anyway she thought it might be more prudent to stand stock- still. The invisibility thing didn't work with Mary, but she was keeping her fingers crossed.

Sr. Clare continued. "Didn't you clean the shoes not a half hour since? Why did you leave these out?"

"But I cleaned them all Sister." Mary began to whine and to do her some justice, Lena though the shoes looked pretty good.

"I can't see my face in them, you little liar! You will clean them until I can." With that, she shoved the shoes into Mary's chest and Mary winced. Lena sympathised, though she didn't yet know of the pain a blow could bring to young, rambunctious breasts. If she had, she would have thought Sr. Clare especially chose that place to shove the shoes into and she would have smiled at Mary's discomfort.

Mary still leaning forward wincing, ran off with the shoes to clean them some more. Lena heaved a sigh of relief, which was not the cleverest thing to do at that very moment.

"Aren't you supposed to be working somewhere, Miss O'Leary?" The cold voice came from a long way up, but the hand approaching her ear was quite near - too close for comfort.

Lena bobbed her head, replied "Yes, Sister" as quickly as she could and thankfully finding the gear for her legs, ran into the house a few feet away. She knew she was safe for the moment, as the nuns never ran outdoors. They could and did run indoors when a child was trying to escape, but she had a few moments. She hurried through the hall, but didn't run there, as it was forbidden for the children to run around the house, though they sometimes did when they were in trouble. They always got extra punishment for that when they were caught. Reaching the other side just as Sr. Clare was entering the building, she slipped outside again and made her way back to the playground. This was her playtime and she wasn't about to squander it on work.

She briefly thought about the nun's queer habit of calling them Mr. or Miss Whoever, as though they didn't have first names. She wouldn't learn until much later, that other places were even worse. Children had no names ... just had numbers.

Finding a corner of the garden close to the house, she sent up a quick prayer. "Our Father, who art in heaven, I don't know if you sent Sister Clare, but thanks anyway. Now that you're maybe listening, could you please send Mammies and Daddies to take me and Daniel and all the little children away from here, but not Mary Noonan, as she's a bad sort. Thank you. From Lena."

Essex, September, 2004

"I don't care! I don't want Maisy staying overnight with her!" Lena screamed at Scott who was looking fed up, understanding, thunderous, sad and perplexed - emotions shifting from one minute to the next. Then his blue eyes were like pieces of flint. He ran his hand through the short fair hair and took a deep breath, his chest heaving up with the effort, and from somewhere deep down some calm returned to him as was clearly seen in his face. He sat down on the bed. He was tired and had an early start the next day, but he had to sort out this business of a baby-sitter with Lena soon. He looked at her, resigned to hearing her out.

Lena paced up and down the room raking her fingers through her long brown hair, clearly agitated. Maisy was asleep in her cot in the next room.

"Honey." Scott said in a quiet voice. "This party is important for me. I might be able to close a couple of decent deals there, but it's the kind of thing where you have to take your partner. My parents are going to be on holiday in Spain and Jenny is someone I trust. I know she won't hurt Maisy. She loves her!"

"And that's the problem Scott. You probably haven't seen her but she is always kissing Maisy, holding her like she's her mother or something, but she's not!" The anger caused her voice to vibrate.

"That's what normal people do with babies. It doesn't mean that they will harm them. Babies are lovable. Everyone likes to hold and kiss them. Why do you think politicians are always grabbing some-body's baby and kissing it? They're not all perverts ... well not that kind of pervert but it's because it is natural for babies to be loved and it does their image good. They look like good family men!"

"I'm not interested in any politician's motives. I'm talking about our child here!"

"So am I, Pet. Jenny won't hurt Maisy. You know that. You used to trust her. What's changed?"

"She .... Oh Scott, she worries me ... ever since the day I saw her playing with Maisy's private bits." "What?" Scott sprang to his feet.

"She had changed her nappy. I didn't see any harm in letting her do it. After she cleaned her up, she put her face on Maisy's buttocks and blew a raspberry. Then she did the same on her stomach. Her mouth was near her ..."

Scott walked over to Lena fighting down his exasperation. He grasped her by the shoulders and made her look at him. "Parents do that to their children all the time. It's just a game. It doesn't mean any ..."

"Game? Game?" Lena exploded. "You think that's a game?"

Too late Scott realised that he'd used the wrong word. He'd heard a little of Lena's childhood 'games' and although he'd understood she hadn't enjoyed all of them, the children's activities hadn't particularly disturbed him, and so in his mind, he had dismissed the stories as childhood pranks.

"But Pet," he continued, "all children play 'doctors and nurses'. Everywhere. It's part of growing up. It's only when a child is forced to do the things adults forced you to do that it's wrong. And changing a nappy ... everyone does what ..." His voice trailed off. Lena was no longer listening to him. She was turned inward like she sometimes is. He led her to the bed, sat her down and sat himself beside her. His arms crept round her and she buried her face in his neck. He felt the wetness on his neck and tears came briefly to his own eyes as he realised the extent of her pain. He knew that he could be in for a long night of difficult stories.

Clifden, 1969 (or thereabouts)

"Fire! Get them out! Get them all out! We cannot have any lost or they'll be baying at our gates!" Sr. Clare screamed at the other nuns who were whacking children with whatever they held to hurry them out of the burning building. There were confused shouts about the whereabouts of this child or that child, but Lena standing outside in the playground felt only happiness as she and numerous other children looked back at the smoke billowing out of the building. She didn't know how the fire started, but she found herself praying quietly.

"Our Father, who are in heaven, burn the place down so we could be sent back to our Mammies and *Daddies*. Burn the divils out so they can't have any more children to torture, and beat, and work and generally make life miser - miser - awful for. I'm sorry I don't remember the big word Our Father who art in heaven, so 'awful' will have to do. Thanks a lot. From Lena."

"*Didja* hear that?" Crumbs O'Connor was three years older than Lena and was nearly her best friend.

"Hear what?" Lena turned to her puzzled. She hadn't heard our Father who art in Heaven say anything.

"Sr. Apainintheear said 'they'll be at the gates'. Who do you think she means?"

"Our Mammies and *Daddies*?" Lena asked hopefully.

"No silly." Crumbs responded by laughing and poking her in the ribs. "The govment that pays for us."

"What do you mean the 'govment'? And what do they pay for? I don't get me share."

Crumbs laughed again. "You are such a babby sometimes. The govment is a big house with a lot of men in it and they give the nuns money for all of us. That's why the place is full up to the gunnels. Sr. Apaininthearse don't want to lose any of us for fear the Govment will take away the money for all the wee 'uns that's burnt up! See?"

"Where's 'the gunnels'?" Lena asked looking puzzled. Crumbs laughed once more and went off to talk with Sally Sheehan.

"Silly Sally Sheehan. Silly Sally Sheehan." Lena chanted below her breath whilst wondering about the gunnels.

"All right! All right! Stop your chattering! Now get together. Two by two. A big one and a little one."

Sr. Apainintheearandthearse, a name that Lena found she liked, was getting them together in a way that worried the little girl. She would rather be with one of the little ones, or with Bridie Gallagher who was okay for a big girl, but many of the other teenagers made you work for them or beat you and some like Mary Noonan made you do smelly things. She struggled through the throng to get to where Bridie Gallagher was and was dismayed to see Sr. Areallybigpaininthearse matching her up with Silly Sally.

Sr. Areallybigpainsomewhereunmentionable said, "Lena O'Leary, come here! You'll pair up with Mary Noonan." Lena's mouth turned down briefly as she struggled with the threatening tears. Mary Noonan's hand fell on the child's shoulder. "Gotcha!" She said.

Lena felt the fear taking hold of her and she began to pray quietly again. "Please our Father who art in heaven, blessed be Thy name and all that, but please don't let Mary Noonan hurt me no more. I don't even like her. If You save me, I'll be a really good girl. I'll eat all me grapefruit peel and I'll stop stealing the rancid butter that the nuns put out for the cats, and I'll work hard and scrub out the kitchen, even under the table in that dark corner where Ratty lives and bites me when I try to steal stale crusts from him. And please our Father who art in heaven, do You think You could send me mammy to pick up me and *Daniel*. I'd be even good for him too, if you could manage it. And ..."

"Quick march you little shit." Mary Noonan's breath was in her nose again as those children at the front of the line, began to move off.

The children were marched down to the gates for buses were waiting there to take them to the boarding school where they would sleep. This would be done every night until the orphanage, which was badly smoke-damaged in the fire, could be made habitable once more.

At the boarding school, Lena looked round with interest, momentarily forgetting who was standing beside her. Some of the children who had no teenagers with them were lucky enough to be linked up with one of the boarders, as they were generally kind to them. The girls' dormitory was separated into a number of cubicles so that the boarders had some modicum of privacy. Lena thought this was quite a good idea until she heard Sr. Clare say, "I've been told that there are not enough cubicles for each of you to have one. Now all of you are in pairs and you will remain in those pairs at bedtime. I expect the older children to take care of the younger ones. Now have a good night." With that she walked out of the dormitory.

Lena's heart felt tight, not least because of Mary Noonan's stinky voice saying, "I'll do exactly what Sister wants and take good care of you, or rather, *you* will take care of me, and I'll have a good night." She smirked at the pale, horrified face staring up at her.

Her hand was tight round Lena's stick-like upper arm and as she dragged her to the cubicle, Lena, resigned to her fate, could see other small girls being dragged to their 'protectors' beds. She knew that in the boys' dormitory, the same scene was probably repeating itself as she'd heard from Crumbs some of the things that the big boys and the priests did to the littler boys. She sent up a brief, silent prayer.

"Our Father who art in heaven, please help Daniel if a big boy tries to hurt him. I know you don't like me much or you wouldn't have fixed the fire so that Mary Noonan could do more bad things to me, but maybe you like Daniel better 'cos he's a little boy and lots of your blessed people like the priests, like little boys too. So please our Father who art in heaven, save him for yourself and when you put your long thing in his arse like I heard the priests do, please don't let it hurt, 'cos he's only got a little arse. Ow!" This last word was said as Mary Noonan got her by the hair and threw her onto the bed.

"Now not a word from youse. Get up against that wall before I choke the life outta youse."

The little girl did as she was told and she braced herself. For months now, Mary Noonan had been after her . in the bathroom when she was having a wash, in the toilets when she was doing her business. Mary Noonan liked to watch and one time she made her lean over when stuff was coming out her arse so she could see it good. She also liked to touch, only when she touched, she pressed hard on her gee or something 'cos it always hurt. Sometimes when a little boy was playing the game with her, Mary would watch them. One time she chased the boy away and made Lena put her hand in her knickers. Lena hadn't wanted to, because Mary's smell didn't get any better close-up, and especially what she had in her knickers. Lena thought that it smelled like something from the 'dead-house', which was how she thought of the mortuary, as the word 'mortuary' sometimes escaped her, but Mary twisted the child's hair until it hurt, so she did as she was told. Lena didn't know what she was supposed to do anyway, for although she scrabbled around as usual, Mary didn't have a 'long thing', like the boys did, and she wasn't too pleased with Lena's efforts. Mary slapped Lena about and when finally the child looked like she was going to cry, told her she'd better

37

shape up and figure out what she was supposed to do. Now here she was, watching Mary as she put some items from her pocket onto the bedside table and took off her clothes. As the full power of her stink was released, little Lena began to feel sick.

Mary was completely naked as she climbed onto the bed and despite her distaste, Lena watched with fascination at the firm young breasts bouncing around on Mary's chest. Just as she was thinking with wonder, 'Will I get some of those?', the older girl lay down and pulled Lena on top of her. She pressed her disgustingly smelly mouth on the child's and Lena struggled until her hair was tugged as a warning for her to be still. Then she took Lena's hand and guided it between her legs, instructing her. After a while, and stinking worse than an alley-cat, Mary forced the child's head down towards her nether regions. "Lick it!" She instructed.

Lena's head snapped up as she looked at Mary, open- mouthed. "What? Lick it?" She squeaked, incredulity written all over her little face, her eyes like big brown saucers.

In response, Mary pushed her back down.

Lena tried to say she couldn't breathe, that she felt sick, but she felt her head pressed further into that strange, noxious place. She licked. She poked and prodded, then licked some more, each time feeling more and more nauseated. Whenever her face was between the older girl's legs, she struggled to breathe, yet she knew if she did, she would probably throw up.

Finally she felt herself being hauled up from that place, by her hair.

"What the hell do you think youse doing? I told you to lick it!"

"I don't want to do this. I don't like the taste!"

"You don't like the taste? Well you'll soon get used to it. Just need a little salt." She reached over to the bedside table, opened a twist of paper she had some salt in and dipped her finger into it before slipping the salty finger between the child's legs. Just as Lena opened her mouth to scream, Mary clamped her other hand over her mouth. "You make a sound and I'll scalp youse." She smiled as the tears welled up in Lena's eyes, but the child made not a sound.

And now Lena knew that God really hated her for he sent the fire, which put her in this hell. Almost like a mantra she felt the thought run through her head as she prayed, "Fire, fire, burning hell. Fire, fire, burn in hell! Our Father who art in heaven, I know now You're not me heavenly father and I'll no more pray to you, at least not for meself, 'cos you're worse than Satan to let this happen to a little child. Fire, fire, burning hell. Fire, fire, I'm burning in hell!"

It was several weeks before the orphanage was ready for the children's return and Lena, now proficient but still disgusted at doing Mary Noonan's bidding, was hopeful of finding a place where she could hide from her. Certainly she hoped that things would get back to normal and all she had to do was cope with the nuns' cruelty and the games she and the other kids her age played. She was thoroughly sick of Mary and even a good beating from the nuns was preferable to what she endured each night in that cubicle. It was bad enough that she had to lick the smelliest gee that the world would ever know. After she survived the first night, she thought she might be able to cope with her new hell, though she knew that she would never get used to the smell. However, that was just the beginning. Mary Noonan liked a lot of really strange things and it briefly occurred to little Lena to wonder how the 'wee divil' learnt it all. Mary liked having her feet rubbed, something the bigger girls called "rooting", and although they were smelly, Lena thought they would be the least of her problems until she was forced to suck the toes. She was also forced to lick other body parts and there was only one thing the little girl could be grateful for. She had eaten loads of shit as the nuns were not good at feeding the children, but at least it wasn't the brown stuff that came out the place Mary Noonan was forcing her to lick, and she would be eternally grateful that she didn't have to lick it when Mary Noonan was having a crap. After this happened for the first time, she realised that she would henceforth think of her meals with gratitude and a more appreciative demeanour.

Less smelly for the child, was Mary Noonan's interest in what was between Lena's own legs. She was constantly rooting around down there, but after that first night, it didn't really burn and so Lena came to realise that, that particular area didn't need salting. Worst of all but only just, was Mary Noonan's promise of what she would do if Lena spoke of their 'little secret'.

"If you tell anyone what we do here, I'll make sure that all the big girls and the nuns that like doing this, know that you like it too … and I'll personally arrange it for youse so that you have to do this to all of us in a single night! I can tell youse, you'll have to lick a lot of butts, and some won't be as clean as mine." She hissed as she pulled Lena's head back so the child could see the intention in her eyes.

Lena nearly fainted with the shock. Her butt was clean? "God bless us and save us," she prayed aloud involuntarily, completely forgetting her oath and Mary sniggered at her.

She didn't know how many of the big girls liked this kind of thing and just the thought that the nuns might, made her tremble with fear. She therefore had no problem making the promise Mary extracted from her. Anyway, she felt dirty, worse than ever, and she was now old enough to know that what had happened to her was wrong. Fire, fire, *burning* hell. Fire, fire, they'll *burn* in hell.

So it was with great relief that Lena returned to the orphanage. "It ends here." She thought.

Mary Noonan sidled up beside her that afternoon straight after lunch. "Come!"

"What? Where?" Lena's heart was thumping. Surely there was no place here where she could do what she did to her in the cubicle.

"We're going down to the fields … back of the laundry. Now! Or you'll have a long night tonight. I promise youse."

The child did as she was told. Fire, fire, *burn* in hell.

"Lena O'Leary! Where are your Sunday shoes?" They were at the back of the orphanage near the playground where some of the boys were playing a boisterous game of football. A couple of girls were on the swings and Lena and a bunch of others were watching a game of hopscotch awaiting their turn, when the nun descended on her.

"I ... I don't know Sr. Clare. I think they were in the fire." Lena trembled. In addition to all her other troubles, she had lived in fear of this moment since they were at the boarding school and realised that she had only her weekday shoes, which were on her feet, but Sr. Clare didn't quite have the same power there and nothing had been said. She had hoped no-one noticed, but here she was, less than a day back from the boarding school, less than an hour back from the fields behind the laundry and she was in trouble again. Fire, fire, *burning* hell!

"Gather round!" Lena heard Sr. Clare's voice and her face fell. She knew she was in for it. The nun repeated her order and waited for the children to make a ragged circle round them. She then produced a hand-brush and gave Lena a thrashing she really did not deserve. The worst part for her was not so much the beating. She was well used to those by now for she was all of six-years-old. What really got her goat was that the other children had to form a circle round them and watch, like she and the nun were the prize fighting chickens in a ring like she once saw near the local market. The only problem was that she was not allowed to peck back, not that it would help her much. The only place that she could reach was Mary Noonan's favourite spot and she definitely wasn't going there ... especially after what Mary said abut the nuns. Why, she might find herself getting punished every day!

The children stared at her with morbid fascination, as she herself had watched many times when one or other of them was being beaten. She realised now just how degrading it was to be beaten in this very public way. She had also not realised before quite how much seeing the relief in some of the children's eyes ... that it was not them this time . would hurt. She promised herself that the next time she was a watcher she would try to look more sympathetic. To add insult to injury, and because she had not cried out enough, she was sent to stand in a corner of the room facing the wall. She could not credit them. Cry out for one nun and you get battered harder. *Don't* cry out for another and the same thing happens. It would be okay if they didn't keep changing their minds so that no matter what you did, you got beat up some more anyway.

She stood in that corner, learning her sums for three long hours as she stared at the cracks in the white paint. Once she asked for a drink. *Denied.* Another time she asked for relief so she could go to the toilet. *Denied.* She was simply not allowed to move and those two infringements cost her dearly as the original punishment was for just two hours.

As the three hours drew to a close, another nun who was sent to tell her she was free said, "If you cannot take better care of your belongings, you will be punished and you deserved this punishment. You have to learn to be responsible and the first thing you must learn now, is to take care of your Sunday shoes when you find them. Now get along. Rosary in fifteen minutes."

Lena left the corner quickly and walked out of the room. She heard the nun leaving the house and looked out of the window at her. "You'd rather I burned in the fire trying to save me shoes, you would, even if the 'Govment' took me money back off you. Well I can tell you. I'd rather be burnt in the fire too, 'cos I know what it's like. Fire, fire, burn in hell, you wee witch, you."

Essex, September, 2004

"I'll try." Lena snuffled in his neck and ignoring the crick in his back, Scott pushed away slightly from her so he could look her in the eyes. They had moved up the bed and were leaning on the bedhead. He held her close to him and did not even try to blink away his tears, for he understood fully now why she had so much angst over her baby.

"I know you will. You always do. That is part of why I love you so much. You're a fighter. Half the time I can only imagine what you went through. The other half of the time you break my heart when you tell me what happened to you and I really want to go out and smash some skulls. I know for sure that if anyone even looks too hard at our Maisy, I'd kill them, and I really wish I was there for you."

Lena kissed the tear filled eyes tasting the salt, briefly returning to the cubicle, and she saw the difference clearly. It had struck her before but was always welcome. Whatever her man wanted from her she would try to give him, for he knew what her limits were and he did not overstep them. His physical reactions to her came from love, not from a desire to abuse and destroy. He knew her exactly as she was, and saw the beauty that was never truly snuffed out by the demons. He knew her exactly as she was. That too was a mantra she repeated often, especially when they were making love.

She smiled. "If you were there for me, I'd be in bed with an old man now."

Scot threw his head back and laughed out loud. He choked back a lewd comment that came to him. It wouldn't be appropriate. It was something he hated, having to be so careful all the time, but if there were any onlookers, it would be clear to them that he thought she was worth it.

"I overreacted about Jenny baby-sitting Maisy. It's not a problem." Lena continued, crossing her fingers behind her back. "I'm a pain sometimes, aren't I?"

Scott looked at her warily and seeing only loving concern in her eyes, he said, "Sometimes it's difficult for me ... frustrating, because I don't have the response you need. If I try to touch you, you push me away, but heaven help me if I lose patience and tell you to pull yourself together. So what I try to do is focus on one time when I was not much more than a kid myself. I was playing rugby at the club and another player kneed me in the goolies. He got me good and I went down in agony. Now if anyone had come to offer to kiss it better, I'd have killed him. Yet if they'd told me to pull myself together, I wouldn't have been too pleased with that either. So what I try to do with you when you are in a snit is pull myself together, find some patience and wait. It's tough, hard to do, but it works. Eventually you come round, and sometimes you even give me the thanks I deserve." He grinned cheekily.

"Really? You think I should thank you? That you deserve something?" Lena replied, pushing him down on the bed and climbing on top of him. "Perhaps I should just beat you up as you lie there." She threw a playful punch at his chin.

"But you won't." Scott laughed up at her.

"No I won't." Lena echoed as she kissed him gently, pushing her hair back out of their faces.

Scott frowned and sighed. Sometimes things were hard for his lady and it was truly painful to deal with. A contented smile spread across his face. "Then again," he thought, "there are times when things are hard for my lady and this is one of those times."

"Life is not always so difficult." He murmured in her ear. "There are times when you're a lucky girl too."

"You betcha." Lena replied, having the last word. Scott reached over and turned off the light.

Four

Let them Eat Grass

Grass and *pee*, who'll
dine with me, Rotten
fruit and veg, leaves
from the hedge,
A good meal we'd make,
before comes *bellyache.*

October, 1967

The light began as faint grey glimmerings on the horizon and the four-year-old lay on her stomach, gazing at the grey line, not quite understanding it. Lena wasn't fond of the dark for her demons were terrifying, but sometimes she woke up and although they remained there lurking in the dark waiting for her should she make a single movement, they never really attacked and slowly her racing heart would be calm again. It was the light that she hated more, for her clearly seen tormentors whose cruelty was equally terrifying as her night terrors, never stopped. Unless she worked very hard, never cried and made her growling stomach still, she could not escape their attention.

She was small for her age, a tiny scrap of a child, with a clear indication of the exotic in her very form, reflecting the heritage of both parents. She closed her eyes tiredly and sleep briefly claimed her.

45

Suddenly with a jerk, she opened her eyes again. It was lighter now, and 'Greylegs' (so called as she always had dusty legs from when she fell over after some abuse or the other) was lying half on her own legs and half off. Ignoring the increasing discomfort, she turned her eyes again to the horizon. The grey line was gone and a grey day was beginning. Hearing footsteps in the corridor, she pushed Greylegs off her, scrambled over the other sleeping and awakening children, jumped out of the bed and scampered to the bathroom. Behind her she could hear others doing the same. None wished to be awakened by the owner of those footsteps!

Crack! Swish! Crack!

"Get up! Get up! And get yourselves dressed!" The nun screamed at those who had not awakened in time to avoid the cruel slashes of the strap.

Lena who until then had been sitting on the toilet straining to listen, now found the urine running freely. *Done*, she quickly put on the white shirt and grey pinafore 'uniform' they all wore at that time and got into the line the others were forming. The nun towered over many of them though not all, as girls of different ages had crowded into the dormitory, the older ones coming over from their 'rooms' to help the younger ones, but often they slapped them too. It was the only way they knew ... the only way they had learned.

"Cailin *Doherty*, you look a disgrace. Straighten up your shirt!" Crack! A startled looking Mairead Sweeney did as she was told. "And you, whatever you're called," the nun continued, "I hope that's not a puddle I see forming below you." Swish! Crack! Swish! Crack! "Go and clean yourself up!"

Greylegs who was actually Cailin *Doherty*, and whose legs were now streaked with the wetness, hurried away as fast as she could, her face twisted in agony and fear. She ran to the basin and in full view of everyone, took off her knickers, wrung them out and put them on again. She had no other, except for the ones that she wore on Sundays and Lena knew that soon she'd be stinking like a latrine. It happened. She watched Greylegs hurry back to the line as the nun began to move in her direction and the march began. They walked out of the building into a very cold morning, which would have been beautiful had their circumstances been different. The sun was beginning to peep over the horizon and sent out a wonderful golden promise for a sunny day, but at this time of the morning it was very cold, and all the children had on were their thin shirts and threadbare pinafores. The nun was of course amply covered.

Soon they were at the Church for morning Mass, and little Lena was on the verge of fainting from hunger, when mercifully it was over and they were marched back to the orphanage. Had she been older, she might have thought about Time being merciful to her, whereas the servants of God who took the title of 'mercy' could not. However, she was just a very small child and she was hungry! Her stomach growled, and she looked up fearfully, but the nun was too far away and didn't hear. It growled again, louder. Terror began to fill her. There it was again. She twisted her fist into her stomach as though that would silence it but it didn't. The thing roared and the nun turned around, her fat face was puffed up round the coif, which seemed much too tight. Her eyes looked like raisins as they scoured the line of girls for the offending creature. Lena's stomach obligingly, but traitorously roared again. It was so loud that the child's whole body seemed to be consumed by it. She stared mesmerised by the approaching nun - a mere rabbit in the headlights facing whatever came. The belt swished. CRACK!

"No!" She screamed and fully awake, she found herself shaking. Looking around, she saw that Scott was still asleep, and her stomach growled again. She slipped out of bed, checked on Maisy, asleep in her room, then still shivering with the power of her dream, walked to the kitchen. She had forgotten a meal before when she was very busy, but in sleep, her hunger had never before transported her back *39* years!

She fried herself some bacon and eggs and was devouring it with some toast and a cuppa when Scott walked in yawning.

"Oh man! That smells good! Some for me?"

"Help yourself. Bacon and eggs in the fridge, bread over there." She pointed with her knife. "Tea in the pot."

Scott sighed good-naturedly and fixed his own. Sitting opposite her, he noticed for the first time that something was amiss.

"Hey!" He reached over and took her hands, "What's the matter?"

"Oh nothing much. Just another dream."

"Want to talk about it?" Scott was walking on eggshells now, for sometimes Lena's dreams caused her to be as unpredictable as a wildcat. Often her horrors were such that she refused to tell him about them, not so much because she didn't trust him, but because she didn't trust herself. This time she just looked at him, tears filling her eyes.

"I was hungry, and she tarred the living daylights out of me."

He didn't have to ask who she was. The horrors of her childhood invaded every part of her life, ambushing her at every turn. He was angry at not being able to fight her demons, but listening helped his girl and he wanted to help all he could. He looked at his as yet untouched plate, and resolutely cut into the bacon, though his hunger was gone. If he threw it out, she would be furious, reminding him of starving children all over the world. As he ate, he said, "Tell me."

"I was always hungry. We all were. After we got up in the morning, we would dress and go to Mass, before returning for 'breakfast'. Sometimes we even got something too - perhaps some watery porridge and a drink of water." She paused, her brow slightly furrowed as she slipped back in time. Her nose reddened, indicating that she was close to tears. Her eyes filled momentarily and she sniffed and blinked a couple of times. Then her eyes cleared and when she spoke, her voice was low.

"More often than not, we would pray before all 'meals' for all the others - the handicapped, underprivileged, for prisoners ... the list was endless and we'd be faint by the time we could eat. There we were - starving, motherless, fatherless, homeless except for what these monsters would provide and we had to pray for those we couldn't help, just as we couldn't help ourselves. When we prayed for ourselves, it was to accept our fate and somehow become better persons for it. I can't imagine how they thought that would happen. They made us compete for scraps from their table, worked us mercilessly so that if the older ones could get someone else to bear some of their load, they did. They abused us in all manner of ways, so that all we knew was to be either the abused or the abuser. Of these options, the more logical would not lead us towards being better people. How could they think that?

Anyway after prayers we would be sent, more often than not, to the dormitory or one of the workrooms for hours on end with no water or food. Lots of us even drank our own urine in desperation."

Scott pushed his plate away and grimaced as he thought what he would do if the right neck was placed in his hands. Lena apparently registering his reaction, but misunderstanding it, continued.

"It sounds disgusting and it is, but you do what you have to do to survive. When they did provide something it was generally peas and lumpy potatoes, and always either too sweet or too salt. Why they put sugar on the peas I'll probably never know. Other times they would lock us up in what was called 'the potato room'. This was where all the vegetables were stored. It was also where the rats and other furry creatures lived. It was dark, damp and cold. We would grab what we could and eat it raw. Because it was so dark, we would be just as likely to grab something rotten or partially eaten by the creatures that lived there and stuff it in our mouths, sometimes swallowing it before the taste hit us. Often we grabbed a rat or some other biting creature by mistake, and to be honest, I don't understand why we didn't all die from some terrible disease." She glanced at Scott who had made a sound of disgust, but he simply looked back at her helplessly.

"I used to find old pieces of bread, stale and hard, and eat them. I'd pick them up off the ground and off windowsills where they were scattered for the birds. They also used to put out bits of dough on the windowsills, again for the birds, and we all used to steal those. Crumbs used to try to cheer us up by saying it was so fresh that it even needed cooking.

We ate out of the pigs' bucket at every opportunity we had. Their food was what the nuns threw away from their own table, which meant that those pigs had the good stuff! Whenever we got to those buckets we feasted like kings alongside the pigs, who were more generous with us than the nuns were. They looked more human than the nuns did too, some of whom had better 'piggy-eyes' than the pigs themselves.

In the nuns' dining room, sometimes they would throw those of us who were serving them, something they didn't want, and I scrambled with the others for their favourite thing sling at us ... the empty half shells of grapefruit and the peel of oranges and other citrus fruit. They were as bitter as hell and my eyes would water eating them but we were just so darned hungry. I remember the nights of stomachache after we had one of those meals.

We were scavengers, pure and simple and it wasn't necessary. None of it was necessary. Even if they wanted to feed us scraps, they could have shared it out equally, not tossed it out to us like the Romans tossed the early Christians to the lions! This was done purely for their own entertainment. They would watch with glee as some of us, more desperately hungry than the others, would begin to fight ... to get the remains of a grapefruit! Then if we got too loud, they'd wallop us. So we learned to fight in silence, digging, biting, gouging at each other. I imagine now the way we must have looked, like human excrement being heaved along by the water newly flushed into a sewer. I've tried and tried to understand, but I can't. What makes a human, any human so inhuman? Isn't a servant of God above inhumanity? Why did they treat us so badly?"

Tears again filled Lena's eyes and Scott moved round to her, kneeling on the hard, tiled floor and holding her close. She held him so tightly that he could hardly breathe, but he accepted that she would slip away from the shore, if he wasn't there to anchor her. After a few moments, her grip lessened and she broke away sniffing. She blew her nose, held him close again and nuzzled his hair before continuing.

"There were times when I would steal food, cooking apples that had gone off, scallions or spring onions as you call them, carrots and so on. Sometimes I would take these from the stores, other times from the nuns' garden and I would hide them under my pillow for a midnight feast. If they hadn't been discovered and stolen from me by one of the others, I would try to eat them silently in the middle of the night so I wouldn't have to share, or lose it all completely." She laughed, and looked at him. "You try eating raw vegetables quietly in the dead of night."

That brief moment of levity passed and she murmured, "We even ate grass, which we would pretend was some type of lettuce. We took choice leaves from the hedges and the few plants we had. Sometimes it tasted pretty good too." She smiled weakly. He looked pale, his eyes bleak. His jaw clenched and unclenched. He was seeing the child who became the mother of his Maisy. He was seeing his Maisy who looked like her mother. He gently detached himself from her, got up and went back to his chair, the jaw still clenching and unclenching.

"There was so very little food for us kids. Have you ever been so hungry that your stomach hurts enough to make you want to pull your hair out to eat it? So hungry that everything looks like it could be food. Everything you could pick up you wanted to put in your mouth to see if it could be eaten. A wet rock looked like a good drink. This kind of hunger was an everyday event for us. When I think back now, I thought that was how everybody lived. Sometimes when I was outside the house, I would simply faint and would be picked up by one of the nuns and taken away. If I was inside, I might be kicked a time or two, judging for the bruises I always collected during these times, before being put to bed.

Do you remember my friend Ann who I went to visit in Galway in 2002?"

Scott nodded, clearly remembering the attractive mixed race woman who was one of Lena's co-'orphans' at the Industrial School. She had a beautiful voice and was trying to make her way as a musician.

"It seems crazy but she told me that she used to be so jealous because I was always being picked up off the ground after fainting. That's how desperate we all were for the human touch.

Sometimes Sr. Clare used to make us clean the older nuns' bedrooms and cubicles. There would be fruit bowls full to the top in these rooms. My mouth would be watering so much that I would drool saliva but I did not steal any of it.

The fear of being beaten was too strong."

"Pity you didn't have some senna to inject into their grapefruit and oranges." Scott said sourly.

Lena laughed. "We didn't have anything like that. In those early days we wouldn't even have known what that was, but later we did try something and got a right hiding for it too. We had to make a chocolate cake one day for their pudding.

One of the older girls got hold of some Brooklax. *Do* you remember it? I haven't seen it for years but it looked like a bar of chocolate."

"Yeah! I do. I think my old Gran used to have some to keep her regular!"

"Well we put that in the chocolate cake to make it extra rich. Anyway, the nuns spent the next day or so producing enough material to fertilise their entire garden."

"So they made riches for the garden eh?" Scott grinned at her and was rewarded when she laughed.

"When they recovered, we got a hell of a hiding. They knew it was us as we made the cake, and they knew it was the cake because only the nuns that ate it had the squits. It was the best of times. It was the worst of times."

"Who the *Dickens* said that?" Scott asked and Lena threw the cushion she was sitting on, at him. He caught it and threw it back.

"Pet, I've always wondered but had a vague idea. Is that why you buy so much whenever you go to the supermarket? Every woman I know buys clothes, jewellery and that kind of thing but you ... well, sometimes I can't get past all the tins and packets in the cupboards. Even the cupboards in the garage are full. We'll never eat it all you know, before we're past the 'use by dates', I mean, and you'll never be hungry again. Neither will our Maisy. I promise you.

She looked at him, uncertainty hitting her like a slap in the face. She got up and began to clear away the table, dumping the remaining scraps of their meal and stacking the dishes in the dishwasher. Scott remained seated, watching her carefully. Finished, she wiped the table clean and fussed around tidying. Finally she said, "Use by dates, huh?"

"Use by dates." He replied quietly.

"Well I suppose I'm not going to spend a lot of money stocking up if it's going to be rotten before we could get to it. I've eaten enough rotten stuff to last several lifetimes. How much tinned and packaged stuff do you think we have?"

"I reckon enough to last us between four and six years." "Hmmm. Well we'd better have a party then. Use it all up.

What is the average life time of the tins?" "Dunno, maybe a couple of years?"

"Couple of years. Is it okay if I buy enough to last us a couple of years?"

"Lena!" He laughed, then shrugged. "I guess two years is better than four ... or six." She was trying to meet him halfway. He would meet her halfway, and anyway, it was good to have something in stock.

"I just remembered something we used to sing for weeks after the chocolate cake episode."

"Go on then;" Scott said stifling a yawn and trying to ignore the kitchen clock which read 03:47.

Lena began to sing, slowly to the tune, For he's a jolly good fellow, carefully at first then with more confidence as the words came rushing back.

The bear went over the mountain
The bear went over the mountain
The bear went over the mo-un-tain
And what do you think he saw?

He saw a tin of Brooklax
He saw a tin of Brooklax
He saw a tin of Bro-ok-lax
And what do you think he did?

He ate *up* all of the Brooklax
He ate *up* all of the Brooklax
He ate *up* all of the Bro-ok-lax
And what do you think he did?

He made another mountain
He made another mountain
He made another mo-un-tain
And that's the end of that
Laughing like two small children, they waltzed into the bedroom humming to the catchy tune.

Five

Wash-A-Bye Baby,
Bloomers and All

The woman sat beside the sleeping child gazing at her with rapt attention. The baby girl had slept badly the night before, her cold making her restless. This morning Lena had taken her to see the doctor and now, having had some syrupy medicine, she was sleeping peacefully, though a little noisily as her cold rattled through her tiny body. The mother looked up startled when the chimes at the door sounded.

She glanced at her watch, which showed 14:30, and realised that she had forgotten Becky was coming over for coffee. Hurrying downstairs, she opened the door to see her new friend smiling at her.

"Becky! Come in!"

"Greetings! I bring you a small token of incipient heart attack." Becky held up a largish package. Her face was grave but there was no mistaking the laughter in her eyes.

Lena took the parcel and the two women walked into the kitchen where she peeked into the package. "Ohh! Cream cakes! You are naughty!"

"But nice." Came the rejoinder, and they laughed remembering the ad for cream cakes.

"I'm glad you did bring something as I had completely forgotten you were coming today." She looked worriedly at the pile of clothing on the kitchen floor in front of the washing machine.

"A problem?"

"Maisy has the flu, poor little mite. I took her to the doctor this morning and she's finally asleep now." She glanced around the kitchen as she filled the percolator with water.

"I'm sorry I'm in such a mess, but yesterday I thought I would have had my washing completed long before now."

"It's not a problem. Your baby's health has priority over all else. I'll help." With that, she got mugs and plates out and generally bustled about preparing coffee while Lena hurriedly filled the washing machine.

A few minutes later, the washing cycle had begun and Becky was pouring out the fragrant coffee. As the women sat to enjoy their coffee and cake, Becky was clearly surprised to see Lena shift her chair, so that instead of the two women facing each other, they were both looking in the washing machine's direction. She smiled, probably remembering how she too found the clothes going round and round to be rather hypnotic ... soothing ... and it seemed that Lena was indeed losing herself in the magic of the machine.

After a brief pause Becky stared harder at Lena, realising that she was drifting away.

"What do you see?" She asked quietly. Lena stirred, then settled again.

"A room. It's large. The interior walls are dirty white and red brick. Huge pipes run in front of the walls and under the ceiling. These carry hot water and always the steam came off of them. Often hot water actually dripped from them." She faltered to a stop, her eyes blinking rapidly.

"Tell me more about the room. What is it? What was it like?"

"Hot! Always very, very hot! It's a laundry. We did all the washing, ironing, and folding of clothes in there."

"Whose clothes? Yours?"

"Everybody's. The priests'- including the vestments for the Church, the nuns' clothing, sheets and other bedclothes like blankets, towels, underwear, handkerchiefs, table cloths, and so on. We also washed what the towns-people sent. This included trousers, dresses, shirts, blouses, winter coats, jackets, etc. We washed our own stuff too."

"Ah yes. I recall that you told me the towns-people paid to have their clothes washed ..."

"Yes. Of course. The nuns weren't at all charitable. They undercut the local laundries, so there was always plenty of washing to do."

"... and that you got paid nothing. Surely they gave you some little treat or other."

Lena broke contact with the washing machine and looked at Becky. "Are you joking? They couldn't find it in their hearts to give us half-way decent food. You think they'd give us anything?"

"From what I've heard so far, I think not, but always I hope that something positive will come out about these nuns. They are so unlike those of my own childhood."

"They weren't the most evil creatures in the world, I'll grant you, but except for this one nun who was the best and would sneak you a hug when no-one was looking, they were never there for us."

"So what did they do with the money?"

"They passed everything on to the Church I suppose, via the priests. I found out later that they never kept many records, not of us children, not of how they ran the institution, not of what income they received other than from the State ... nothing. And they worked us like dogs."

"And when you began to do this laundry work you were..."

"Six. I remember how proud I was to be going to work there because it meant that I was a 'big girl'. I had no idea what awaited me. The heat was unbearable. I remember taking the mickey out of the nuns' bloomers. Each one had their names on labels sewed on the garments and some were so large, and I suppose we, as half starved children were so small, that four of us would get into a pair of them, two in each leg. We did once attempt three in each, but one leg began to rip and terrified of the consequences, we abandoned that attempt ... It was hard grafting in that heat, and dehydration was a common thing."

May 18th, 1970

Lena walked eagerly alongside the other girls as she made her way to the laundry. At the age of six she stood at 3'7" tall and was very underweight for her height, but she walked with an energy that belied her frail form. The day before yesterday, Saturday, was her birthday, though she hadn't known it. All she knew was that she was now a 'big girl' and that you had to be six to be a big girl. She felt a sense of pride at this achievement, and thought to herself.

"It doesn't even matter that smelly Mary is going to be in the laundry too. There'll be too many others around for her to try anything stinky."

The laundry was in a separate grey and cream building within the industrial school complex. It was the same colour used for all the fronts of the buildings, though the backs, which were not seen by passers-by, were a dirty, dark grey. She walked through the door of the laundry and stopped suddenly as the heat first hit then engulfed her. A couple of the girls crashed into her and she was pushed roughly forward with the words, "Get a move on, Titch."

Within seconds, she could feel the sweat running down her back. The noise was tremendous as machines rumbled in the room. Pipes, which seemed to run everywhere overhead hissed, shaking and knocking alarmingly. Her first thought was that the place was on fire as she could hardly see through the 'smoke' and although she had been pushed into the room and the other girls showed no fear, she peered into the murk to find the red glow that would signify fire. Instead a large girl emerged from it.

"What do ya think youse doing standing there? Get to work."

"B-but there's a fire!" Lena stammered.

Bridie Gallagher began to laugh. "Yer first day, ainit?" Lena nodded nervously at the older girl.

"S'not smoke. It's steam. Comes from the pipes, see? Them pipes is hot. Ya mustn't stand under them or hot water will fall on yer bonce, you hear?"

"What's my bonce?" The child asked nervously.

"Yer head." Bridie explained obligingly. "Now youse'll start on the table over there 'cos the machines are full. I know. I just filled 'em. Come 'ere."

Lena followed her into the steamy atmosphere and was surprised to see that it was clearer at the back of the room, even though it was unbearably hot. She looked back and saw the steam like a moving curtain behind her.

"Here's where youse'll start." Bridie said.

Lena looked at the high table with interest. It was the strangest one she had ever seen. It was almost as tall as she was, had a wooden section, which was about three feet wide and it ended with a huge round roller, which ran along its entire width.

"This here is an ironing table. That round thing there is what presses the clothes. Like everything else in here it gets hot, so be careful. Now youse stands here … hmmm." She paused as she looked at the small girl whose chin hovered just above the table. "Youse'll have to lie on here." She pointed to the table and lifted the child onto it. Next time use the chair over there to climb onto the table. Lena obediently looked over to where she pointed.

The girl walked off leaving Lena staring at the roller which was so hot that the child found herself pushing back away from it, too afraid to get off of the table. Bridie seemed friendly and helpful, but if she got off the table, she might get belted, but then again, the roller was so hot!

The girl returned with some pillowcases. "Here I'll show youse what youse hafta do."

She lay one of the pillowcases flat and smooth in front of Lena and pushed the edge into the bottom end of the roller. She then walked round to the other side of the table and began to turn a huge spoked wheel. To Lena's delight, the pillow case disappeared into the machine and came out the other side beautifully ironed, Bridie folded it and put in on a stack of other clothing that had clearly gone through the same process. "Alright, do the next one … and be careful not to touch the roller or youse'll get a nasty burn!"

Lena took a pillowcase from the pile beside her and lay it flat as she was told. Bridie turned the wheel but nothing happened.

"Ya hafta put it under the roller so it will pull it through." Bridie instructed.

After a couple more attempts, Lena managed to get the pillowcase through the roller without burning herself. She looked at it proudly as Bridie held it up, and was dismayed to see the look of disapproval on the older girl's face. "It's got too many creases. Youse'll have to do this one again or we'll get a larruping. Now I've helped you enough. Got my own things to do. When youse done with these, come and get me to check them, and if they're good enough, I'll give ya another pile." Bridie smiled as she walked away.

Lena took another pillowcase, made it smooth, poked it as best she could under the machine, then she realised that she would have to get off the table to turn the wheel on the other side. She wriggled backwards until she could drop the last foot or so off the table, ran round to the wheel, but couldn't reach it properly to turn it. She went over to the chair, staggered with it back to the wheel, climbed up and found she couldn't turn it even then. It had looked so easy when Bridie did it! Knowing what problems awaited her if she didn't work well, she pushed and struggled until she got the wheel turned and the pillowcase slid out from under the roller, onto the floor. Her heart in her mouth, she jumped off the chair, picked up the pillowcase and was horrified to see that it was dirty. Bridie who had clearly been watching her came over and took the offending article. She looked at it, sighed and tossed it onto a pile of dirty laundry. She turned her eyes on the child and Lena suddenly found grey-blue eyes staring into her brown ones and she shivered in fear.

Seeming to notice, Bridie touched her arm briefly and said, "Youse sure youse six? Ya hafta be six to work in here. Youse look like four."

"I'm six, so I am." Lena replied. "Howja know?"

"Sister Clare said so."

"Well she'd ought ta know. But youse too small for this work." Bridie asserted as she looked around. "Alright. Come here. This machine is nearly done. When it stops, open the door, and put all the stuff in these baskets. Somebody will take them away when they's full."

She pushed Lena towards the machines. The brief gentle touch on her shoulder caused Lena to look up, quick tears spring into her eyes before darting away again.

"Why are you nice?" She asked.

Bridie paused for a moment, then looked down at her. "I remember." She said.

"What? What do you remember?"

"They came and took me and me sisters and brothers away from me mam."

"Who's they?"

"A man come. He said he was some kind of inspector but I think he was from the polis or something." "Why didn't your da stop them?"

"Me da's dead. Me mam had a new man but Father O'Connell didn't like it ... so he sicced the polis on her and we wuz took away."

"And that makes you nice?"

"I was nine when they took us away. Me sisters were ten and five. Me brothers twelve, eleven and seven. I thought we'd all be together, but I come here and I don't know where they send the others. I like to think somebody is watching out for my sisters and brothers, especially the baby. She'd be nine now herself. Here. The machine stopped." She showed Lena how the door opened, flashed her a quick smile and was away again.

The child smiled back and set herself to her task, lifting the heavy cassocks out of the machine and quickly filling the plastic containers. As soon as one was filled, someone dragged it away. She worked for what seemed like a long time filling and emptying the machines and after a while, she felt weak and realised that she had a raging thirst. She looked around to see if there was a jug of water or a cup but there was nothing. She caught sight of a row of sinks along a wall and was making her way there when Maeve Quigley stopped her.

"You on holiday?" The grip on her shoulder was firm and Lena sensed the cruelty that could be unleashed on her. "Please, can I have a drink of water? I feel busted bad." "You can drink later. I have a job for you. See these doors?"

Lena looked at what she thought were skinny cupboard doors. They were the size of the lockers she'd seen when she had visited the community school with Bryan and Clare. As she stared, Maeve pulled open a door and to Lena's amazement the room got even hotter. The 'cupboards' were a huge dryer. The long narrow oven doors pulled out like stacks in a library. When the doors were out the oven, Lena could see transverse rods upon which clothes had been hung to dry.

"These are the drying ovens." Maeve continued. "Take the dry clothes out, fold them and put them on the batch over there for ironing. When it is empty, take the wet stuff from the basket there and hang them on the rails."

Nodding quickly, Lena found her chair and dragged it over to the oven. Even so, she couldn't reach the topmost rail.

She tugged at the heavy sheet hanging there and it fell away on top of her, engulfing her. Hands helped extricate her and Bridie called over three other girls to help. She watched the four youngsters fold the large sheet, before moving away. The girls made quicker work removing and folding the laundry, but even so Lena found herself getting light-headed. She didn't realise it, having no watch, but she had been working in the steaming laundry for almost three hours without a drink, and her meagre lunch was a long time past. She took the white cassock one of the girls handed up to her and tiptoeing on the chair tried to hang it on the highest rail she could reach. She heard herself cry out, but that was all. She never realised that Bridie, still keeping an eye on her small charges, saw her sway and as the child began to fall into the oven rails, she dashed over and grabbed her as she fainted.

Bridie was worried as she fanned the little girl. She had laid her down in a corner of the room near the door where it was cooler and had used one of the nuns' wet handkerchiefs to cool her arm. It had briefly made contact with the oven door as she fell, and although the skin had blistered, it hadn't broken. It wasn't serious. Certainly Bridie had seen worse, some of which she'd collected herself, and they all fainted when they came down here so small. Even bigger ones tended to faint on the first day. Still, she worried about her, for there was a vulnerability about her that she should have lost a long time ago. She remembered seeing her as a toddler when she herself arrived in this hell.

"Aw. Leave her be. You baby them too much. She'll toughen up. All this one needs is a drink and she can get herself one when she wakes up." Maeve pulled Bridie's arm roughly and the girl pulled it away. She was as tall as Maeve and could hold her own against her even though she was the younger by a couple of years. Maeve took the hint and stood back, but she watched until Bridie left the child and went back to work.

Lena wondered why her bed was so hard and unyielding as she opened her eyes. She looked around with surprise at the small girl lying asleep against the wall beside her. Her face was beet red and she had water running down it. At the sight of the sweat, Lena licked her lips realising how dry her mouth felt. Then she remembered that she was in the laundry and was trying to get a heavy, white priest's dress onto the rail in the oven. She sat up slowly and saw that other girls were still working. Too weak to stand, she sat for a moment quietly observing them and saw a girl they called SlobyMoby behaving rather oddly. Instead of walking directly from one place to another, she seemed to be taking the long way round all the machines, hugging the walls opposite to the big washing machine in particular. She then noticed Bridie at the sink with her sleeves rolled up. Almost as though Bridie felt her eyes on her, she looked around and seeing that Lena was 'awake', she smiled. She turned away and when she turned back, Lena saw that she had a cup that she was bringing to her. Lena took the water gratefully, and gulped it down.

"More?" Bridie asked and at the child's nod she went to get her another cupful. "Drink more slowly." Bridie instructed her.

After Lena had finished the second cup, she noticed Sloby Moby again. Sloby whose real name Lena didn't know, was in everyone's opinion, so slow and stupid at doing anything that they gave her the nickname.

"What is Sloby doing?" Lena asked.

Bridie looked round at Sloby then back at Lena. "Don't call her Sloby. Her name is Maureen," she said.

"Why not?" Lena asked.

"How would youse feel if everyone called youse Lazy Lena 'cos youse lying here doing nowt?"

"That wouldn't be fair 'cos I was feeling bad. I couldn't help it."

"And she can't help being what she is either. So don't youse be calling her names if youse don't want to be called names."

"Okay ... but why does she walk around so funny? She's always like a scaredy cat and she's bigger than me."

"She's eight or so I think, 'cos she came down here a couple of years ago. There was another girl here. I won't say her name ... she was maybe fifteen or sixteen at the time. Anyway Maureen couldn't get the hang of working the washing machine. It was only her first day and like most of us when we first come down here, had never seen machines like these before. That brute of a girl forced Maureen into the big washer there and switched it on. I remember her saying that she was so slow maybe a good wash and spin would make her think quicker. Maureen was howling like a banshee, and one of the girls who was standing outside run in and said that a nun was coming. They hauled her out the machine quick smart and by the time the nun got here, Maureen was in a corner crying and falling about, and everyone was working like nothing happened. The nun asked her why she was crying, but Maureen knew full well what that brute that put her in the washer would do if she spoke, so she said nowt. She collected a battering from the nun instead. After that a couple of us would watch out for her, help her like, and luckily for us, the brute of a girl got preggers and was sent somewhere else like a week or so after that. Since then, Maureen is scared of the machines and I know it's hell for her to come in here. But she does it and that tells me something good about her. You'll have to fight, like her, fight the demons that make you scared."

"I can't fight the nuns. They'll beat me something terrible … and what's preggers? Can I get some? And if I get some, will they send me somewhere else too?"

Bridie laughed. "You don't want some of that neither. Not yet anyway. As for going somewhere else, I've heard there's places worse than this."

"Worse! I don't believe that. There couldn't be." Lena said boldly.

Bridie laughed again. "And surely youse right, but no matter how bad this is, it's home. It's what we've got and it's better than some other places."

"… and as we've since learnt, there were worse places." "Many of us were lucky not to have attracted the priests'

attention for there were those who abused many more, including some of the boys. Some of them used to get their kicks beating up the boys, when they weren't forcing them to entertain them in their bedrooms or wherever. They were thugs pure and simple." Lena sighed and got up to put the load of washing in the tumble dryer and the second load in the wash. Becky made a fresh pot of coffee. Seated again, Lena said, "I am always amazed at how similar doing laundry work is, except that now it is quieter, a lot cooler and generally far more comfortable to do. Here I just stuff the clothes in the machine. Badly stained clothes get extra soap over the stain but generally it's just a bit of powder and off we go.

In the convent laundry, we used to hand wash some items in the sinks. There were these big scrubbing brushes we used to get stubborn stains out, and blocks of soap that we rubbed on the clothes. There was even an old, ribbed board we sometimes used to literally scrub a particular item of clothing on. We smaller ones spent much of our time scrambling on and off chairs we dragged behind us, so we'd be tall enough to reach the work surfaces. Occasionally there would even be a fight as there were never enough chairs around. The nuns didn't want us resting too much and the laundry room was too hot for them to spend time in, so it was the older girls who supervised us. The nuns would inspect the clean laundry later. If they found any stains or other blemishes, or if the ironing wasn't perfect, we'd be punished. If anything had gotten ripped in the wash and hadn't been repaired so they didn't really notice it, we got punished. There were so many things they looked for. It wasn't just the washing and ironing ... before we put anything into the machine, we had to check the material for possible weaknesses and repair it before we washed it and made it worse. So we had all these smelly, dirty clothes to inspect and mend ... the underwear was the worst! And we did this for every wash, whether from the Church, the convent, the townspeople or our things.

We got 'new' stuff only once a year, and we only had the two sets, for everyday and for best. As you can imagine, the everyday stuff was often tattered by year-end. Our clothes were generally sent to us by outsiders and often they had been worn for years before we got them. We were always having to explain why our dresses were torn, and we were knocked about no matter how good the reason we gave, that is, those of us who were smaller. The bigger girls weren't beaten. I think the nuns were scared of them, but they also cultivated them to keep an eye on us. They even seemed to like some of them ... On reflection, I think that although the 'uniforms' we used to have marked us as different, at least they were comparatively new to start with and could be let out or taken in as they passed from one child to another. When we got 'normal' clothes, most were donated, mostly after several children had worn them.

When I got used to laundry work, I worked on all the machines, even one that is similar to a modern trouser press. This machine was as tall as I was when I first started using it and I was always running from here to there with a folding chair. Sometimes the chair would collapse when I was running with it and I'd get my fingers trapped in it. Other times it would fall over when I standing was on it. I got burnt so many times at the 'trouser press', the 'table press' and the drying ovens that I soon learned to shrug them off. When we weren't getting burnt by hot equipment, hot water dripping on us, or hot steam, we got chemical burns. We often had to bleach the whites so they stayed white and you had to get the mix right. Too much bleach, they turned a funny yellowish colour and you got a hiding. Too little bleach, and the clothes weren't white enough, so you got a hiding. And when you were working with these washes, your eye had better not itch. I remember the first time I rubbed my eye and started yelling. I was lucky that Bridie was there. She literally shoved my head under the tap and washed the stuff out my eyes. I was trying to squeeze them shut tight, she was trying to prise them open. Eventually the stinging settled down, but it was days before I could see right."

"Have you ever been back?"

"Yes. I have. I was hot on the trail of my past and in September 2002, Scott and I visited Ireland and the convent, which was by now converted to luxury flats. I think the premises were sold to private builders. To my amazement, although the industrial school was shut down in 1983, the laundry was still there and full of equipment. A large, old washing machine was still here. So too were the ironing table and the trouser press, which was outside the door.

There was so much stuff. We made a video. Would you like to see it?"

"Yes. I would." Becky answered enthusiastically.

In the primrose yellow lounge, Lena busied herself with her DVD collection. Becky sank onto a soft leather couch and made herself comfortable. Lena soon joined her, the remote control in her hand. The television snapped on, and the laundry came into view. In addition to the equipment Lena mentioned, there were racks of various sizes lying around on the floor like discarded children's toys. A couple of fold-up metal chairs rusted in the middle of the room. Over by the wall were the sinks she'd spoken of, the windowsill still holding scrubbing brushes and blocks of soap. Beside the sinks was a stained glass window with an alcove in which had once stood a religious statue. On the video, Lena picked up a scrap of discarded linen, which she folded and put in her bag, explaining to Scott who operated the camera that she wanted a souvenir. Out in the garden stood the discarded piece of equipment, which looked like a huge trouser press. Judging from the now 5'4" tall woman, standing beside it, it was as tall as the average, healthy six year old today. Another part of the laundry consisted of a room so dark that it looked like a coal shed. On the film Lena was saying, "This is the generator room, which provided the power to the laundry."

The film cut away suddenly, and Lena was hugging a large stone out in the middle of nowhere. "I used to come out here and hug this rock. I used to pretend it hugged me back. It was my mother ... my father ... someone who loved me. It kept me sane. There was no-one else to hug." She said wistfully, her long hair whipping around her face, flying free in the wind, as she never had.

Six

Wee Willie Winkie

Loughrea, Co. Galway, Summer, 1967

The man walked into the room where the two small girls lay in bed and said cheerfully, "Wakey, wakey! You're not asleep yet are you?" He spoke with the soft melodic tones of a Northern Irishman.

Crumbs O'Connor sat up in her bed and looked at him expectantly. She was about six or seven years old and she smiled at his appearance. The nuns' had sent her and her younger friend Lena to this family at Loughrea for their holidays. They had been with them for only one day and the father in particular made sure that they were comfortable, had lots to eat and he bought them presents, interesting things they had never eaten before. He'd said that he knew that kids like them were always hungry. She didn't know how he knew and didn't ask for he had given both some taffy and Crumbs had been busily trying to 'unstick' her teeth. She looked over at the other bed in the room and saw that Lena was beginning to sit up too, a broad smile on her face. In addition to the food and sweets, which were a great treat for them, they had beds ... one for each of them! They would often sleep in one of the beds together, as this was what they were used to and it felt more comfortable, but tonight they were relishing having a bed to themselves.

Although the furniture was old and pretty basic, the two girls had never had such luxury before. Lena was in the bed on the right near the window and Crumbs' bed was across the room at right angles to hers, so that as they lay in their beds, they could clearly see each other. In addition to the two beds, there were bedside tables, one each, a small wardrobe and a dressing table. Crumbs looked again at the man, and at the plates in his hand.

Michael Finney danced cheerfully from one foot to the other, balancing the plates as he whistled, and making the smiles on the children's welcoming faces grow wider. A bespectacled, well-respected man in the community as befitting the head teacher of the local Catholic School, he was a wiry looking individual whose thinning, curly hair lay shiningly flat against his narrow head. Despite his position, and the fact that he was well into middle age (at fifty-four years old), he was a 'young' sort and dressed as was the fashion. In the summer months, he generally wore just jeans and T-shirts to work, unlike the other men of his stature in the area who sweltered in their suits, and at home he liked to wear baggy shorts.

He walked over to young Crumbs and offered her a small plate with some bread and jam on it. She briefly looked at the other plate in his hand which also contained bread, but the spread on it was not the red of her raspberry jam ... it looked more like blood. She smiled to herself. Lena had asked for tomato ketchup on her bread, the silly baby. She had never had tomato ketchup before today, and had fallen in love with the taste. Of course she, Crumbs, had been out with other families before, and knew quite well that ketchup went on chips, and very good it was there too, but on bread? Well, she supposed that Mr. Finney will give them chips tomorrow or sometime during the holiday so the baby could learn what ketchup's for.

She bit into her bread gratefully, and watched as the man walked over to Lena's bed with her bread. To her astonishment, instead of giving Lena the plate, he put it on the bedside table and sat on the bed beside the little girl, who was craning her neck round him to see the tomato ketchup bread.

Crumbs was a pale, but sturdy child who recently had her dark blonde hair cut short. She was a bit of a tomboy and looked it, even though the eyelashes, which protected her grey-blue eyes were almost as long as a camel's. She was completely opposite to Lena who had her dark brown hair cut in a neat shoulder length bob and who tanned easily. Lena was pretty too, much prettier than Crumbs believed she herself would ever be.

As soon as they had arrived, she'd noticed that Mr. Finney was taken by Lena. He'd picked her up and put her on his shoulders and generally fussed over the smaller girl, as he hadn't over Crumbs. She was a little downhearted by this memory, but not too much. First she had a plate-ful of bread and jam to see off and second, she knew that the younger children always got more attention than the older ones. It was so with her too and now that she was becoming a 'big girl', she mustn't be a baby. But sometimes she wished she wasn't becoming a 'big girl' so fast as the nuns never hugged her and she only started getting hugs from adults when she began her 'holidays' about a year ago.

Lena was downhearted too. She didn't know what she had done wrong but it looked like she was not going to get her tomato ketchup bread, and just the sight of it made her so hungry! As she struggled to see round the man who brought it to the room, he laughed and said, "You're hungry! Aren't you? *Didn't we feed you enough at dinnertime?*"

Lena felt a little ashamed of herself. She had indeed been well fed, better than anything that she got 'at home'. True the meat was a bit hard to chew but it was the first time she had eaten it and she reckoned that she would get the hang of it, as it tasted good. The potatoes were good too. She didn't have a big thirst after, and instead of being full of water like she often was at the orphanage when she could get to the tap, she was full of food. She wasn't even very hungry when she thought about it. She just wanted to eat and eat as the tomato stuff tasted so good!

"*Don't you worry, girlie girl. You'll get your bread, but first you have to give me a big hug!*"

Lena was amazed. A hug! From her! And she would get the tomato ketchup bread? Wow! She threw her arms round the laughing man and hugged him as tightly as she could. She was even more amazed when he hugged her back, pulled her from under the sheets and sat her in his lap. Then came a further surprise. He had some hard, yet not too hard lump (for it didn't hurt her) in his trousers, and he jigged her up and down on it for a while as he sang what she recognised as an Irish jig. They had to learn them at school with Sr. Concepta. She joined in and bounced around even harder on his lap, sometimes feeling his lump by her arse sometimes by her gee. He laughed out loud, clearly delighted by her enthusiasm and they jigged around in this fashion for some time, Lena even temporarily forgetting her treat. After a brief period of time when the jigging about was so frantic, that the by now slightly scared Lena knew she would have fallen off his lap had he not held her across her legs so firmly, he made a funny sound and was still. Almost immediately Lena noticed that the lump in his trousers was no longer there and was puzzled, but she didn't stop to wonder about it when he said, "You're a good girl. Now eat your bread and go to sleep." He kissed her on the cheek, slid her back in her bed, and handed her plate of food to her.

"Will you play the jigger with Crumbs now?" Lena asked, noticing her friend staring at them and realising that the older girl was close to tears because nobody was playing with her.

Michael Finney smiled at her and looked briefly over at Crumbs. At that moment, Lena stole a quick look to see if his lump had come back and saw instead a wet patch on his jeans. That she understood, as she had seen small boys who wanted to pee but were not near the toilet and their 'long thing' often stood up like it was saying, 'Hurry! Let's go' to it's owner. Then after he peed, it was back to normal. Maybe next time Mr. Finney will pee before he came to play jiggers with her.

Michael Finney walked over to Crumbs, took her empty plate, patted her on the head and said, "Go to sleep now. There's a good wee lassie." Then he walked out of the room.

Mr. Finney's home was like most other houses Lena had seen in her short life, except that it had two levels. Downstairs was the living room, a dining room and a kitchen. Three bedrooms and a bathroom were upstairs. It was about a half mile away from the school where he taught and was a typical white-painted, slate-roofed Irish house. It had a large garden and was surrounded by fields, which were often occupied by the huge black and white cows from the neighbouring farm. When Lena first heard them lowing, she was scared out of her wits, but the more 'worldly' Crumbs laughed at her and told her that 'they were only cows' and not to 'be such a baby'. So Lena learned not to be afraid, and would watch the animals avidly as they lumbered across the fields back to the farm at milking times.

Although it rained a lot, there were days when the sun would come out and huge white fluffy clouds would hang around waiting for something to happen. Lena loved these days, as it meant that she could get out into the garden, which she thought was beautiful as it had lots of flowers.

The girls often found themselves alone with Mrs. Finney during the day, and she was a hard taskmaster. The flower beds outside needed to be tended, jobs inside the house had to be done, but hard as it was, it still seemed a holiday to the two youngsters and they generally thought life was good.

Often when they were having a break in the kitchen and perhaps a drink of lemonade or some such, they sat at the table with Mrs. Finney who would look at them with her mouth turned down. Occasionally she muttered something about 'perverts and wee colleens' but although they figured that they were the 'wee colleens', neither girl knew what 'pervert' meant and really didn't care. The woman didn't beat them and her turned down mouth didn't hurt so that was okay.

Lena never looked much at her anyway as she sensed the woman didn't like her or Crumbs much. Why on earth she allowed children to come to her house was a mystery. She clearly didn't like Mr. Finney spending so much time with them, but Mr. Finney would stare at his wife in a funny way, and she would just leave the room. Lena's eyes roved beyond the kitchen sink, out the window to linger on the pretty flowers, which always seemed to her to be in bloom. She wondered when Mr. Finney was coming home.

Both children often couldn't wait for him to come back from wherever he was, as he always brought some treat, crisps, chocolates, boiled sweets, even chewing gum which Lena swallowed the first time she had some and Crumbs laughed her head off. Even so Crumbs was a little less enthusiastic about Mr. Finney than Lena, but Lena just knew that it was because Mr. Finney played the 'jigger's' game only with her. He didn't seem to want to play with Crumbs at all. Lena didn't mind. It was the first time she had so much individual attention, and she basked in it.

Bryan and Gaby who lived near the convent and who she saw sometimes, loved her but didn't see her for such long periods and she never got to sleep over with them so she hadn't known before that bedtime could be so much fun. She did wonder about Mr. Finney never going to the toilet to get rid of his lump before playing with her, but it never mattered. She straddled him as he'd instructed and had more than once thought she might hurt him, but he whispered to her that she must jig and jump as hard as she could, so she did! It became her goal to bash that lump exactly as he wished, to see if she would make him wet himself again, and to get her treats. She had once suggested bashing it with a piece of wood or with a big stone, but Mr. Finney didn't like that idea at all. He wanted her to sit and jig, so she sat and jigged.

The next week she learned the Malteasers game. This was an easy game for Lena, made better by the prize of a Malteaser every time she correctly identified Mr. Finney's various body parts, starting with his eye and ending with his 'long thing', though he would jump around so she had to find his knees, toes, and thighs before she got to the 'thing'. Lena noted that it was longer than any she had seen before, fatter than any she had seen before and almost always hard. She came to understand that playing with it made it 'stand up', for sometimes when Mr. Finney showed it to her, it was just hanging there.

He would make her take it in her hands and play with it, kiss it or even pretend it was a lollipop. Sometimes Mr. Finney put a sliver of chocolate under the skin (which to Lena's amazement he could roll back in a way she had never seen before), and she would have to find it, doing exactly as she was instructed. She became proficient at taking the long thing in her mouth, probing for the chocolate with her tongue, while Mr. Finney tried to stop her finding it by firmly holding her head so she couldn't move it around, while he jiggled in and out her firmly closed mouth. He jiggled so much that she gagged and almost threw up, and he became angry.

His fierce blue eyes bored into hers like gimlets, and he instructed her again exactly what she must do. Fearful that she might be made to go hungry, that she would no longer have treats and that she might lose her new 'daddy' to Crumbs who watched them with narrowed eyes every time Mr. Finney was busy with Lena, she did her best. It took a while, but finally one morning, she did things to Mr. Finney's satisfaction, for he pulled himself out of her mouth and to her great surprise, spilled milk from his long thing all over her face and hands. He told her she was a little witch who made magic with him and turned his golden pee, white, and he rewarded her with a tube of smarties and a packet of opal fruits.

Even so, Lena was never very good at this game for she threw up more often than not, which annoyed Mr. Finney a lot, but it wasn't until the day she involuntarily closed her teeth on Mr. Finney's long thing, that he stopped putting it in her mouth and began putting it elsewhere.

When Mr. Finney was not at home, sometimes the children would play in the garden and they tried to guess what the names of the flowers were.

"Mrs Finney said that one is a pansy," Crumbs said pointing, "and that one's a nennomoney."

"A nenno money? That don't look like no money to me." Lena replied.

"Not money silly ... a nennomoney. It's a flower."

"I can see that it's a flower stupid, and I'm not so silly that I think it's money - nenno or no!" With that Lena flounced away to the fence to gaze in the distance at a big black cow, which looked like it wanted to jump over a black and white one. Some men stood by near the milking shed watching.

"Crumbs" She said, "Come 'ere." Crumbs went over and the girls stared.

"Bettcha that black cow will never jump over the black and white one, especially if the black and white one keeps running away."

Crumbs stared hard as the animals turned and she could see them side on. Quick as a flash, she understood something of what was happening and she glanced at the smaller girl. Lena's eyes were open wide, as was her mouth.

"Is that a boy cow?" Lena gasped. "Now he's got a 'long thing'."

"Lena!" Mr. Finney was calling from the house. Lena and Crumbs looked back but couldn't see him.

"We'd better go." Crumbs said pulling Lena along. Lena looked back to see the 'boy cow' bucking around the black and white's arse with a movement she recognised, and a sudden knowing look came into her eyes.

The children rarely saw the two girls they thought were the Finneys' daughters. They slept in another of the three bedrooms in Mr. Finney's house whenever they were there. It is possible of course that they were his children, but their frequent absences might have been accounted for, if they had been other little girls sent to him from some convent or other. Perhaps they were his granddaughters as he was already in his fifties when he began his abuse of the young Lena. She believed that they were Mr. Finney's own children, and was puzzled that he didn't seem to play with them much either. Just like Crumbs. She didn't think too much on this conundrum, because he loved her! She was his 'girly- girl' and he was a boy cow, and she was immensely grateful that he wasn't using his long thing to buck around her arse. She had already heard about priests and other children and what happened to many of their arses, but she had never truly understood what went on till she saw those cows.

One night, Mr. Finney went to Lena and Crumbs, bearing gifts of chocolate. He gave Crumbs a 'Milky bar' and walked over to Lena with a box of Malteasers. Immediately Lena understood that she was going to have to play longer this night for she'd only ever had small packets of Malteasers before and here he stood with a box in his hand! As always she was wearing a long, yellow and white striped, long sleeved flannelette nightdress and he sat on the bed, tickling her ears.

"Time for you to learn a new Malteasers game, girly-girl." He said holding the box of Malteasers just out of Lena's reach.

Lena waited good-naturedly. She knew she would get her chocolates, just like she got everything else he brought her. She moved over to sit on his lap but he stopped her.

"Didn't I say it was a new game?"

She nodded and waited. "Now gimme a kiss."

She kissed him on his cheek and was rewarded by him opening the box of Malteasers. He took one out, said 'open wide' and when she did, he popped the chocolate in her mouth. She grinned. He laughed. Over in her bed, Crumbs chewed her Milky bar slowly and watched.

"Now gimme a kiss here." He pointed to his mouth.

The little girl planted a kiss on his mouth and he popped another chocolate in her mouth when she obeyed his command to 'open wide'.

Lena stared as he put the next chocolate in his own mouth. "That wasn't fair! He didn't eat any of Crumbs' chocolate." She thought.

"Find it." He said, opening his mouth to show her the chocolate between his teeth.

She immediately reached up to take the chocolate but he backed away. Bit by bit she understood that she had to find the chocolate with her mouth and soon was probing his mouth with her tongue to find it. The 'game' progressed in this fashion until there was no part of him that she hadn't explored with her hands or her mouth, to find her chocolate.

Then it was his turn to explore her. He worked his way round her body then he pulled up her nightdress. After pulling her knickers off, he made her spread her legs wide open. As he examined her with one hand, he reached over to the box for another chocolate ball. Lena felt a sharp pain in her gee and almost cried out, her mouth open, but it was quickly gone. She had the odd feeling that Mr. Finney's finger was somewhere inside her, but was distracted by him popping the Malteaser in her mouth. In time the game would progress, and by the time that Lena was a week older, she knew for sure that not just one, but two fingers could slide into her, when Mr. Finney used a lot of the stuff he took from a jar, but she had to struggle not to cry out. She didn't like it when Mr. Finney was angry.

Early the next morning, before the children were awake, he returned to Lena's bedside. Crumbs was sleeping in Lena's bed, as she often did after Mr. Finney had left the room. He poked her awake.

"Time to get up. Go to the bathroom and get yourself washed and down in the kitchen. Start breakfast."

Lena, awakened by his voice, looked at him warily. He sounded like he was angry and she didn't know what she had done wrong. However he said cheerfully, "Good morning girly girl. *Did you sleep well?*" With a flourish, he brought his hand round from behind his back and Lena saw that he held a plate with a fried egg sarnie on it.

He watched as Lena devoured it, all the while stroking her legs, working his way up under her nightdress.

"What's this?" He said suddenly, his voice hard.

Lena stared at him, her mouth full.

"I don't want you wearing these." He said as he pulled her knickers down. She had put them back on after he had left her the night before.

She swallowed the egg and bread and said, "Okay." Her mind was racing. The nuns would do their nuts if she went to bed without her knickers on. She didn't like it either. Somehow having her knickers on made her feel secure. She didn't tell him any of this. Instead, finding that the bread seemed to be sticking in her throat, she whispered, "Can I have some water?"

He went to the bathroom, filled the plastic cup that held the toothbrushes and returned to her. After she had drunk, the 'game' began.

He produced some sweets from the pocket of his baggy shorts and sat down. The sun was shining and although her bed was not in it's full glare, it was getting more light than she' ever remembered before. The man released his long thing, which Lena saw for the first time in full daylight. It was a dark reddish colour and she looked at the long blue things under the skin, which forked this way and that, and throbbed in a way she had never seen before. He placed a couple of sweets on it like crumbs on a windowsill. When they fell off, Lena was allowed to feel around in his shorts for them. She scrabbled around eagerly in his underpants and his thing twitched and stood up straighter. She thought it was hilarious, for she was only four years old and although she had played with many 'long things' before, none were quite as strange as this one.

Another twist to the 'game' meant that when he played with her gee, he usually tried to put his tongue in it, which tickled her. He was so silly ... there was no place for his tongue to go. It was too wide, not like his fingers. It did make her remember Smelly Mary at the convent and although she hadn't as yet washed this morning, Crumbs had made her have a quick one after Mr. Finney had gone last night. She was glad of that as she didn't want him to think she was stinky too, for by now she knew that she was Mr. Finney's 'special girly girl'.

Whenever Lena was at his house, Finney went to the child every night, many mornings and occasionally during the day when he was at home. He insisted that her bedroom door be always left open which did not bother the children too much as they were used to open spaces, but it worried Crumbs that he could just stand outside and watch them as they slept. Sometimes, when Crumbs pretended she was so fast asleep that she couldn't be easily roused, he let her lie where she was (the children usually slept top to tail) and he'd slip between them as though to shield what he was doing from the older child's eyes. Once he even took the smaller girl to his wife's bed. He lay her down between himself and his wife who turned away from them, clearly not wanting to see what was happening to the child. For some reason Lena didn't understand, she felt odd, uncomfortable. She had never before been in a bed with two adults ... never before played the game with another adult around. She squirmed with discomfort, but Mr. Finney simply laid his hand under her nightdress and said, "Now stop worrying. We are only just like a real family." For some reason, Mr. Finney just pulled her so she lay with her bottom against his long thing and he rubbed himself against her. After a while he grew quiet and Lena, who lay awake for a long time after he'd stopped moving, heard him snoring. Sometime later his wife began to snore too, and even later yet, Lena fell asleep. It was the first night she didn't have to play the game, as she had come to know it.

And so her holidays and her life moved on, day after day - sometimes slowly, sometimes quickly. They all went to church on Sundays where Mr. Finney would take Holy Communion then hold the children's hands and introduce them to many large and seem-ingly important men, and to the priest with whom he shared a couple of jokes they didn't understand. Many people came up to them and congratulated him, and Mrs. Finney too, on being such wonderful, generous people. For it was known that the couple's house was always full of abandoned and orphaned children, mostly small girls. Mr. Finney said his wife couldn't cope with rowdy boys and preferred to 'mother her daughters'. Lena and Crumbs didn't know anything of her 'mothering' but were too smart to open their mouths. Their motives however, were becoming less the food and treats they got, and more their growing concern, and especially that of the more mature Crumbs, about the way Mr. Finney's games were progressing.

Later, he would go with these men to the pub while Mrs. Finney, looking quite sour, would take them back home. Some days Crumbs would be sent out to play without Lena, or on Saturdays, to shop with Mrs. Finney. Lena would be kept back to 'play' with Mr. Finney and she learned a number of adult games that didn't involve actual pen-etration. They still jigged sometimes, and until the day accidentally

Lena bit him, he liked playing 'Mr. Lollipop'. There was also his favourite game still to be learnt.

One night he came in with plates of bread and crisps. "This is a good game. You'll like this game, you wee girlie girl. It called wee Willie Winkie. I have the 'wee Willie', though I grant you it's not so wee. Not even wee enough for my wife, but it always likes a good tight fit and I think parking in her is like putting a flea in an aircraft hanger. And you are so small I just know that just laying it between your legs and getting you to squeeze will be a tight fit. So it's my 'wee Willie' game see?"

Lena nodded although she did not really listen. She was interested in nothing but the large slice of bread he'd brought her, smeared with lots of ketchup - on nice, soft bread. He spoke nonsense sometimes anyway. She had no idea about 'parking' or what 'fleas' and for that matter what 'aircraft hangers' were. If he'd said midges or 'wee bugs', she would have had a third of the story and would have wondered about them and Mrs. Finney.

"And you my pretty," he continued as he kissed her forehead and gave her the bread, "what you've got is the 'Winkie' and wee Willie needs his Winkie, you see?"

Lena nodded again as she bit into her bread. Crumbs across the room, was eating too, but Lena could see that she was paying attention to them. Although Lena was sad at first that Mr. Finney didn't want Crumbs to play too, she began to understand that Crumbs was jealous, as she was getting all the attention from Mr. Finney. She shrugged. She thought one day Crumbs would get lucky too. In the meantime, there was lots of bread and ketchup, crisps, chocolate and other goodies for them to eat ... as much as they wanted, and all she had to do was play his games, including the one she was playing now, even if she thought it was silly ... a grown man wanting her to squeeze his 'long thing' tight between her legs while he did what he called 'push-ups' on top of her.

During these years, Sr. Clare farmed many children out to whichever families would take them in and Lena stayed in various places, sometimes alone, sometimes with Crumbs. One time she was sent to another family ... man, wife, two young children. There too, she found that explicit fondling was expected by the man of the family. He liked his 'long thing' to be pumped up and down with Lena sometimes imagining that she was doing it so hard and fast that it would fall off because that's what her hand and arm felt like. His thing didn't of course, and there were no treats for her here, so she longed to be sent back to Mr. Finney's house instead.

She got her wish. Every summer holiday for three years, she was sent to Mr. Finney whose games became more and more innovative. He was a highly sexed man who abused Lena almost non-stop every time she stayed at his house and as the girls became older, Crumbs grew more and more perturbed at what she was seeing. Something told her that what was happening wasn't right. She was now nine years old and had come to understand that the reason why the older children didn't want anyone to know what they did to the younger ones, was because it was wrong, dirty, sinful. If it was so for children, was it also not so for adults? She had tried to warn Lena, but her friend told her that she was only jealous because Mr. Finney didn't want to be her daddy. It was true that she would have liked to have a daddy, but not one that was always doing the kinds of things that Mr. Finney did with Lena. Still, uncertain, she kept her mouth shut, but she was bursting to ask someone for advice. Lena was still so small for her age and it was like she felt she had to please everyone. Crumbs understood that but the feeling that Lena was being made to do something wrong was becoming all pervasive.

Crumbs was tidying up in the kitchen when Mrs. Finney came in. Lena was upstairs with Mr. Finney. She had wanted to stay and watch but he'd sent her to work down here. Mrs. Finney banged a bag of groceries on the kitchen table, pulled a chair out and sat down heavily.

"Where's she? She servicing him again?" The woman's voice was a little slurred and Crumbs realised that she was either drunk or sick and she really didn't care which. She didn't speak and the woman looked at her, hostility pouring out of her.

"Put them things away." She ordered. Crumbs obediently did as she was told, keeping a wary eye on Mrs Finney who was muttering to herself.

She didn't hear everything the woman said and some of what she'd heard she didn't understand, but some words made her realise that Mrs. Finney thought that she, Crumbs was lucky to look like a boy, that he (Mr. Finney) was the 'divil incarnate' who was going 'straight to hell' and was 'taking the poor wee colleen' (Lena) with him, and her (Mrs. Finney) too, as she 'hadn't the strength to stop him'.

Alarmed, she looked at Mrs. Finney who had lain her head on her arms and the child was horrified to see she was crying. Not knowing what to do, Crumbs slipped out of the house, found a quiet spot in the garden so she could watch the cows, and she stayed there until she could hear Mrs. Finney calling her in for dinner It was after the summer holidays ended and Crumbs and Lena were back at the school for almost four weeks. Lena was now six years old, and was reluctant to go back to the Finneys next summer, because she knew that what he was doing was not good for her. This time she had come home with pains in her gee and she was beginning to smell as bad as Mary Noonan. Then she got a bad cold and her throat hurt. She saw the doctor who made her take some tablets for a week and to her surprise when she had finished the tablets, the funny smell from her gee had gone too. She found Crumbs.

"Hey Crumbs! Guess what!" Lena spoke excitedly

"What?" Crumbs looked at her while poking at one of her teeth.

"The stink from my gee is gone."

Crumbs stopped poking her teeth and grinned at Lena. "I heard Sr. Clare telling Sr. Bridgette that you had a chest infection and the doctor gave you medicine for it. So the infection must have started in your gee then it moved to your chest and that was twice lucky for you."

"Lucky for me? How could it be twice lucky for me?" Lena demanded.

"You're lucky 'cos the doctor looked at your chest and didn't go rooting round in your gee too. The medicine he gave you killed all the germs in your chest and your gee."

"That was lucky, but that's still only once." Lena replied thoughtfully.

"Well if the doctor did poke around in your gee and find the infection there, he would have told Sr. Clare that."

"On my!" Lena stood stock-still.

"Aye. They are stupid ignoramuses at everything else, but them nuns know a lot about gees."

The two girls fell silent for a moment, perhaps reflecting on what new hell Lena would have had if she told the nun about her activities at the Finney house.

Crumbs spoke again. "You mustn't let him do these things to you anymore. I think he gave you that smell you got."

"How?"

"I don't know, but didn't you notice he was a bit smelly last time?"

"No, but he did use to wear something he said was 'aftashafe'."

"Well he didn't wear no 'aftashafe' when he was near me and I thought he was smelly. And what's more, I think he made you smelly too."

"But he said he would be my 'daddy'" Lena was close to tears. "He said he would always give us nice stuff to eat. I wanted to go back to the pictures with him." Lena recalled the Saturday treat last summer when he took them to the cinema to see 'The Sound of Music'. "It had nice nuns in that picture."

"We both want to have a family, but you're my best friend and I don't want you to end up like smelly Mary Noonan."

Lena face was a picture of shock. She too didn't want to become a smelly Noonan making small girls put their faces in that smell.

"*Do* you really like the games you play with Mr. Finney?" Lena thought a moment. "At first I thought it was okay, but I don't feel comfortable about them. I play them so we could have our treats. I don't get treats from anybody else, even when I still have to play the game."

"Where else do you play the game?" Crumbs asked, surprised. She'd thought that it was only Mr. Finney who did these things to Lena.

"Remember when I was sent to that fat man's house? The Connors? You didn't come with me 'cos you were sick" As Crumbs nodded, Lena continued. "Well he made me play with his long thing and when I didn't want to, he hit me. He said he knew you and me went to the Finneys house, that's why he specially asked for us."

"God bless us and save us!" Crumbs said. She understood even as Lena didn't, that her attack of the 'flu had saved her.

January 18th, 2007, Essex, England

04:37

The car passing on the road outside backfired loudly. The woman grunted and opened her eyes briefly before falling back, into the deep sleep she was roused from.

Summer 1970

Crumbs folded the large sheet, grateful for the helpful hands of Bridie Gallagher and Moira Sheedy. In a week's time she and Lena would once more be on holidays with Mr. Finney and his wife and she had a lot on her mind. She was only listening to the two sixteen year olds with half an ear when she heard a name from the past.

"Did you hear? They sent Mo to the Magdalene laundries. She's only fourteen or so!" Moira was saying.

"Aye! I heard. I thought she was younger you know." "Nah! She just looks it."

"They couldn't have picked a worse place if they wanted to frighten the bejesus out of her. She won't last long there. She'll soon be leaving in a box." Bridie replied.

Crumbs had not seen the girl they called SloMo since she had disappeared a few months earlier.

"Why did they send her there?" She asked, sweat dripping from the end of her nose unto another sheet they were folding. It was late afternoon and the three girls were alone in the laundry finishing up. Outside, the other children were enjoying their break.

"It's where they always send them after they got their babbies. They take the babbies away and they send the left- overs to the laundry."

"The worst part for Maureen is that they sent her to the same place they sent that auld bitch that put her in the washing machine." Bridie added shaking her head.

"*Did* the auld bitch have a babby too?" Crumbs the inquisitive asked.

"Sure did."

"That Josey Conway had more than one." Moira added nodding knowingly.

"She never did!" Bridie asserted.

"Aye. She did so too, surely to God aye." Moira asserted. "In fact she had two with another on the way is the way I heard it. They took the first away and that one was sold to some American, like they haven't enough babbies over there to abuse. Then the priest saved her soul by sticking his willie in her to drive the divil out and show her the error of her ways. When that child was born, it too was sent to America. Now the priest must try harder to save her soul, so he filled her up with another babby."

"Shysters. Them priests must have ants in their pants that they must always be shoving their willies in us." Bridie said.

Crumbs' eyes open wide. She too knew what the priest could do. She had made her First Holy Communion already. "*Did you get a babby?*" She asked Bridie nervously.

"Nah! *Don't* be silly. I was lucky though. I reckon I was too young. It happened before my bloods come. After that, I knew to run and hide when that old goat was around. He only did it the once."

"And is that how girls get babbies, when men put their long ... willies in their gees?"

"Sure is, so you be watching your little gee." The older girls laughed uproariously.

"Especially watch them priests and never get sent to the Magdalene laundries ... you'll either leave in a box or the way that two and a half baby bitch did." Moira added.

Bridie put the folded sheet down and looked at Moira. "How did she leave then?" She asked.

"The stupid eejit decided to tell on the priest. Now she is in the madhouse where they sent her. Bad things happen there too. When her babby is born, they'll likely sell that one too and when the men in the madhouse are done with her, they'll likely give her electric shocks."

Crumbs gasped, and Bridie looking at her saw her fear. She put her arm round the girl, led her to the basket of folded sheets and as she did so, spoke over her shoulder to Moira.

"Get away!" She said. "You're just saying that to scare the wee kid here." She turned to Crumbs and continued gently, "you'll be alright. Just don't get yourself sent to the laundries, 'cos I know for a fact it's a hard life. I knew someone who was sent there for a short time as punishment and she told me this place is heaven compared to the laundries."

Lena and Crumbs were packed and ready for the journey to the Finneys. Crumbs had already repeated to Lena all she had heard from Bridie and Moira but she suspected that Lena remained unsure. On the one hand, she liked having a 'daddy'. On the other hand, she didn't like playing the games anymore. On the third hand she was worried that she would get another infection and this time Sr. Clare would find out and on the fourth hand, Sr. Clare might send her to the Magdalene laundries even if she didn't get preggers.

Crumbs looked at her hands and wondered if she could get a fifth hand in there somewhere. She knew that she didn't yet have her bloods so she was safe, and that therefore Lena was safe too. Neither of them would get preggers yet, and she intended to run whenever she could, just like Bridie did … but Mr. Finney was putting Lena in danger. She was alarmed, and desperate to speak with someone who could help them, but she was now just ten years old and scared. She knew telling an adult was going to mean trouble, so she said nothing.

It was the last night of their vacation. All summer, Mr. Finney made Lena play games with him in exchange for treats. In addition to the usual, he took them to the cinema a couple of times and to the circus too, but Crumbs didn't enjoy them as she worried about the girl who was the closest thing she had to a baby sister. Now his figure filled the doorway, and Crumbs, who was lying in bed with Lena, in their usual top to tail position, closed her eyes and feigned sleep. Finney walked over to the bed and kissed Lena on her mouth. He took off his trousers and underpants then he got into bed with them. After a while, he began to move about and suddenly finding more room in the bed, Crumbs ventured a peek. Lena was lying on her back with her legs spread wide. Mr Finney was between her legs on his knees and on one elbow. She could see Mr. Finney holding his willy, guiding it toward Lena's gee. She heard Lena gasp, but not cry out and would learn later that just as Lena got a painful fullness such as she never had before, Mr. Finney had pressed his mouth on hers, stifling any possible cries. From her viewpoint near the bottom of the bed, Crumbs watched as Mr. Finney moved up and down on her friend. She felt the bed shudder and tremble as he moved harder against Lena. Then all went still as he lay trembling on top of the girl. Later, she watched as he pulled his limp willy out of her, and he staggered out of the room.

She saw Lena curl herself up into a ball, and realised that she was crying silently. She hustled up beside her and they clung to each other until Lena stopped crying and said.

"It hurt, Crumbsy. It hurt so high up inside. It was like he was trying to poke my heart out with his thing."

"We won't come back here again," Crumbs said stroking the girl's hair. "It won't happen again. I won't let it."

It was late in the afternoon when they returned to the convent but that morning Crumbs was forced to go to town with Mrs. Finney leaving Lena behind. She had tried to stay, but got such a stinging slap from Mr. Finney that she thought she could see stars. Mrs. Finney hustled her away before Mr. Finney could hit her again. The whole time she was shopping with Mrs. Finney, she thought of what she would say when she got back 'home', and now here she was, in Sr. Clare's office telling her what went on at the Finneys' house. Before she could even finish what she was saying, the nun got up and walked over to her. Crumbs tensed for she had seen this demeanour before and knew that she was in deep shit.

Sr. Clare hit the girl in the face with her fists. She also used a stick she kept nearby, and even with the long rosary beads that hung by her side. Crumbs staggered against the desk as she fell when a fist bashed her mouth. Down on the floor, the nun kicked her several times and the girl curled herself up into a ball crying silently. Lena who was outside the office had no idea what Crumbs was going through. When the nun's rage abated somewhat, she opened the door of the office and Crumbs heard her say, "Miss O'Leary. Come in here. Now!"

Crumbs was crestfallen. She had hoped that she wouldn't get a beating, but she'd been sure that her friend who had already suffered so much at Mr. Finney's hand, would have been treated better. She tried to wipe the blood from her mouth but ended up smearing it over her face and hands instead. There were already large spots of blood on her clothes.

"Close the door." From her vantage point on the floor, Crumbs saw Lena look at her fearfully as she closed the door.

"Were you in bed with Mr. Finney?" The nun's cold voice rang out loud in the room.

"I ... I ..."

The nun's face looked like she had a lump of shit on her top lip. "You'll turn out to be just like your mother, you wee divil. *Just like your mother!* She jumped into any bed as long as it had a man in it. You little slut! You'll burn in hell as sure as eggs is eggs. You'll burn in hell!" Her mouth was a thin, tight line when it was shut ... a black hole when it was open.

She continued to upbraid the child, her finger wagging as she spoke.

"You'll be down to the Magdalene laundries, mark my words. It's just your good fortune that you are only seven and too young to go there now. But I'll see to it that you learn your future vocation well in the laundry here. We'll work the divil out of you if it kills you. Furthermore, you will forget everything that's been happening to you in that house or I'll beat it out of you. *Do you hear me?*"

Spit flew from her mouth and Lena had no trouble nodding her head, so terrified she was of the kind of beating Crumbs clearly had. Already her friend was showing some nasty bruises and her mouth was a bloody mess.

"Now get out, the pair of you ... before I give you both a sound thrashing."

Lena and Crumbs hurried out of the nun's office. They were never again sent to the Finneys even though Mr. Finney had asked for them. No other girls from the convent were sent to his house either. Sr. Mary Clare did not call a doctor to see if Lena needed medical attention ... and as far as the girls knew, she did not call any of the other schools or orphanages to warn them that Finney was a predator of young girls. She had done her best.

January 20th, 2007, Essex, England

20:48

Scott was asleep in bed, recovering from a road traffic accident that left him with a mild head injury. Maisy was also asleep and Lena, at a loose end, sat down with her cigarettes and the remote control. She had finally settled on a film and after a few moments her eyes narrowed, partly because of the smoke from her cigarette, and partly from the couple's antics on the television. He was stroking his lover's leg ... she had reached over for some chocolate, which she was using to lay a trail for him.

As she watched, Lena's eyes hooded and she was transported back to the sound waking her, a sound like a shot. It had awakened her briefly when she was with Mr. Finney! She sat still for a long time, as the pictures behind her lids flickered rapidly and memories long buried burst their way into her consciousness. What happened to her at the Finneys had lain the foundation for all that would be destructive in her life.

"He raped me! *Dear God how could I forget that?* The bastard raped me. He took everything. He took my innocence, my body, my soul, even my memory. He made me a piece of filth! How could I have wanted him to be my father? How could I have liked him? How could I? What kind of eejit am I? I know I was a child but even so I could have stopped him, couldn't I? I should have stopped him.

Somehow! And why did I forget so much? I thought his abuse was just confined to touching, bad as that was. How could I forget the horrific things he did? *Dear God!* When will this pain end?"

As though in a dream, she stood up and walked to the bathroom. She opened the cabinet and found vials of some unused medication. They contained anti-depressants, sedatives and all manner of cures for her problems. She gathered the vials together and got a glass from the kitchen. Back in the lounge she put the vials and glass on the coffee table before moving over to the drinks cabinet. She picked up the first bottle she saw and went back to the sofa. After filling the glass with the cognac, she sat staring at it as the pictures began to replay themselves and she relived the horror over and over again.

She reached over and snapped the top off the first vial. It was full of blue pills. She slowly turned the vial over letting the pills drop onto the tabletop. Then she reached for the next vial. White pills joined the blue ones and she herded them together.

"Ma-mi? Can I have a drink of your apple juice?" Lena started, realising for the first time that a small girl stood before her, hands reaching out to the full glass of cognac.

"No! No!" She said pulling the glass towards her. "That juice is no good. We'll get you some fresh from the kitchen."

"M&Ms." The child said happily reaching over to the pills. "Not those baby. I have some bigger ones in the kitchen for you."

The little girl put her hand in the woman's and the two of them walked to the kitchen. Lena gave Maisy a couple of M&Ms while she poured the child some juice and she squatted beside her as she drank. She too was drinking - she drank in the sight of the healthy little girl beside her. This is a dream, she thought.

"Must go pee-pee." The child again took her hand and they walked to the bathroom, Lena almost in a trance ... entranced and led by the child.

Finished and hands washed, the child threw her arms around the woman, kissed her and said, "I love you Ma-mi."

Tears came to Lena's eyes as she picked up her almost three year old and held her close, basking in her love. The child turned her head to the side and was preparing to fall asleep again, so Lena took her back to her bed, tucked her in, returned to the living room and switched the TV off.

Do you always depend on your baby to ease the pain? The words floated into her head and she smiled wryly. It's a big burden on a small girl.

She looked at the cognac and vials still waiting patiently for her and she poured the cognac back into the bottle, which she replaced in the cabinet. She scooped all the pills back into a large bottle and picked up all the other vials muttering, "I don't know why I keep these things." Just then her eyes fell on a note at the side of one of the bottles. She quickly looked at the others and began to giggle. "They're almost all past their 'use by' dates. I don't believe it. Now I'm trying to take rotten, old pills."

She returned to the bathroom with the vials, but instead of putting the bottle now containing all the pills back in the cupboard, she opened it and poured its contents down the toilet, flushing several times to ensure that everything had gone. She didn't want her baby girl finding any of them.

It was still not yet midnight so she returned to the living room as she didn't think she could sleep. She heard the child's voice in her head again. I love you Ma-mi. She whispered, "I love you too baby, and you and I are going to learn to fight the bastards. Tomorrow, I'm going to look for marital arts classes for us to join. No-one will ever hurt you. I'll see to that for as long as I live, and you'll see to that for as long as you live. I love you Maisy. I love you Lena ... I love you both."

Seven

Witches and Monsters

Foster care – Mrs. O'Shaunessy 1974 – 1976

It was a late summer's day, which was threatened by dark grey clouds scudding quickly by. The wind, suddenly cold hurried the two children into the car. Summer holidays were over, and they were being given a chance, or so they believed, to have a life, get an education. Lena was 11 years old when she and her brother were fostered out to a woman called Mrs. O'Shaunessy a schoolteacher who at sixty odd years old was fast approaching retirement. She was a stout woman and may have been related to one of the nuns. She drove to the industrial school herself to collect Lena and Daniel. She had fostered at least one child before and now was alone as her own children, then her foster child had grown up and left home. Having visited the industrial school to familiarise herself to the children, she was now taking them away with her. For their part, Lena and Daniel were just happy to be leaving the industrial school. The nuns cheerfully waved the two children off on their journey into what they had told the children would be a better life.

It was the first time that Lena and Daniel had been sent anywhere together. They knew that they were brother and sister of course, but as they had spent so much time living virtually separate lives, even though they inhabited the same buildings, they weren't really that close. Boys and girls had separate dorms and worked in different places, for example Lena was proficient at laundry work and Daniel was fast becoming a good baker. They were also sent to different places for their 'holidays'. Lena knew that her brother spent much of his 'holidays' working on the farms the Christian Brothers ran, and that terrible things happened to the boys. Daniel didn't speak much of his experiences and Lena didn't ask. She was now of an age when she didn't want to speak of her experiences either.

It was a long, cold journey from Clifden to Ballybay in County Monaghan and the grey clouds had opened up and evacuated a heavy rain on the travellers. Lena looked out of her window at the thick mist of rain as the windscreen wipers swished and scraped at the torrent running down the screen. Daniel poked her leg and pointed to their driver. The woman had her nose almost on the inner side of the windscreen as she drove slowly into the gloom. Daniel mimed the car moving so slowly that someone walking beside them would overtake them and disappear in the rain. Lena pulled her lips together so as not to laugh out loud and the car moved on.

Sometime after, both children were still sitting quietly in the back of the car with their thoughts. Lena was wondering about her new foster family. She wasn't sure what awaited her there. What was Mrs. O'Shaunessy like? Were there menfolk in the house who would be a problem? She and Crumbs had spoken about what she would do if any men wanted to 'do things' to her. Crumbs, who had grown a lot faster than Lena - the latter was still only four foot six inches tall - advocated kicking them in the willie, but unless they were lying down, that was a tall order for Lena. She remembered Mr. Lollipop and knew she would bite anything that was in her mouth, even if it wasn't food, but it wasn't always so easy.

She hated them ... all of them - the nuns, the priests, the men, all those who controlled her and the other children. Sometimes she felt that she would burst with all the feeling that sometimes welled up inside of her, especially when she hated herself. It was all her fault, the whole sorry mess. If she wasn't such an awful child, her mother wouldn't have given her away to the nuns. If she wasn't such an idiot of a child, the nuns wouldn't have given her such a hard time.

They would have loved her and she knew that they could, as they really seemed to care for a few of the other girls. If she wasn't such a beastly child, Smelly Mary wouldn't have had her do what she did. If she wasn't such a stupid child, the dirty old men wouldn't have done the things they did to her and she wouldn't have let them. If she wasn't such a disgusting child, God would not have abandoned her and she wouldn't have had to abandon him 'cos he was a useless lump when it came to protecting her and most of the kids she knew. If she wasn't such an awful child, just about every nun and many of the adults she knew wouldn't think she had the divil in her. Having temporarily run out of the words she had heard used all her life to describe her, she concluded that it was all her fault and one day she would burst open and all the evil would spill out.

"Okay everybody out. Time for a cuppa!" Mrs. O'Shaunessy's voice startled Lena out of her reverie and she saw that Daniel was already stepping out of the car. She looked around as she too got out and was surprised to see that they were before a small tea shop in Claremorris, according to the nearby sign.

"Are we here already Mrs O'Shaunessy?" She asked nervously, for she had no idea where in the world they were being taken to.

"Granny! Have you forgotten already? You're to call me Granny!"

"Sorry Mrs. ... er ... Granny."

"And no. We're not there ... just stopping for a drink." Mrs. O'Shaunessy replied.

It was the first of several stops 'for a drink', and the children soon spotted that before each drink, which they also had in Carrick-on-Shannon and Cavan, Mrs. O'Shaunessy asked the waitress where the toilets were. Even so, they were delighted as they filled up on sugary drinks while 'Granny' emptied herself. Despite the lemonade and cakes, Lena was worried. The journey was too long and the rain had not let up even a little. Furthermore, the police would soon be after Granny O'Shaunessy because whenever she stopped the car for a drink, she just left it any auld way, not neatly in a space like the other cars. Sometimes she just stopped in the middle of the road. Luckily, there were few cars about. In addition, the dark, dirty day and incessant rain suggested to her that where she was going was so bad that even the sky was crying for her and *Daniel* ... even the heavens were defying God.

As they reached journey's end, Mrs. O'Shaunessy pointed to her house, which was near the top of a hill. It was a huge house which Mr. O'Shaunessy, a builder who had died some years earlier, had built for his large family and it had two reception rooms. It was too big a house for her and she had a maintenance man to take care of it. Her seven adult children all had homes of their own and led busy lives holding down respectable jobs - one was a teacher, another a priest, yet another a bank manager, and so on. The married children were bringing up their own young families. Mrs. O'Shaunessy needed for nothing except perhaps for two young children to help her with the daily chores while she provided for their education. Even as she was stopping the car in the drive, Mrs. O'Shaunessy was explaining that across the road from her house lived a family of Protestants and she had a few unfriendly things to say about them, telling the children to keep away from their kind.

"Kneel!" She ordered them almost as soon as the front door closed. "Thank the Lord for a safe journey!"

Daniel and Lena obediently fell to their knees as Mrs. O'Shaunessy began a long, monotone. When they heard the words, "through Christ our Lord", they obediently said, "Amen" and watched the old woman. When she crossed herself with the familiar words, "In the name of the Father ...", they knew the prayer was over and they crossed themselves too.

"Now! I'll tell ye once more! You're not to call me Mrs.

O'Shaunessy as you've been doing. You're to call me 'Granny'."

When both children nodded, she added, "Come. Let me show you your rooms."

Although delighted at the space they would have, the children had no time to 'settle in' at their new home. After putting their belongings in their rooms, they had to help prepare supper, and to pray. They prayed before their meal, and that eaten, they said the rosary before bedtime. Lena's heart sank. She didn't expect to have to pray at every turn. This was going to be as bad as being back with the nuns. They were ordered to bed after the rosary for the next day was the first day of school.

Lena found herself in the 6th class, which Mrs. O'Shaunessy taught herself. Her first day was an eye- opener and told her immediately that she was not going to enjoy living with this woman. Her new-found 'granny' walked from the front of the room and stopped beside a desk just two rows away from where Lena sat.

"Aileen Mawhinney! What is the square root of 256?"

A dark haired girl sitting opposite the woman began to fidget. Lena had noticed her earlier, because she had a pale face with bright, laughing, blue eyes looking out of it and she had winked at Lena when she walked into the room. She was the only student to have looked in her direction, the others looking frozenly ahead, for Mrs. O'Shaunessy had walked into the room behind Lena.

"Er ..." Aileen was clearly taken aback by the question and from the red flush Lena could see on the back of her neck, she didn't know the answer.

Neither did Lena. Square roots? She had been told that this was a math class, not biology or botany or whatever.

Whatever did roots have to do with numbers, square or other-wise? Her thoughts were interrupted by a loud 'Swoosh, ker-ack!' and Lena realised that although she was looking at both Aileen and Mrs. O'Shaunessy, she had not seen the cane appear in the woman's hand, or crash down on the girl's shoulder. She just heard it.

Aileen flinched and was rewarded with two more swipes. Lena wanted to cower in her chair but was afraid of catching Mrs. O'Shaunessy attention. Fortunately the woman walked slowly back to the front of the class repeating her question to various children and swiping at them until mercifully one of them got the right answer.

Lena knew then that it would only be a matter of time before the auld witch's heavy hand would fall on her and she was right, for Lena was hopeless at math ... and scholastically, at everything else besides. It wasn't really her fault. She had simply not had enough schooling having spent most of her schooldays working in the nuns' laundry. It was in those moments that she resolved never to think of the woman as 'granny', though she was smart enough to realise that she would have to pay her 'lip service.'

After school was finished that day, Lena looked over at Aileen hoping to catch her eye. She didn't know anyone and she hoped Aileen might help her meet the others so she could become a part of the crowd. To her astonishment, Mrs O'Shaunessy tapped her on the shoulder.

"Come!" She said.

Lena obediently followed her out the school buildings and realised that she was to get into the car, whereupon Mrs O'Shaunessy immediately drove her back to the house. Daniel was not collected. He would find his own way 'home'.

Once back at the house, 'granny' made small talk while she and Lena prepared the evening meal. Although she had not yet hit the girl, and appeared to be friendly, Lena simply could not bring herself to trust her. She didn't even want to talk with her or hear her voice, but there was nothing she could do ... yet. After Daniel returned to the house, the three of them sat down to their meal after a lengthy grace, and as they ate, they listened to Mrs O'Shaunessy's cold voice telling them what she expected of them.

"Lena. Each day you will return home with me. I know something about how girls like you behave and we'll have none of that here. During breaks at school you will have plenty of time to play with your friends but I don't expect to hear that you spend the entire free period playing ... and I will hear! Those 'free' periods are for private study or religious contemplation." She fixed a cold stare on Lena's face, for the girl had made no response.

Lena's thoughts were racing. What does she mean by 'girls like me'? And why do I have to come home with her every day? She let Daniel come home by himself. Why can't I come home alone?

Even as Lena was contemplating these things, Mrs O'Shaunessy continued.

"Daniel." She said. "You will be able to spend time with your friends after school but I expect you back before dark ... before dinner! If you're not here for your dinner, you'll get none. I will not be waiting on you children. I've already done my shift. Instead, you, and particularly you Lena, will have to learn to wait on me. My children and foster child have all grown up and gone, and it's only because Sr. Clare said what good workers you two were that I took you on. *Do you understand?*"

The two children nodded.

"After dinner, you have chores about the house to do.

You Lena will do all the cleaning up including dusting and the dishes, as well as the household laundry. I understand that this is work that is not unfamiliar to you. You will also help me in the kitchen preparing the vegetables for me to cook. I do not trust you to prepare my meals, but you must watch me and learn. *Daniel*, you will bring in the peats, wood and coal and have the fire laid up fresh every morning before you go to school. You will also do any work in the garden that I require. Lena, if you are finished your chores or *Daniel* isn't here, you will fetch the coal and so on. There is a handyman *Daniel* ... Mr Hugh Quinlan, and he will do the heavier jobs about the house - repairs and such. If Hughie needs your help, you are to give it."

"Yes Granny." *Daniel* said looking at Lena who was still not saying anything.

Mrs O'Shaunessy didn't seem to notice anything or realise that Lena was deliberately being non-responsive. If she did, she probably thought that the girl was overawed by everything. She continued giving them their instructions and when the meal was finished said, "Alright you know what your jobs are for tonight. *Do* them quickly now, then get your homework done." With that, she led them in a 'grace after meals', pushed away from the dining table, went into the big room with the television and sat down to watch *Coronation Street*.

Lena quickly learned to hate living with Mrs O'Shaunessy. She was always being punished for something, both at the house and in school. Mrs O'Shaunessy was a hard taskmaster who also happened to be the teacher of Lena's weakest subject. Why kids had to *be* taught math is something I will never understand, she thought. Arithmetic was bad enough, geometry was worse, but algebra was like learning a whole new language which would be okay if it made sense. How can a + b = c, when they were all three different? It was stupid and Lena found a whole new relationship with Mrs O'Shaunessy's cane, ruler, sweeping brush, bath brush, or anything else she could lay her hands on and often the auld witch came up behind her for the attack. After each beating, the girl would then have to get on her knees and pray for 'God's forgiveness'. This hurt Lena more than any beating, because she knew that He didn't give a damn! If He didn't care enough to protect her from the evil like she used to really pray for, why on earth would He forgive her, especially when it was the auld witch that needed forgiveness from both Him and her.

Despite these hard times, Lena considered that had she been a younger woman, Mrs O'Shaunessy might have been better at being a foster mother, at being a true 'granny', for just occasionally a kindness would emerge from her rather large breast. She sometimes took the children swimming and once she even took them by aeroplane from Shannon to Dublin. Even so her cruelty could not be hidden or ignored and Lena thought she was easily the most wicked person she'd ever met, as the strict old woman pulled, pushed and beat her into what she said was 'submission'. Lena had by then heard this word often before and she knew it meant danger for her. She did not believe Mrs O'Shaunessy to be a Mary Noonan, but she also knew that submission to a stick was not good. What she didn't as yet know was that as she moved closer to her twelfth birthday, her hormones were beginning to pick up and she was about to change from a quiet child to a 'wild young woman'.

Lena had learnt from Crumbs about her 'bloods', for the two girls shared their secrets and Crumbs wanted Lena to understand that when the 'bloods' came, she must fight anyone who tried to stick his willie in her. "Tooth and nail." Crumbs had said, "Tooth and nail". Crumbs' blood had come just before she was twelve and Lena was warily watching for when hers would come. Her twelfth birthday came and went, and she was just getting worried that she was somehow damaged by her 'badness' in the past when the monthly bleeding made it's first appearance.

It was early on a school day morning when she woke and realised that her big day had arrived. She quickly checked the sheets and was relieved to find that they hadn't been stained. Running to the bathroom, she cleaned herself off then knocked on Mrs O'Shaunessy's bedroom door to tell her that she was bleeding.

Mrs O'Shaunessy ordered her into the bath where her brother was already taking one having laid the fire before breakfast, even though it was early summer. She did this as the children were allowed one bath a week and Lena had already had hers two days earlier.

Lena protested, "I can't bathe with him!"

Almost simultaneously, Daniel knowing that Lena expected her bloods to arrive any time soon and understanding her posture, stood up and said with consternation in his voice, "I'm not going to bathe with anyone bleeding from her c**t!"

"What!" Mrs O'Shaunessy face puffed up like a bull-frog's as she grabbed the long handled bath brush. "How dare you?" She hit him hard. "How dare you?!" She hit him again. Every time she said 'How dare you?', she clobbered him. Then she moved on to, "Wash your mouth out with soap! Wash it! Wash your mouth out with soap!"

When Daniel simply cowered, she grabbed the soap and shoved it in his mouth. She hit him again and again. Finally as Daniel spat out the soap, she cried out, "And you would bathe with someone not bleeding, would you? You filthy little brat! Pray! Pray for forgiveness. Now!"

Daniel fell back under the blows raining down on him and cracked his head against the tub. This did not stop the beating, which Lena hoped would not fall on her too. Finally exhausted, Mrs O'Shaunessy stomped out of the door, and Lena helped Daniel out of the bath, onto the floor where he lay for a few minutes. Hearing Mrs O'Shaunessy returning, Daniel grabbed a towel, wrapped it round his middle and ran to his room across from the bathroom, shutting the door behind him. Lena immediately sat down in the bath, found the soap in the water and began to soap herself.

Mrs O'Shaunessy walked in, placed a sanitary pad on a nearby chair, instructed Lena to 'stick that between your legs before you put your knickers on', and told her that there was a packet of the things in her room. There was no explanation of what the bloods meant, although Lena didn't need one. A couple of days later, she found a leaflet called Every woman, on her bed. It had diagrams and 'pictures', which showed how babbies were made. So she was a big girl and now her bloods had arrived she could get a babby ... and maybe she would, she thought. If she had a babby, surely it would love her. She could find a way, as soon as she was old enough to be free. She would have a babby and there would be nothing they could do, for she would be free. She would find a man her own age. He would stay with her. They would get married and no-one would be able to take the babby from her. She truly believed that, for she was still young enough to believe that she would be different. She would be the one.

Soon after this episode, Daniel who had collected a couple more beatings from Mrs O'Shaunessy for not doing some tasks he'd been set, and who was petrified of collecting another beating, began bed-wetting and sleepwalking. He too, was small for his age, and after the bathroom incident, and following some perceived mis-deed, Mrs. O'Shaunessy had taken to him with a old fishing rod of Mr. O'Shaunessy's, which stood in a corner of the hall with other stuff he'd left behind when he died. However, Daniel had one advantage that Lena did not have. Each day, he could go out to play with his friends whereas Lena could not. Except for activities approved by Mrs O'Shaunessy, she was a virtual prisoner.

So her first year with her foster parent ended and Lena became more and more sullen and truculent. She began to find herself suppressing the flashes that simmered just below the surface and although she didn't know it, it was almost a repeat situation of the anger that boiled and often erupted from the young Frances O'Leary who had bashed her head on a *Dublin* sidewalk years earlier. It was an anger that almost erupted when Mrs O'Shaunessy spoke to her in the garden, after they had driven home at the end of the school year.

"You are one of the dimmest children I ever had the cause to teach. Nothing seems to go into your head. I know because I've spoken with your other teachers. One or two of them seem to have faith in you for some reason. They think you only need a chance to settle a little. As a result, I'm going to give you another year to 'settle' in my maths class. You will be repeating the year." With that she walked off into the house, leaving Lena staring after her with her mouth open. The child turned away from the house, kicked the flowers in a nearby flower bed, and headed for the gate. She would not live here a second longer. She began to march down the road and had gone about half-a-mile when the car pulled up beside her.

"Get in! Or I'll scalp ye!"

Lena had never seen Mrs O'Shaunessy look so mad, really mad, like a lunatic. She was even spitting everywhere when she spoke. Lena looked down the road. It was a long walk to the village, plenty of room for Mrs O'Shaunessy to run her down, and she looked like she could. Lena got into the car. Mrs O'Shaunessy turned the car around and drove quickly back to the house. She rushed out of the car and dragged Lena out by her long hair. Walking to a sapling, she tore a branch off it and began to lay into the girl, whilst holding her firmly by her hair, dragging her into the house.

"*Do* you think I'll have you broadcast to the neighbours that I cannot handle a child like you?" Whack! "What do you think that will do to my reputation? Eh?" Whack, whack! "I will teach you respect! I will teach you obedience! I will have you submit!"

The enraged woman hurled Lena into a corner of the room the children did their homework in. "Get on your knees and pray! Pray for forgiveness. You'll stay there on your knees until I say otherwise." She walked out the room briefly and returned to see Lena sitting back on her haunches.

"On your knees!" She ordered as she flung the rosary beads at the child. "Two decades!"

After twenty minutes during which the child said the two decades of the rosary, watched by Mrs. O'Shaunessy and hit if she got any of it wrong, she was ordered to work on her algebraic equations ...

"... or I'll clatter you until your brains .... what little you have ... fall out."

She slammed the door and Lena heard a key turn in the lock. She looked at the window and considered getting out of it, but Mrs O'Shaunessy was not a fool and no doubt would be watching it. In any case, she was hurt and had no place to go. She looked at the algebra and sighed. It still made no sense. Her eyes fell on her maths box containing her geometric tools. She took out the compasses and stared at it wondering if it would hurt, then she had a better idea.

Just over an hour later, Daniel walked into the room. "Granny wants to know if you've fini..." His voice tailed off and a look of horror ... panic came into his eyes which opened wide.

On Mrs O'Shaunessy's fine mahogany furniture, Lena had scratched her name several times, and had included a number of pointed insults about her 'granny'.

It was several days before Lena was well enough to move without wincing. Mrs O'Shaunessy had laid into her with a back scratcher, which had pierced her skin in a number of places. Daniel helped her by putting a large number of plasters over the worse punctures whenever she had a wash, and even Mrs O'Shaunessy made her sit each evening in the bath, laced it with Dettol antiseptic to help the holes heal over without becoming infected. During those days she prayed so much that she felt she should have been elevated to some very high place. Sometimes Daniel would join her and as the children said the rosary, they changed the words to suit themselves, as the children at the Industrial School often did. As long as they kept their voices to a low murmur, the auld bat didn't know exactly what they were saying.

Daniel:	Hail Mary full of grapes, the Lord is a tree
	Blessed are you amongst women
	And blessed is the fruit of your womb, Jesus
Lena:	Holy Mary mother of God Hooray for us sin-
	ners, now and at the hour of our deaths Amen

Quiet, in terms of beatings, for the next few weeks Mrs O'Shaunessy allowed Lena to join the youth club, which Father Finnegan ran and where Lena discovered a love of basketball. Mrs O'Shaunessy drove her there and collected her later when the priest was done with them. Stifled by this intense attention, Lena began to run away whenever she could, and the few friends she managed to make, would hide her. When she was found she would be returned home to whatever punishment Mrs O'Shaunessy could provide. If she had managed to get into the house before Mrs O'Shaunessy's anger spilled over, the woman would grab the nearest 'weapon' to beat her.

Some months after her 12th birthday, Lena was allowed a little more leeway and could actually meet up with her school friends, away from Mrs. O'Shaunessy's eyes. She met up with Aileen Mawhinney's older brother, Donal, who was 13 years old. He was her first boy friend, despite the fact that Lena was dressed in old-fashioned hand-me-downs that Mrs. O'Shaunessy had forced her to wear.

"If they were good enough for my children, they're good enough for you." She had said. Now Lena was entertaining her first real friend-ship with a boy, dressed like his mother did when she was a kid. She quickly changed into the t-shirt and shorts she was allowed to wear for sports and the two young people played basketball together, occasionally held hands when no-one could see them and gener-ally enjoyed being in each other's company. When Mrs O'Shaunessy somehow found out about their friendship, several days later, she put a stop to it, banning Lena from meeting him. It was the first male-female friendship she'd had, that had not involved playing adult games ... and now Lena knew that there were people watching her. They were reporting every move she made, back to the auld witch. She had suspected it before as the woman seemed to know everything she did, but now she was sure, and the dam welled up further inside her.

She responded by running away again. Chloe McNulty who sat next to her in Mrs. O'Shaunessy's class, lent her some of her clothes and 'hid' her in a shed at the end of a field near her house. Lena was 'free' for exactly three and a half hours and later took her punishment and said her prayers stoically. The next day, Chloe got a wacking in Mrs.

O'Shaunessy's class for not knowing her sums even though she'd only gotten one wrong, and both girls knew that the punishment was for her helping Lena.

That evening after school, Lena saw Chloe and began to run to her to apologise for the beating she got.

Lena O'Leary!" Mrs. O'Shaunessy's voice rang out.

"You're a young lady! Not a wild Indian. Walk!"

Lena duly slowed to a walk and when she reached her friend, her first words to Chloe were "And she's an auld bitch from hell. That's why I run."

Chloe grinned at her. "She's always been that way, but she can't beat me too bad 'cos my mother knows what she's like. She used to be in her class too, and if she beats me too bad, she'll be in trouble with her. She don't like her much either. Next time you run away, come over. I know a place to hide you where she won't find you so quick."

Lena would run away several more times and always Mrs. O'Shaunessy's spy network ensured she was found.

One evening, she ran again, but it was cold, wet and soon dark too. When she spotted Mrs. O'Shaunessy's car, she hurried towards it and gave herself up. Mrs. O'Shaunessy cackled loud and long and although that night her beating was not too severe, she spent several hours, until after midnight, on her knees, praying, while Mrs. O'Shaunessy interrupted her television viewing periodically to come and cackle over her.

Both *Daniel* and Lena showed some talent on the athletics field, a talent that may have been developed by their constant running from some adult or other. Having discovered it, Mrs. O'Shaunessy allowed both of them to improve on it by ensuring that their recreation time was limited to practise, and that they focussed on hard work and prayer, as she was convinced she could help both children to amount to something. Even so, although she wanted both of them to do well academically, and she had high hopes for *Daniel*, she was less sure about Lena. The nuns had assured her that the girl would be useless scholastically, but she had never failed with a child and would simply have to beat it out of her. *Daniel* was determined to prove his worth and did his best to please 'Granny'. He appealed to Lena to improve her ways.

"Come on. She's not so bad ... and we've never had family before."

"She is not my family!"

"Look, like it or not, she now our Granny. She's giving us an education. We never had that before. Anyway the nuns told her you'll be a harlot so you have to prove them wrong! You can't let Granny come to believe that too."

"I couldn't give a shit what the auld cow or for that matter, the nuns think, and if my fate was to be a harlot, then I'll be the best in the world, whatever a harlot is."

Lena was now almost thirteen years old and in the two years since she had lived with her foster mother, she had become completely sick and tired of Mrs. O'Shaunessy who she now privately called Mrs. More-Holy-Than-Righteous. The auld bat was in her sitting room speaking with one of the priests who was always at her house. If it wasn't a priest, it was a nun or some other individual from the Church. One day a Canon arrived and he was constantly putting his arm round the child, often turning her so that no-one could see his hand creeping under her armpit to firmly latch onto one of her now clearly obvious breasts.

After that, Lena avoided most of the religious folk who visited. She was only in the house for this priest's visit as she quite liked him. He was one of the few adult males who treated her like a human being, rather than as an object for his pleasure. He understood something of Lena's problems as she often spoke with him in the confessional about the abuse she'd suffered at Mrs. O'Shaunessy's hands. She'd never told him of the abuse she suffered at the hands of the nuns, as she felt that to do so would be to lose his friendship. Neither did she tell him of the sexual abuse she suffered from Michael Finney. She trusted him, but not so far and she didn't know if, once he'd heard about her sexual experiences, he might assume that she'd be 'easy game'. Having said that, he'd never attempted to abuse either her or Daniel and was generally lots of fun to be around. He always tried to see her point of view and he prayed with and for her.

It was partly because of him that Lena had become twisted and turned around where her beliefs were concerned. She had turned away from the Church at a young age, but he was making her believe in something again. He knew that some adults were evil, divils even. He said so himself. He also knew that some children who were said to be bad weren't bad at all, just hurt and hitting out where they could. So she waited to see him, wondering what Mrs. O'Shaunessy was saying to him. She moved closer to the door of the sitting room.

"She's virtually unmanageable." Mrs. O'Shaunessy was saying. "She never seems to be able to do what was expected of her. What am I to do with her? Daniel is improving and is by far the better behaved child."

"Have you tried reasoning with her? I'm sure that if you did she would be more obliging. I have always found her to be easy-going."

"You are the priest! She has to respect you. It seems that a school-teacher doesn't command so much respect these days, and that little brat ..."

"There now, Mrs. O'Shaunessy." The priest interrupted her. "She is a child, not a brat. If you treat her like a child, she will most likely behave like one. Now let's pray together that this problem can be resolved."

As the priest and the old woman began to pray, Lena felt hot tears come to her eyes. She quickly left the house and wandered down to the bottom of the garden where she allowed her tears and her thoughts to flow freely. *Daniel* ... O'Shaunessy liked *Daniel* who was improving, the traitor ... while she, Lena, was the brat ... "well," she thought, "I'll show them!" She dried her tears and settled down to wait for the priest's emergence. She could see his car.

"Ooh - you're no longer a wee colleen are youse? Your titties are getting quite big aren't they?" Lena was startled by the voice beside her. She hadn't seen Hughie Quigley creeping up to her. She stared at him, eyes wide. Hughie was a thin man, not much taller than Mrs. O'Shaunessy, and about sixty years old. He was partially bald, had a big red nose and watery looking eyes. It was the first time he stood so close to her and she could smell the stink of tobacco and alcohol on him. His face was lined with grime and dirt as he often worked in the garden. He also took the delivery of coal when it came, and it looked like he had just finished shovelling it all into the 'bins' for Mrs. O'Shaunessy.

Just as she was about to speak, she saw the priest by his car and tried to brush past Hughie who was blocking her path. Hughie grabbed her arm and as she tugged it away from him, the priest backed his car out the drive and drove away.

"*Don't* you ever touch me again." She screamed at the handyman, "Or I'll tell Mrs. O'Shaunessy on you."

"Oi've been 'er Nibs handyman lang before you come 'ere. Oo do you think she'd believe? She already noos that youse for the 'ot place down below. So whenever you got somat 'ot 'tween yer legs that need coolin' down, jus' com to my room." His hand strayed towards his crotch.

"Over my dead body! And you come near me again and it will be over your dead body too. Like the auld bitch knows, I'm due for a hot place downstairs and I'll send you there first to announce my arrival!"

"What you need is my tongue stuck inside you." He leered at her.

"You can stick your tongue and anything else you've got, where the sun don't shine."

The anger pumped through her as she walked away from the handyman. She would ensure that she was nowhere near his room in the future. He apparently had no family and lived at Mrs. O'Shaunessy's since her husband's death. Maybe he even stuck his thing in the auld demon. Mrs. O'Shaunessy didn't seem to know about his drinking or if she did, she didn't care. He was always in church taking Holy Communion and that made him a damned angel as far as Mrs. O'Shaunessy was concerned. She would surely take his word over hers. By the time she reached the house, her anger had throbbed its way into her head.

What was it about her that attracted these divils? What was it? Well, she wasn't going to take it anymore. She still couldn't kick them where it would do the most good, even though she had grown a good bit taller these past two years ... but she was handy with any number of utensils both inside and outside the house, and she knew just where to strike to cause the most pain. She had served her time as a whipping post. Now if anyone came near her intending to do damage, they'd just better look out! And if Creepy Hughie came anywhere near her, she would do him, then do herself, but no way was he going to stick anything inside her.

Her steely determination must have shown for although Hughie continued to make remarks about her breasts and was always staring at her ... although he often grabbed his crotch when she was around and no-one could see him, he never tried anything else. Even so, Lena was relieved for she knew that deep down inside, she was afraid of him, and she avoided being alone with him.

Lena had dressed carefully. She had tried binding her breasts so they would not seem so prominent but that proved more uncomfortable that she could handle, so instead she wore two of her baggiest t-shirts, followed by the white school shirt over which she pulled her blue uniform. She was now looking critically in the mirror to see if anything showed. She couldn't get the handyman's words, or the Canon's deeds out her head. She remembered Mary Noonan's breasts. In those days she had wondered if hers would be as magnificent. Now she had them, she didn't want them. She was also distressed about her increasing hairiness ... the stuff was under her arms, above her gee, even on her arms and legs, though it wasn't too thick on her limbs. She had seen pictures of the divil. He was hairy too.

As she gazed at her reflection in the mirror, which faced the window, she saw the reflected image of the bus going past.

"Jesus!" She yelped as she grabbed her bag and ran out the house. She had to get the school bus to the Convent of Mercy secondary school at Castleblaney, and if she missed it she would be trapped 'at home' with her foster mother and the handyman. *Daniel* had already left. She ran as fast as she could and was dismayed to see the bus pull away from the stop. She screamed, but no-one heard. None of those she could see at the back of the bus looked back. As she reached the stop, she slumped on a large stone nearby and began to cry.

After a few moments, she stopped, dried her eyes and considered hitching. She saw a car approaching and stuck her thumb out, but the car drove on. Two more cars passed in the next five minutes without stopping for her. As she looked up the hill, she saw Mrs. O'Shaunessy' car come out the drive towards her. Sick with apprehension, she watched the car approach, stop and she got into it. Without a word, Mrs. O'Shaunessy drove on until the bus, which was still stopping to pick up students was in sight. She drove past the bus, stopped directly in front of it and looked at Lena, who muttered "Thanks", got out of the car and got onto the bus.

As she did so, she heard *Daniel* say, "Jesus! Where did you come from? I didn't miss you till we were well gone."

The holidays had begun and that evening after prayers, Mrs. O'Shaunessy told the children that they would be going away for a couple of weeks' break. *Daniel* was going on a trip with the priests and a bunch of boys, and Lena was being sent to visit Mrs. O'Shaunessy's daughter Mary McKinley, who lived in Ballymahon, Co. Longford, with her bank manager husband and two adopted babies.

Whilst she was there, Lena ironed, cleaned, did all the other household chores and played nursemaid to the tots, while the woman of the house spent time at her hobby which was cooking, with her husband when he got home or with the children who after a hard day getting under Lena's feet were almost ready for bed.

Ten days after her 'holiday' started, she ran away but not far, only down to the town of Ballymahon. As she walked, a strange man fell into conversation with her, and after almost two weeks of just the company of small children Lena was happy to be talking with some-one who could string two words together. The man was happy to show Lena around the sights of the town and as they were on foot, in public, Lena thought nothing of anything. Before she'd realised where she was, they had walked through the town and the farmland spread out before them. She turned to go back but found herself in an arm-lock she couldn't get out of, and as usual when she needed help, there was no-one around. As the man forced her onto the farmland, she struggled harder, only to be punched hard in the face.

She was not clear what happened then, but she woke up alone in the field, and in pain. She managed to stagger to the road and after a few minutes had recovered sufficiently to begin the walk back through the town. Moments later, a Garda car pulled up beside her.

"Are you Lena O'Leary?" The Guard asked.

"Yes."

"It's time for you to return to Mary McKinley's as she's searching for you."

"I ... I don't want to go there." "Why not?"

"I'll be in trouble. I'm always in trouble."

"Then you should try harder to stay out of trouble." He said. "Get in!"

At the house, Mrs. O'Shaunessy, Mary McKinley and a doctor were waiting for Lena. It was almost as though they knew what had happened to her. Without asking any questions the two women dragged her to her bedroom and held her down while the doctor inserted a speculum and began a vaginal examination.

Lena was struggling, screaming with terror. She struggled, as she would have done had the man who attacked her not knocked her out. She tried to get up. They too struggled, to hold her down. Eventually the examination was over and the two woman forced the girl into the bath. They used a brush and scrubbed her like she was a dog as she howled her anguish against the world.

For the next four days, Lena refused to leave her room, crying with the despair and shame that overcame her. If she was in pain after she woke up in the field, what the women and the doctor did to her was more brutal than anything she had ever experienced. She refused to eat or drink and finally one morning, worried about her survival, if not her sanity, Mrs. O'Shaunessy called Father Finnegan.

That afternoon, the priest arrived and persuaded Lena to have a drink, to tell him what really happened. Although he listened to what had happened from the time the man spoke to her until the time the police returned her to the house without showing much emotion, there was a look of horror on his face when he heard what the doctor and the two women had done. He sat with his hands clasped and his head down, so that Lena could only see the top of his head, and after a moment of reflection he asked wearily, "What do you want to do now?"

"I don't know." The girl replied. "But I don't want to go back to Mrs. O'Shaunessy's. She's too cruel and I hate that creepy handyman. He's always staring and talking about what he'd like to do to me. I can't go back there!" Her voice rose and the panic in it was clearly heard.

"I'll talk with Mrs. O'Shaunessy … but you understand, I can only make suggestions. Your stay with the O'Shaunessys was arranged by the nuns at Clifden, and with the tacit approval of the Bishop. I'll do what I can to intercede for you, but that's all I can do at this stage. Don't give up hope. We'll work something out."

"Father, they all hate me, even that doctor who'd never seen me before or since that day." Lena cried in anguish.

"Of course he doesn't hate you. Why would he? As you said, he doesn't know you."

"I saw it in his eyes when he was done hurting me and looked at me. His face was sour, like he was sucking a lemon. He looked at me like I was dog mess on his shoe. Why would he look at me like that? Why?"

The priest said nothing, but Lena saw his jaw clenching and imagined that she could see the gleam of tears in his eyes.

Lena learned later that the police were informed of what they called 'statutory rape' as the doctor had suggested. He had found the bruise on Lena's chin where she had been slugged and apparently said that he'd give her 'the benefit of the doubt', though as Lena was well under the age of consent, he really had no other option. She never heard anything else about the attack or the man who attacked her, but years later when she had managed to track down papers of the assault, she found that her social worker had written a damning report of her and her behaviour 'with a married man'. Still that day was nearly thirty years into her future and her concern was about the now.

She returned to Ballybay with Mrs. O'Shaunessy.

"Now that you are back here, there are lessons for you to learn." Mrs. O'Shaunessy said as she grabbed the back scratcher with her right hand and Lena's hair with the left. "You are nothing but a little whore and I will beat it out of you. Repeat those words after me. 'I am nothing but a little whore ...'" She hit the girl as fast as she could swing her arm.

"No! No, you auld bitch. I don't know about you but I am NOT a whore, little or no!" The rage began to swell.

The words halted the onslaught briefly, but Mrs. O'Shaunessy renewed it with vigour.

"Old bitch, am I? Well you are a whore! Let me tell you! You filthy little whore!"

By the time she was finished with the girl, Mrs. O'Shaunessy was exhausted and Lena just wished to die.

Instead she survived. Day after day, she survived. The regime under which she lived reverted to the 'normal'. She dodged Hughie and ignored his comments when she couldn't. She tried to accept the restrictions of her life, but it was hard and ever so often she would run away to hide with a friend for a few hours. She was being beaten less, but that she thought, was because she was growing more, and Mrs. O'Shaunessy was growing less robust. Even so, the auld bitch could still hand it out if she was enraged and Lena tried not to make her angry.

She didn't see that much of Daniel anymore, even though they lived in the same house. After school, he was allowed to spend time with his friends, then he'd come home, do his chores and his homework, watch a little television with Mrs. O'Shaunessy, then go to bed. As he too grew older and bigger, Mrs. O'Shaunessy punished him less and allowed him even more freedoms. On Saturday nights, he was allowed to stay out until midnight. It seemed to Lena that the more freedoms he garnered, the more restrictions were placed on her. It simply wasn't fair! So she changed tack and tried to be less confrontational.

However, much of her new-found meekness came as a result of the rape. Before she had thought that it was only men in whose house she was, who were a threat. Now she knew that she could be grabbed off the street just as easily ... and so she tried to be as hardworking as she could, but sometimes the demons drove her. When this happened, she would run off, or exhibit what Mrs. O'Shaunessy called 'destructive behaviour'.

During the two years that Lena lived with Mrs. O'Shaunessy, she'd tried to observe how 'normal, people ... good people' lived. She listened to the gossip of the older women whenever she had run to one or other of her friends, and she wasn't impressed. She heard of Paddy This- O'Body, or Finbar Something-or-other or John Joe What's- His-Name, amongst several others, good Catholic men all of them, who beat and raped their wives, and sometimes their kids and drank every penny they earned. This happened every day of the week including and up to 'confession time' on a Saturday night, when they would confess their sins, secure in the seal of the sacrament, attend Mass, receive the Host that was 'the body of Christ' and generally present to the world what 'good' men they were.

It was a new thing in those days ... if you attended Mass on Saturday night, you needn't attend on Sunday. This was perfect for these men and stole from their beleaguered families the one night of freedom they used to have on Saturday nights. Previously, confession on Saturday nights would be followed by Sunday Mass and the men had to refrain from abusing their families until after they had received Holy Communion. Now they could do the lot in about ninety minutes on a Saturday night. After Mass, they would be down to the pubs with their mates, and on return home, for the wife and wains, it would be business as usual.

Lena herself observed one of these men who was big with the Church. During the Mass, he would even pass around the bag on a stick for the collection, so all the world could see what a saintly man he could be, for ninety minutes a week. With these examples of 'goodness', Lena decided that she'd have none of it. This godforsaken world, so full of His servants, was pure evil, she thought. She believed in the deity, thanks to Fr. Finnegan, she believed ... but not in what she was learning of real life.

There was nothing else to do and Lena and her friend Louise were climbing trees in the field next door to Mrs.

O'Shaunessy's garden. It was one of the few visits she had been allowed, and she suspected that Mrs. O'Shaunessy knew that she'd planned to run off to be with her friend, so she'd telephoned Louise's mother to ask if the girl could visit.

"I've invited your friend Louise McGinnis over." She said. "You're free to help yourself to some pop and biscuits. Play outside, but do not, I repeat, do not do anything to annoy me, or you'll be in big trouble."

"Yes, Granny." Lena replied, wondering if dropping a quick curtsey would bring her 'big trouble'. She decided not to chance it. She didn't want her friend's visit to be cancelled, and she certainly didn't want Mrs. O'Shaunessy wielding the flexible, and rather painful 'branch' the woman had cut from a tree in her garden. It was about three times as thick as the cane she liked to use at the school, and broke the skin badly, leaving thick, long weals wherever it hit. There was no use Lena complaining to anyone. Corporal punishment was part of daily life in those days, and Mrs O'Shaunessy beat all the children who displeased her. Her obsession was to provide a good education, and she believed she could whip any child into shape academically. It was just unfortunate that she believed that she could do so more though the skin rather than through the brain cells.

Less than a half hour later, the two teenagers, were enjoying their cherryade and some cookies they'd found in the cupboard. Louise was wearing jeans and a green and white striped polo-necked sweater, which Lena was much taken by. Lena was dressed in her cast-offs as usual.

"How come Loony O'Shaunessy's letting you have visitors?" Louise asked.

"I don't know." Lena frowned at the sobriquet Louise had bestowed on Mrs. O'Shaunessy. She didn't mind saying the 'auld witch' or any of its derivatives, or even Mrs. More-Holy- Than-Righteous, but Loony O'Shaunessy reminded her of Maureen in the laundry, and she'd never forgotten that these kinds of names could be used on her too. She wondered briefly if any of her pals ever thought of her as 'Loony Lena', or some such thing. She said nothing though, as she didn't want to be fighting with any of her friends. She needed them as a balance for the ogres in her life.

"So what do we do now?" Louise asked.

"Let's go down to the field. We can talk better there." Lena was suddenly suspicious that Mrs. O'Shaunessy was nearby listening to their every word.

The two girls were too old really to be playing in trees, but Lena suggested it for she sensed Mrs. O'Shaunessy lurking behind every bush, every tree in her own garden. They had gone into the field next door, having jumped over a small stream and were now in one of the trees which marked the border of the field. From this vantage point, they should be able to see Mrs. O'Shaunessy if she approached.

"Hey!" Louise suddenly cried out, and Lena, who had been scanning Mrs. O'Shaunessy's garden, looked round to see that Louise had slipped and was in danger of falling out the tree. Lena reached over to help her, but Louise's sweater had been snagged and she slipped even further away.

Louise began to scream. Lena began to laugh for she could see that her friend was in no real danger. Even if she fell out of the tree, she would likely not be hurt as the ground was not so far away. Lena had tumbled out of trees much higher without harm.

"*Don't* be such a baby!" She was still highly amused, and shouted over the screams, "Give me your hand!"

Either Louise didn't hear or she wasn't pleased about Lena's mirth. In any event, she continued to scream shrilly. "GET *DOWN* FROM THERE!" The stentorian voice brought both girls back to the reality of their situation. Lena remained where she was. Louise had no option as her sweater was truly fixed.

Mrs. O'Shaunessy's gimlet eyes quickly assessed the situation.

"Hughie!" She bellowed. The handyman was so quickly there that Lena wondered if he had been spying on them. "Bring the ladder!"

As Hughie returned with the ladder, Lena quickly got out of the tree. She didn't want him saying any of his sleazy words to her in front of Louise.

Standing on the safe side of the stream, she watched Hughie negotiate it, fix the ladder near Louise, and as he un- snagged her sweater, he managed to 'accidentally' grope her breasts. Lena was aghast, especially as she could see first the confusion, then the horror in Louise's eyes. When Louise looked at her, she knew that she had lost a friend.

"Let me go! Let me go! LET ME GO!" The rage burst like a dam and Lena managed to rip herself out of Mrs. O'Shaunessy's grasp. Even the sight of the long strands of hair in the woman's hand didn't deter her. "You're a bitch ... an auld divil and you'll burn in hell. Fuck you! Fuck you! FUCK YOU!" Lena eyes darted about for a weapon as she hurled the words out. She saw the fear show in Mrs. O'Shaunessy eyes and knew that the auld witch knew!

Never would she ever be able to do Lena any more harm, for she was wild, completely dangerous.

Somewhere with her words and the fear in the old woman's eyes, some sense came back to Lena and she knew she would really hurt the auld cow if she stayed in the house with her. She whirled and ran, never stopping until she was down the hill and at the Church. She found Fr. Finnegan who listened sombrely to what she said. His eyes showed understanding as she spoke and he examined the bare patch on her head , wiping the blood clean with his handkerchief. She showed him the nasty looking weals on her arms and would have shown him her back, where Mrs. O'Shaunessy had beaten her with the cut branch, but he said he'd seen enough. He spoke with her in his usual gentle way, asked if there was anything she could have done better, prayed with her and finally took her back to Mrs.

O'Shaunessy's house.

There he sat with the two women - one in her early twilight years and the other, still in the dawn of hers. He listened to them both, but at the end of it all, suggested to Mrs. O'Shaunessy that she was not the best person to be caring for Lena. Finally the old woman relented and she drove Lena back to St. Josephs, Clifden.

The girl was surprised at how happy she was to be returning 'home'. She later told the tribunal which was assessing her case for damages, that "at Mrs. O'Shaunessy's I was living on egg shells, afraid all the time. I just had to get away from there. I hated it! I do not believe that any of these people were vetted before (being allowed) young kids in their care. I only wish Sister Clare had told them that I had been sexually abused previously and that I might need extra care or therapy."

She got her bag out of the car and turned towards the house. The front door opened and Sr. Clare emerged. As the eyes of the nun and the young woman met, there seemed to Lena to be a crackle in the air, and she could almost smell the sulphur emanating from the woman. A brief glance it was, just seconds long, and as she turned to Mrs. O'Shaunessy, Sr. Clare's thunderous face broke into a welcoming smile.

Eight

A Thirst Unquenched

" . . . Iam truly ashamed of you. You were expected to show our convent in a good light by having some decorum. You have let us down very badly."

"I'm sorry Sister. I didn't mean to." I apologised yet again for something that was largely not my fault. I knew that I should have tried harder, but it seemed to me then, and now, that there was little I could have done to please Mrs. O'Shaunessy.

I was back at St. Joseph's after leaving my foster 'mother' and had endured a rather prolonged, blistering condemnation from Sr. Clare. I didn't care really. I was away from the auld harridan and although I had very few happy memories of St. Joseph's, it was home.

What surprised me, was that Sr. Clare had opted for a tongue-lashing, rather than the usual lashing with a weapon. It was some hours later when I looked around and saw that at least half of the children from my childhood were no longer there, that I began to understand why this was. There were also very few boys left and they were all under the age of eleven or twelve. With less children getting under their feet, perhaps the nuns had more patience. I changed my mind again later when I saw that beatings had not been eradicated, or even reduced. It was then the truth struck me. In the time I spent away from St. Joseph's, I had grown. I was almost as tall as many of the nuns, and I had grown stronger. No matter how difficult Mrs. O'Shaunessy had been, she had fed both me and my brother well.

She had played no favourites with our food. I was taller and stronger, and with aggression bubbling just below the surface, the nuns clearly recognised that hitting me could be hazardous to their health.

Even so, I was surprised on my return, to be recognised and be treated like a 'big' girl. At thirteen, I would now have the responsibilities of a grown woman, for as long as I stayed at the convent. However a few days later, Sr. Clare gave me a choice.

"You may stay here if you wish, and continue to work in the laundry, or you may choose to go to school, in which case I will make the arrangements for you."

"I would like to go to school, Sr. Clare."

"Are you sure? Mrs O'Shaunessy didn't seem to think that you had any scholastic ability."

"Please Sr. Clare. I am sure."

"Very well. I will arrange what I can. In the meantime, you are to make yourself useful here. You will continue your laundry work, and I understand that Mrs. O'Shaunessy taught you to cook. She also said that you can lay a beautiful table, so part of your duties will be to wait on us when we eat. Understood?" "Yes, Sr. Clare."

I was surprised that Mrs. O'Shaunessy had anything good to say about me, but as I was now away from her petty dictatorship, I began to see her in a better light. She did try to teach me what she called 'social skills' like how to answer the telephone in her prescribed manner and to give me a decent education. It was a matter of professional pride for her and I recalled her words in the classroom to all her students.

"Without an education you are nothing. Without an education you might just lay down in the street and die. Without an education, you can never undo the chains that bind you to whatever lowly station in life you may be destined for. So no matter what else you may do with your lives, make sure it includes having an education."

In the classroom, I had joined my friends to quietly snigger at her. Now here, back at the convent with a life of servitude waiting for me if I did nothing to change it, I remembered Mrs. O'Shaunessy's words and I took them to heart. At last, now that her yoke was removed from my neck, I could make sense from them. She had tried to help me academically, I decided and years later, when I had a chance to get copies of my school reports, I saw that my best grades generally were obtained in the time I was with her, though never in her subject, math. It was as though I decided to work harder for everyone else but her. However, even so I clearly learned something of math, for the in next school report I got, from the Community School in Clifden, I had managed my highest score in Math (70%) during my schooldays.

After keeping me back for that year in her class, I had learned to work harder. School was to be my saviour, so I suppose that although I had sniggered at her words, on some level I must have taken them seriously. I worked harder, but it was sporadic, depending on the other events going on in my life. If I was unhappy, I found I didn't care, and this was reflected in the comments from various teachers, sometimes for subjects I was generally thought to be reasonably good at. Comments ranged from 'very good worker' to 'shows great interest' to 'has plenty of ability but must work harder' to 'giddy and inattentive'. These comments might be for the same subject from one year to the next. It was only when the terrors of my life were asleep, that I found I was able to concentrate on schoolwork. I remember thinking that I just wanted life to hurry up ... to do what? I'm not entirely sure, but I knew when I was in control of my life it would be better. Little had I known.

The last year I was with Mrs. O'Shaunessy, I attended secondary school at Castleblaney Convent, but this was just before I was raped and although my end of year report was quite good, this was largely due to course work done during the year. My examinations followed the rape and my exam marks were nothing special as you would expect. Out of the ten subjects I took, I collected a single 'B'. Of the remaining nine, four were assessed as 'E', one as 'D', and the rest were 'C's. I simply had no concentration left following the assault.

After I left Mrs. O'Shaunessy, I realised that I really wanted to do well at school. I was not a troublemaker. I would start each term doing quite well and I would say to myself, 'right I'm going to start working. This time I will do it', but it proved to be very hard and I was not generally successful. I lacked the energy to concentrate on lessons. The damage was too deep.

Even so, when I look at those old school reports, I found that I was at times quite good in one or other subject. However the teacher's comments made me see quite clearly how up and down my work rate, attitude and aptitude were. Perhaps it is because I knew what had been happening in my life that I could see so clearly the pattern of a seriously disturbed child in my school reports, but they were trained teachers who interacted with hundreds of children. Why couldn't they recognise that something was seriously wrong and try to find out what it was? Why didn't they help?

Again years later the answers became clear. That was how they viewed childhood generally. Children were disturbed little people for whom discipline and severe handling was the only therapy ... the only way to produce happy, well-balanced adults. Spare the rod and spoil the child, they said. It was the same with the nuns too. The devil made work for idle hands to do, they said. So to stop the devil taking over the children, work them mercilessly, thereby deny-ing the devil and saving the soul of the 'would-be' fallen. Yet their hypocrisy becomes clear when we learn that many of the children of the Industrial Schools and the laundries who died through overwork, debility and abuse were not given the grace of a Church sanctioned grave. They lie in ground unconsecrated.

Lena looked far away across the Virley Channel towards St. Peter's Flat on the Essex coastline. The woman beside her waited quietly knowing that when she was ready she would continue her story. A moment later, Lena spoke again.

"It was while I was at Castleblaney that I discovered athletics to go with my love for basketball. Both my brother and I found we had a talent for it, and with the better food we were getting access to, we were to be winners. Mrs. O'Shaunessy who had previously consid-ered banning me from playing basketball and indeed doing anything connected to sport, suddenly found herself getting praises for my sporting performances, for the school was run by Mercy nuns, some of whom visited her regularly.

At the time, I thought her change of mind regarding me and sport was simply a face-saving exercise. After all, people would wonder why she wasn't encouraging us. Later I learned that it was not so much what people would think of her severity that mattered to her, for she was already universally known as an exceedingly strict person. Rather it was the kudos she acquired for 'dragging the two heathens' to a point where they could actually be winners, and we did win! She also found that the training sessions we needed to attend kept us out of trouble. Mrs. O'Shaunesy took great pride in the fact that she was the 'granny' of the child now collecting this or that medal. She was a show-off and we stood out in Balleybay. To my amazement, after my first win, she even bought me a new pair of spikes! I was always grateful for this attention, but the harsh regime I lived under never endeared her to me. Anyway, when I returned to St. Joseph's, I had a number of medals in my belongings, which proclaimed my victories, second and third places in the 100 metres, the 200 metres, the hurdles at both distances, the 400 metres and the long jump."

The two women paused their languid stroll along the beach to wait for the small child to catch up. Maisy was fascinated by a small crab scuttling away from her, across the sand and pebbles, into the sea. When she made as though to follow, her mother called to her.

"Come on over here. We'll build a sand castle." Lena persuaded the little girl to join them. Becky, the other woman, glanced at the preparations for the sand castle building then stared out to the water. They were on Mersea Island on a clear, crisp day, which had beckoned them to the outside. There wasn't a cloud in the sky, which was bluer than of late and high above a 'silent' aeroplane was leaving a vapour trail. On the land side, all along the beach were pretty little huts where people changed their clothing into swimwear. Further back, they had strolled past a caravan site, normally busy during the high season, but largely deserted now, as were the small shop and cafe they had passed earlier.

There were colourful wind-surfers and sailboats going by, and in the distance a water skier was being pulled along by speedboat. Becky sank to the sand and joined Lena and Maisy building the sand castle. The little girl had definite ideas about what she wanted to do, and after a while, the women let her get on with it while they sat back to continue their conversation.

"So how long were you at St. Joseph's before you went back to school?" Becky asked as she wrapped the beach blanket she'd brought with her round her shoulders.

"Just a couple of weeks, but that was long enough for me. Sr. Clare had to go off somewhere ... I'm not sure where she was, perhaps negotiating with this other group of Mercy nuns to admit me into their school. Her deputy in those days was Sr. Bridgett who was left in charge on my return. I don't recall if I told you about this nun before, but she was another cruel, cold woman. One of my most vivid memories of her was from when I was ill as a very small child, and she tried to force-feed me. Other memories are of her beating me for some 'wrong-doing' or the other. While Sr. Clare was away, she made sure that her authority was to be taken seriously. She would beat any child who had an extra slice of toast in the morning and would sooner see that you did not get it.

She was always beating someone, and like all the nuns did, she would tell you what each blow was for. 'This is for a, this is for b, and so on.' But this time, not me. I was no longer beaten. She did approach me one day with the narrow piece of wood she used to like carry around with her, but I turned to face her and she clearly saw something in my face, because she turned away and after that never attempted again to hit me. I think I must have become a real hard case, and I'd learned that these people were basically cowards. I also understood how some girls had become their favourites. They were those who stood up to them, but otherwise did nothing to harass or embarrass them.

Within a few days of Sister Clare's return to St. Joseph's, she sent me to a boarding School in Kinvara, Co. Clare, another Mercy-run school. It was a lovely place in secluded grounds, but life was very mundane there, even though my co-orphan and friend Susie *Doherty* was there too. The hard times were when all the girls went home for holidays and weekends or when their families came to visit them. I was always just left there alone, because Susie was usually staying with a family and I had nowhere to go and no visitors ... except one time when Fr. Finnegan came over from Monaghan. He even brought me a parcel containing chocolates and an Elvis record. Then he took me out for a drive and gave me some money so I could buy myself some treats. He was wonderful and the only reason why I retained some hope that God existed and had some great plan for all of us. I thought His plan for me was pretty shitty, but as long as there were priests like Fr. Finnegan around, I would be able to cope somehow. In any event, for that one time, I didn't stand out like a sore thumb.

The boarders were very nice and never bullied me, thank heavens. Their families used to send them food and gifts and they used to share with me. I was frustrated and bored, and the nuns never gave me any kind of leeway. I used to get hunky pin-ups from the women's magazines and pin them up in my cubicle. They would rip them down. As soon as I'd saved up for a new magazine, I'd replace the pin-ups and they would tear them down again. It became a challenge for me to see how long I could get away with having these pinups. On the whole, I still felt somewhat alienated, and that got me into more hot water."

"What happened?"

"Not enough really ... that is why it was so boring ... but that was my problem, I suppose. Anyway, one evening after class, about halfway through the school year, I was playing alone on the basketball court, practising getting shots into the hoop. A boy came walking towards me and spoke to me. I'm still not sure who he was or where he came from, as this was a private school. I can only assume that he was one of the people who worked to keep the grounds in order, or perhaps he was from a nearby farm. Anyway it was nothing much. We were just talking, no big deal ... We may have spoken for ten minutes ... not much more ... then he went on his way. There is no way that he could have come close to me or enter the basketball court without a long walk round to the gate, because there was a eight-foot wire fence between us.

The next morning at assembly the Reverend Mother announced that a certain 'young lady' should attend her office, due to the fact that she was seen talking to a boy on the basketball court. Well, we all had a giggle, including me.

I did not seriously think for one minute that she was referring to me, because the boy I spoke to was not on the basketball court but on the other side of the fence that surrounded it. After assembly, I went to my classes as usual, but at around eleven o'clock that morning, the Sister in charge called me to her office.

It was awful! She asked me and I admitted that I had exchanged a few words with a boy who was standing on the other side of the fence from me. But she went on and on asking about how we met, how often, whether I spent any time alone with him ... clearly thinking that perhaps we were in a shed somewhere. I can still hear her voice ... 'knowing young men is against the rules ...' I couldn't believe it! I didn't know at that stage that knowing could have another meaning but I guessed what she was hinting at and I was incensed at her cruelty. I found it so hard. What was it? Did I have Little whore in action branded on my forehead? ... anyway I was given some household tasks to do as a punishment. She just did not believe that I was simply practising throwing the ball into the hoop when he wandered by and spoke with me. When I refused to change my story she ridiculed me in her office calling me names I never imagined a nun would know! She really thought I had done something terrible.

For my part, I was wondering what crime had I committed now. So I spoke to a boy of my own age as he passed on his way to somewhere. For me, the danger was men! ... particularly much older men. Anyway, it wasn't until she told me that she was reporting the 'incident' to Sr. Clare that I began to wonder if she had known about what had happened to me when I was spending time at Mrs. O'Shaunessy's daughter's house. In any event, after that episode, I knew I was in big trouble. I saw my chances of being kept in school slipping away from me, and I begged her not to tell Sister Clare of my 'breach' in speaking with this boy. She smiled a terrible smile and told me she had no option. Sr. Clare had to be told."

Lena paused briefly and looked out to sea. When she spoke again, her voice was low. "I became very anxious, worried and afraid of what was in store for me this time. I just could not cope anymore. I told one of the nuns I needed to see the doctor. When I spoke with him, I told the doctor that I had pain when I went to the toilet and he put it down to a kidney infection. He gave me antibiotics along with some analgesic pills from the pharmacy. That same day, I took almost all of the pills, believing that the overdose would end my miserable life. I would feel no more pain and not be the evil child they made me believe I was. I could not bear the thought of Sr. Clare's reaction and what she was going to do with me.

After taking the pills I made my way to class, sat at the piano and began hysterically banging the keys any old way. Then I remember feeling faint and I collapsed. They found a couple of pills in my clenched fist, and I believe now, as they did then, that the overdose was a cry for help. I had let them know what pills I'd taken.

They took me to Galway's Regional Hospital where they tried to pump me out but I was not having any of it. In the end they forced me to drink some horrible tasting concoction and I vomited profusely. Later Sr. Clare arrived and took me to a psychiatrist, which was terrifying for me. 'You've let me down again! What is the matter with you?' She said.

Sr. Clare banged on and on about her loss of face with the other nuns not seeming to know or care that I was gripped in terror. I had heard the stories of children who ended up as users of the mental health services, of girls and sometimes boys, who had been repeatedly raped there, often by the so-called 'carers', other times by madmen who managed to get hold of them. Again, I cannot help but wonder ... did these eminent psychiatrists, trained as they were in understanding the human psyche, not see that many children from the Industrial Schools needed their services? Could they not put two and two together? Why did they not help?

Anyway, I was expelled from the boarding school and returned to St. Joseph's. By this time the children there were attending the new local community school but I still wanted to self-destruct. I felt so ashamed of attempting suicide at thirteen years old, not that it is better at any other age. But something told me that in attempting suicide I was a completely lost cause. I had learned by then from Sr. Clare and any other religious person who had spoken to me in those days, that suicide was a direct chariot to hell. Suicides were buried in the devil's plots - those unconsecrated graves. Suicides were carried out by the devil's children. They went on and on and instead of getting the help I needed, I found I was being pushed deeper and deeper under.

Now I know that the attempted suicide, the self-injury I would do later and the strong sense of what I call 'toxic guilt' were effects of the sexual and physical abuse that I had suffered. At that time though and despite the frightening information I was flooded with, I felt I could not take living any more. I know I was weak, doing what I had done. I am not proud of it, but I was thirteen and in a right state."

"Lena, stronger people than you would have killed themselves years before you made your first attempt. You have shown amazing resilience and tolerance, as most children do, because it is all they know. It is only when we realise that our 'selves' have been damaged, that the despair overwhelms us. If the kind of sexual abuse that happened to you had happened to an adult, especially one who has been taught to have a high opinion of 'self', like a man for instance, he would have either murdered his attacker(s) or himself long before you made your cry for help."

A few moments of silence passed between the women, and when Lena started again, her voice was stronger. "Social services had sent social workers to help us at St. Joseph's and they in a way provided some safety for us, as the nuns could no longer beat the children too severely as the marks would show. However, on an overall level, they were absolutely useless. They wrote reports that put the blame for everything, firmly on the child. They could see clearly from our behaviour that all was not well. One of the things I did that should have been a signal, was that I talked about sex all the time. For me and most of the children at the orphanage, it wasn't taboo.

Why didn't they pick up on the fact that we had intimate knowledge of the sex act? They should have anyway. They are trained to do this. That is their job! They were worse than useless. I saw their case reports recently and couldn't believe what they had written about me. My outspokenness about sex was seen as a sign of my degeneracy, not of abuse. They were absolutely pathetic. Apparently, I was the instigator of everything that happened to me, by my bold and promiscuous behaviour. How could they subscribe to this? We were young children? Why didn't they help?"

Becky shuddered and Lena seeing it assumed that the wind was picking up.

"It's getting cold. I think a warm drink is in order. Come on." She said, before calling to Maisy who was hitting what looked like a large sandy pancake with her plastic spade.

Collecting their things and the child, the women made their way back to the car and Lena drove through the town with it's picturesque shops, over the B1025 bridge and out to the countryside. She expertly navigated the narrow, twisting lanes towards the village of Peldon. Although the land was rather flatter than she liked, it was still pretty and Becky enjoyed the short ride. Lena drove into the the Peldon Arms' car park and with almost indecent haste got Maisy out her bucket seat and hurried into the pub, explaining to the bemused Becky that the food was wholesome and 'scrummy'.

With two large mugs of coffee before them and a warm, milky drink for Maisy, the women spoke desultorily while they waited for the Shepherd's Pies they had ordered for all of them, to arrive. Having eaten, and with their drinks replenished, Maisy climbed onto her mother's lap and began to doze.

"Oh this is so much better than the apple and sandwich lunch or the sausage/black pudding dinner we used to get at the convent in my teen years ... where did I stop?" Lena asked as she cuddled her child close.

"You're at the psychiatrist." The reply came.

Lena laughed. "Well I must say you're doing a better job than he did. I had the sense that he was bored with me. The sessions I had with him were just under an hour long. Sometimes we would sit there the whole time saying nothing! It was a while before I realised that he was waiting for me to say something, and eventually I did. Even then, he didn't really come alive until I started talking about men and sex. Then it was like he was galvanised. I hated him. I felt, rightly or wrongly, that he was getting his kicks listening to young girls talk about sex. So I clammed up again. Eventually the sessions ended. I'm not sure why, but I suspect they had perhaps paid him for a set number of sessions after which I would get no more therapy.

By this time I was settling in at the Clifden Community School, which was run by a mixture of nuns and lay people, and also had good sports facilities. The school is pretty ordinary by today's standards, I suppose, but in those days it was new. The buildings had lots of glass so it was light and wonderfully airy. It was situated in beautifully landscaped gardens and from some of the windows and various parts of the grounds, you could see the ocean. I felt a sense of freedom from the darkness that blighted me and seemed destined to remain deep inside me, a darkness that even then, I managed to transcend somewhat, at least externally, for with my fluctuating grades, the one thing that stands out in just about every report I have seen of my young self are the words 'Lena is a very pleasant child'.

There were now fewer children at the 'orphanage', perhaps about forty or so, probably less than half than I was used to seeing. This meant that we had more space and I was, as a 'big girl' now in the second dorm in my own cubicle. My tasks included looking after the younger ones, cleaning the convent, working in the kitchen and also in the laundry. This despite the fact that I was also more or less in full time school. And miracles of miracles, Sr. Clare one day asked us older girls what we wanted ... that's how we began to get some free time on Saturdays. It was the only time we had to ourselves and we made up for it by working hard all week.

At the convent everything was locked up and we had to be in bed by 9 p.m. If we wanted to do anything after that time, we used to get out the window and shin down the waste pipes. Cailin Doherty, previously known as Greylegs had discovered alcohol, and she introduced me to it. We couldn't drink at the orphanage and there was nowhere to go other than on the peat bogs. Cailin also used to dissolve Anadin in Coke which she said gave it a buzz. I don't know whether it did or not, for whether I drank it with the Anadin in it or not, I never got a buzz. I just thought it was horrible. I did get one when we managed to buy a small bottle of whiskey. I also got a nasty headache the next day. It was a bit of a lark for us. If we got caught, we always got some kind of punishment, like standing facing the corner, ... can you imagine it? We were teenagers! Anyway, mostly we lost 'privileges', but sometimes when we weren't looking, we'd collect a clout on the back of the head.

In those days, I would run away a lot ... sometimes to the moors, sometimes to a favourite place of mine, which had a huge tree growing by the roadside. In the summer, when I was up that tree, I couldn't be seen, and I used to hide there and watch the nuns, and sometimes the police, driving up and down the narrow road looking for me. One time, I had been caught before I reached the tree and the nuns - Sr. Clare was driving and Sr. Bridgette was with her - stopped the car. I knew that they wouldn't be able to turn the car round quickly, partly because the road was so narrow and partly because Sr. Clare was not the best driver in the world. Her three-point turns were more like six or seven point. Anyway, I ran back in the direction they came from and even took a little time to watch her trying to turn the car round. When she succeeded and had caught up with me, I dodged round again in the opposite direction so she'd have to turn the car round again. I had a lot of fun that day."

"Why didn't one of them just get out of the car and grab you?"

"Are you kidding? I was the school champ at both 100 and 200 metres and these were two nuns who were at least in their sixties then. Sr. Clare was the younger and she is in her nineties now. Sr. Bridgette is stoking coal for her boss way down below. Anyway, nuns do not run in public. That was my trump card!"

The women laughed and had their coffees refilled, while Maisy who had climbed down from her mother's arms was alternately reaching out to and backing away from a large tortoiseshell cat. After a moment's reflection, Lena continued.

"Sr. Clare had also encouraged me to re-make contact with my old friends Bryan and Gaby, and for the first time that I could remember, I began to feel like a normal child I often visited them at the weekend and for me it was a freedom I had never known before. At Bryan and Gaby's, I could watch TV and often we'd sit up late chatting. We used to watch the Late, late show with Gay Byrnes and that was followed by Dallas. It was great! They used to buy me crisps and chocolates, and the first time Bryan gave me some, I was transported back into the Finney household. Bryan's gifts were unconditional though, and I sometimes wondered if he was normal. He simply didn't seem to like me as other men did. He also used to let me go to the local teen-disco after getting permission from the nuns for me. I always begged him to ask because I knew that if I did, Sr. Clare would have said no. He always dropped me off, then came back for me later, so I had some time in a party atmosphere with some of my friends.

Clifden Community school was some distance from the orphanage and we used to go there by bus. That was another freedom for us. I made friends with a local girl I'll call Mairead whose mother had ordered her to keep house for her brother Jimmy who was a priest. I called him Fr. Jim. Some days I was sent to work for him, helping with the cooking and cleaning. I didn't get paid ... I believe Fr. Jim paid the nuns direct, but he did allow me to eat with them and the food was great! After the work was finished, I could spend some time with Mairead and she taught me to smoke. You could smell that smoke everywhere in the house, but her brother, the priest, never said a word." Lena grinned her face lighting up with one of the few pleasant memories she had of life in those times.

"I remember one day I was supposed to cook steaks for all of us, but there was plenty of time before he would be back to eat and Mairead suggested a bike ride. We weren't away very long but when we got back we found a very satisfied looking red setter, who should have been out in the garden, lying on the kitchen floor and the steaks were gone!

I was horrified! It was one of my nicer jobs and now it looked like I would lose it."

"Come on." Mairead said as she grabbed my arm. "We're not here." With that we ran out and hid waiting for her brother's car to return, which eventually it did.

We sauntered over to him and he greeted us cheerfully saying "Is dinner near ready?"

Mairead said, "Nope." and when he looked at me, for it was my job to do the cooking, I blurted out, "The dog ate them." At first he looked annoyed, but then he must have seen something of the fear and shame in my face and it seemed that he was beginning to relax. Just then Mairead said. "You always did like that dog having the best of everything, but he didn't even leave the bones for us!"

Father Jim began to laugh. "Want a Wimpey?"

"What's that, Fr. Jim?" I asked timidly, wondering if it was some new kind of punishment.

"Jump in." He opened the car door, and drove us to a local restaurant. It was not like one of the posh places I had seen pictures of. The seats were red plastic and the tables were fixed to the floor. The menu was also plastic but there were interesting pictures on it of what the food would look like ... and there, I had my first ever burger. It was delicious!

It was here in Clifden that I spent the longest time in a single school. We used to go there by bus and that was another freedom for us. The Principal was a Christian Brother who was always talking about sex but not about sexual abuse, usually to one or two girls alone, but he didn't do anything physical. He would stand outside the door to the classroom with his foot in the door so you couldn't close it. He was pathetic ... and he reminded me of my brother, who'd had to work on the farms they ran.

I never had any contact with *Daniel* after leaving Mrs. O'Shaunessy's, though she wrote occasionally to tell me what a super boy he was and how well he was doing without me disrupting his life and hers. We didn't meet again until I was eighteen years old.

Despite all this, my grades at school began to improve. I would never be top of the class, but I didn't go to rock bottom either. It was here that I did both my group and intermediate certificates, which I managed to scrape through. It was here that I truly became aware of my thirst for knowledge and understood that where education was concerned, my cup was less than half full. I wanted more, was desperate for more, but the time I had at absorbable education was fast coming to an end. In a couple of years time, I would be sixteen and free! Free from the control of the demons in my life! Free to discover who I really was! Free to make my own choices about how I would live! And yes, free to fill my cup with knowledge, to sate this unquenched thirst!

Nine

Freedom is a
Scorpion's Tail

Free at last
Free at last
Thank God Almighty
I'm free at last

June, 1978

Lena stood at the bus stop waiting for the bus to Galway, when the words shouted their way through her brain. It was strange she thought, but she hadn't considered those words since she had heard them for the first time, almost four years earlier. She was living at Mrs. O'Shaunessy's at the time and it was during a history class that she heard the American's words. She recalled feeling jealous of the man. He was free - she was not. It wasn't fair that anyone should not be free.

She had listened attentively as the man's history was explained to them. She wondered if, how and when she could emulate him and even as she did so, she heard with a heart-stopping fear, how this man was assassinated. For her, the moral of the story swiftly

138

changed, from 'fight for your freedom' to 'keep your head down and hope for the best!' It was not hard for her to accept this change. She was, after all, only eleven years old then.

It was a gloomy, wet day and her light jacket was not sufficient to keep both the rain and the wind from her. She didn't mind so much because it was only June 1978, and she was suddenly free, almost one year early for she was just fifteen years and one month old. She had to fly as quickly as possible before they changed their minds. She peered into the mist and saw no sign of the bus, but didn't dare try to find shelter somewhere as it might not be far away. She explored the American's words again and tried to remember what he looked like. He was an African-American, had a moustache and wanted only for people to be free. Some thought that he wanted freedom only for other African-Americans, but she had considered even then, that he was speaking for her too. Then some nutter shot him.

Why must life be so hard for some people? It is always so ... if you looked different like some of the kids at the convent who had bandy legs or some such thing, if your brain was a bit addled like Maureen from the laundry, if your skin colour was different like this man's, whose name was on the tip of her tongue but wouldn't be spat out, even if your education wasn't good, you were seen as different and exploitable. Your options became laundry work or cooking and cleaning - slaving for someone. Why? Why couldn't those people who were lucky enough to have decent homes, decent jobs and good lives understand that they were just lucky? Why didn't they help the others? Why did they have to exploit everyone else? They wouldn't be so well off if they didn't have us doing all the things they didn't want to do ... That's it! That's why they are so horrid. If it weren't for us, they wouldn't have so much.

As revelation hit the girl, the bus stopped with a screech of brakes and the doors shuddered open. Lena got in, paid her fare and found a seat at the back of the bus. She took off the wet jacket and wiped her face dry. A moment later, she put the jacket back on. Even though it was summer, she had begun to shiver and needed its warmth. She tried to focus on her new-found thoughts to go with her new-found freedom, but instead her thoughts turned themselves to where she was going. She didn't know the family she had been sent to. Sr. Clare had made all the arrangements. It was typical of the woman! There was no consultation as to where she would stay ... just 'here is the address. These are good people. *Don't* let me down again!'

Lena had been surprised at the conversation they'd had about two weeks earlier. She turned it over in her mind again. The nun had sent for her and as usual Lena had gone to her office feeling some trepidation.

"Miss O'Leary. Have you considered what your future is to be?" Sr. Clare asked. Just like that! Of course she had wished for a future, but she hadn't planned anything yet as she had no idea when she would really escape this life. She had hoped it would really be by her sixteenth birthday, just another eleven months away, but she'd heard enough stories and met enough people to realise that it mightn't happen for her. She was vaguely planning an escape too but the plan wasn't taking proper shape. It was just that every time she ran, she ended up in the fields or the peat bogs, for if she ran to the town, she was quickly found and returned to the convent. One time she got pretty close to one of the 'twelve Bens' - a nearby mountain range, and she hid among the rocks for hours. Invariably however, hunger would find her and she'd return to the convent and the extra chores she would have to do as punishment. So no, she hadn't really been able to 'consider' her future as she had no idea where she could go. *Despite* that, she wasn't about to explain that to this individual in front of her.

"Yes, Sr. Clare." She replied.

The nun's eyebrows raised and her mouth turned down and suddenly Lena just knew for sure that this woman believed that she would amount to absolutely nothing. "Oh really?" She said almost sneering at the girl, "and what might your plans be?"

"I thought I would go to college." The words popped out before Lena had time to think.

There was a harsh bark of laughter, then the nun said, "*Do you have any realistic plans?*"

"I ... I ... um ..."

"You have two choices. You could go out into the world now and make your way however you can, or you could sign these articles that will see you provided with work until you are twenty-one. Consider this carefully. You will have a job which will provide you with whatever extra training you'll need for your life after you leave."

"If I sign, could I leave before I'm twenty-one? I mean I mightn't like the job." The girl asked nervously. She liked the idea of a solid job that would give her some training.

Perhaps she could make something good of her life from this. However, what the nuns had demonstrated to her all her life made her think that this job mightn't be as good as it sounded, especially as Sr. Clare made no mention of payment.

"If you sign, you are bound by this contract. You will have to remain there for the specified time of the contract. As for liking the job, does anyone ever like their job?"

Lena frowned. She hadn't considered that people hated every job there was. It didn't make sense to her. Why - she knew some girls that liked cooking and wanted to work in a restaurant when they were freed. "What's the job, Sr. Clare? And how much will it pay?" She asked.

"You'll be joining the Magdalene laundry in Dublin and they will discuss your terms and conditions when you get there."

Lena was appalled. There was no girl at the Clifden Industrial School who had not heard of the Magdalene laundries and not one wished to end up there. It was where they were sent as a punishment. It was where many died, either by their own hand or through sickness or worse. Why was this demon trying to make it sound like a good place? It was a place of punishment and she had done nothing wrong. In a flash she responded.

"I think I'll make my own way, Sr. Clare."

The nun's face was as sour as anything Lena had ever seen. "Very well." She said, "I will make arrangements for your board and lodgings. You'll be gone in a couple of weeks."

"Weeks? But I thought I would be here until I was sixteen. That's ages away." Lena was both excited and scared. She wanted out but she didn't how to survive in the outside world. It was true that she had been to many places here and around, but all had been strictly controlled one way or another. She wanted to go, but now realised that she was scared of leaving 'home'.

"We expected that you would be in the laundry system by now." The nun's voice was dry. "But somehow, despite your sluttish behaviour, you have avoided becoming pregnant which would have guaranteed your being sent there without further ado. Even so, you are an embarrassment to this convent and we want you gone. Now get out of my office."

Stunned, Lena had left the office and now, here she was sitting on the bus, which had already arrived in Galway City and was slowly making its way through the traffic to the bus terminus where the family who took her in would be waiting. Lena continued to reflect on the nun's words. She had not become pregnant because she had not behaved like the slut they were always referring to. She'd had just the one boyfriend when she was fourteen, and the nuns had put a stop to that when they'd found out about it. Even so, they had been seeing each other for about six months before they found out ... plenty of time to become pregnant!

She had been in Clifden town one afternoon and was walking past the pub when she happened to see this rather handsome fellow looking out the window at her. He had long, dark hair and a droopy moustache as was the fashion in those days and Lena thought "Ooooh!" as he waved at her.

His name was Gary and at twenty-one, he was seven years her senior. He also had the brightest blue eyes Lena had ever seen. She soon discovered that his older brother was her science teacher, and she had liked him a lot. He was sweet in a bumbling kind of way and when he kissed her, it felt comfortable. They would sit in each other arms for ages, sometimes kissing, sometimes not, and Lena felt no need to do any more than that. It seems Gary didn't either, or perhaps he really liked and respected her. It may be that he understood that she was underage and that sex with her would be illegal or perhaps he was too shy, a virgin himself and didn't really know how to proceed. What he probably didn't know was that if he had proceeded, Lena would have thought nothing of it and would have co-operated whether he had given her any sort of pleasure or not. It was what she expected from men. However, he did nothing and neither did she, and for those six months, Lena had enjoyed a caring friendship with a young man which did not involve sex.

One evening Lena had clambered down the drainpipe to meet him in the local pub. She had not been there long and both were drinking cokes, when the nuns walked in. They had been informed by one of the regulars that Lena was there drinking with a man. When Lena saw them, she jumped up and began to run, leaping on chairs and tables, trying to evade them and get out of the pub. There were too many of them however, and they soon had her with the help of some of the pub's patrons. Winding her long hair like a rope, one of them twisted it around her arm and in this fashion, they dragged the hapless girl through the Clifden streets and back to the convent where they ganged up to give her a severe beating. Later, she was dragged to Sr. Clare's office.

"You are one of the older girls here now and should have a sense of responsibility, but you are poison ... pure poison. You are a bad influence on the younger girls and I know that you are the reason why so many of them are cheeky. Now when they are to be punished, they are fighting with us. Fighting the nuns! And even some of the children from the town! ... and you can wipe that smirk off your face."

Even though Lena was shocked, she tried to remove the natural look on her face. She had been blessed with lips that turned upwards, but to these nuns it signified smirking and cheekiness. She considered the nun's words. She'd heard of the fighting of course, but had nothing to do with any of it. How could they blame her? She wasn't even there!

"I don't want you infecting the other girls with your filth. I know you've been telling them about your promiscuous activities and several of them have reported that they are quite disgusted by you.

Now if there is one more episode of this kind of behaviour. Just one more, we will send you to the Reform School in *Dublin* where you will remain until you are twenty-one years old. *Do* you understand?" The nun's voice was strident.

Lena nodded, unable to respond. It was true that she had spoken explicitly of sex, but partly it was because she wanted to show that she knew something of the world and partly because she was trying to warn them of what could happen to them. She was no longer surprised that she had once again behaved in a criminal manner. She didn't care anymore. If she was evil, pure poison, so be it. She will do what she must to earn the names they give her.

Later, she tried to contact Gary and learned that he had moved away to Galway, pressured to leave by the good citizens in his life. She managed to find out where he had gone from her teacher, and ran away, taking the bus to Galway to find him. As she took her seat, she glanced out the window and immediately cringed. Mrs. Maggie Fahey was staring straight into her eyes. Maggie was one of the women who sometimes came to the convent when an inspection was due. She would help with the cooking and cleaning and generally making the industrial school look as it should for inspections, and also for one time when a television crew came to film the children when Lena was about four years old. She was also one of the nuns' snitches. No child could get away with anything when Maggie Fahey was around. The woman turned and headed for the telephone box nearby.

"Shit. Shit. Shit." Lena said as the bus pulled away. She didn't know what followed her boarding of the bus, but she imagined that it went something like this.

"Hello Sr. Clare? This is Mrs. F."

"Aye Mrs. F. What is it?" Lena heard the crisp tones in her head.

"It's jest that I saw that little madam Lena O'Leary, that's always causing you so much troubles, getting on the bus. I didn't see where it was going though."

"Where was the bus stop?"

After getting all the information she could get from the woman, Sr, Clare would have checked the huge timetable of buses she kept on the bookshelf in her office, found where the bus leaving from that stop, at that time, was going, gathered her posse of nuns together and set out after the runaway.

Lena kept looking round the back to see if she could spot the nuns, and mercifully the bus arrived in Galway before the nuns did. She managed to get to Gary's lodgings and persuaded him to come out with her as the nuns were looking for her. They had just hit the sidewalk when the nuns' car pulled up and Lena was forced into it. Gary was given a warning which he accepted without comment and Lena was returned 'home' for her punishment.

She managed to avoid being in further trouble for a couple of weeks more, until the day they caught her smoking. She was in the toilet enjoying the cigarette when the nuns smelled the smoke and got her. She was punished again, but still not sent to reform school. She suspected that as long as her 'crimes' were fairly insignificant they might find it hard to 'put her away', and since the ferocious beating the nuns had collectedly given her, she was never physically harmed by them again, though she had to endure standing with her face 'in the corner' and the sniggers of those who went by.

The bus she was now travelling on pulled into the station and stopped. Lena was glad to get off, as the brakes, which screeched every time they were used, were getting on her nerves. She was also feeling nauseous and had a headache, which she suspected came from sitting at the back of the bus. As she got off the vehicle, she felt in her anorak pockets for five of the £20 Sr. Clare had given her.

She had divided the money up into small denominations and had hidden the remaining fifteen pounds in her bag and various pockets as instructed by Sr. Clare. The nun had also provided a couple of items of nearly new clothes, which were in the shabby backpack she carried.

"Lena O'Leary?"

Startled Lena looked around at the severe looking woman staring at her. "Y- yes." She stammered.

"I'm Mrs. Mulcahy. This is my husband Mr. Mulcahy. Sr. Clare arranged for you to stay at our boarding house. Come!"

Lena obediently hefted her backpack and followed the middle-aged couple into her new life.

Although Lena worried about where she was going, she was very excited. The fear she'd had originally at hearing that she would soon be free had dissipated like cigarette smoke in the wind, as soon as she'd left the nun's office.

Now she could hardly contain her excitement, but didn't wish to speak as she wasn't sure about this couple.

The man parked the car in front of a large house on the outskirts of Galway City and said loudly, "This is it!" He got out of the car and opened the back door for Lena to get out, before hurrying round to open his wife's door. Lena got her backpack and waited for the couple to walk round the car towards the house.

"Come!" The woman said. Lena followed them.

The inside of the house surprised Lena. She expected it to be as shabby as the outside did, but it was shining with cleanliness. Mr. Mulcahy disappeared somewhere towards the back of the house whilst his wife spoke to a young woman who was standing just behind the door, with her hands behind her back and a respectful look on her face.

"Everything in order?" She asked.

"Aye, Mrs. Mulcahy." The girl replied sounding like she'd said those words a thousand times this day and it was not quite lunch time yet.

"Be about your duties then."

The girl turned and it was then that Lena saw that she had a duster in her hand. As the girl went back to her chores, Mrs. Mulcahy walked to a cupboard, took out a key and turning to Lena said "Come."

Lena hid a smile as she followed the woman up the stairs. If the woman had not introduced herself and spoken to the girl downstairs, she would have thought the only word she knew was 'come'.

"This is your room."

This time Lena allowed the smile through. The room was small, smaller than the one she had at Mrs. O'Shaunessy's, but it was way bigger than the cubicle at the convent where she had been sleeping for the past two years.

"I can see it pleases you. Now we have certain rules here." The woman continued and Lena looked at her, her cheerful mood becoming uncertainty.

"There is no smoking anywhere on the premises. It affects my allergies. No smoking especially in the privacy of your bedroom. It is a fire hazard."

Lena nodded. That was easy, she didn't smoke that much anyway.

"You will keep your room tidy at all times. I do not inspect rooms, but I will do if strange smells are detected coming from here."

Lena nodded again. She was a tidy person ... you had to be living with people whose credos included 'Cleanliness is next to Godliness'." That one was also easy.

"No loud noises from radios, record players, or conversations."

Lena had no radio, record player or friends, so her head kept on working.

"No alcohol or drunken behaviour on the premises. You will do nothing to damage the walls, ceiling, floor ..." The woman went on and on and Lena felt that she could easily deal with the rules. She tuned the woman out and looked around the room. It was painted a pale green (including the ceiling), with white skirting boards and door surrounds. The door was also green so the white surround was lucky, Lena thought, or she might never find her way out the room.

It was already occupied by a single bed, a wardrobe and a chest of drawers which had a mirror on top. There was also a small table and two chairs. An old armchair was stuck in the corner. The window which she had edged towards looked over the back of the house onto neat gardens and a sudden surge of happiness flashed through the teenager. Her eyes roved beyond the garden and across the road beyond she saw a huge building she would later learn was the army barracks.

As though she had followed Lena's eyes to the army building, Mrs. Mulcahy said, "No men allowed, at any time. I understand that you are partial to male company and we'll have none of that here. One lapse and you're out of here, Sr. Clare or no Sr. Clare. *Do you understand?*"

Lena spoke for the first time. "Aye, I understand, and whatever you may have heard about me will mostly be untrue."

"Sr. Clare is a nun. Nuns do not lie. If she says you're a little harlot, I believe her and if you as much as put one toe out of line, I'll come down on you like a ton of bricks!" She looked at Lena reminding the girl of a photograph of an eagle she'd seen.

Lena sighed and said, "Aye, Mrs. Mulcahy," realising that as she said so, she sounded exactly like the girl downstairs. "The room will cost you £10 per month in advance. There is also a £5 deposit against damages. Sr. Clare said you'll pay on your arrival. You've arrived."

Lena fished in her bag and found the fifteen quid needed. She gave it to the woman who produced a small book from her skirt pocket and wrote in it. She handed the book to Lena.

"This is a rent book. Each month when you pay, bring the book so I can record that you've paid." Lena took the book smiling. Paying rent was the first 'independent' thing she done.

"Now I understand that you have some money from Sr. Clare. How much?"

"Twenty pounds minus what I just gave you." Lena replied truthfully.

The woman pursed her lips. "That won't last you long. Now Mr. Mulcahy was asking around the town and he may have found some work for you. It's in a local restaurant and bar. Are you interested?"

"Aye, Mrs. Mulcahy!" Lena was beaming with enthusiasm, and the woman's mouth relaxed into a small smile.

So it was that Lena found her first job shortly after she arrived in Galway. She was enchanted with the city, which was full of students, some of whom were studying to be deacons at a nearby monastery. She met a young man named Francis, who was one of these would-be deacons and they fell into an easy friendship.

She was now a waitress earning the princely sum of £55.50 per month and as she would say later 'was beside myself with my new found freedom'.

If Lena thought that working in the restaurant would be a piece of cake, after all she had worked hard all her life and had served the nuns at their tables, she was soon to find that she didn't have a clue.

Orders came fast and furious and Lena simply couldn't cope. There were just a couple of them doing the waitressing work and at lunch times especially, the restaurant was crowded. She got all the orders and the change mixed up and was driving the boss and other staff nuts. One day, having collected a pile of dirty dishes from the table, she backed into the swing doors leading to the kitchen. However, there was a system the management called 'keep right' where movement in and out the kitchens were always on the right so that incoming dirty dishes were brought in one side of the double swing doors, and outgoing food was taken out through the other. Lena failed to back into the correct side, and crashed into the other waitress who was hurrying out her side of the door with a tray of steaming dishes.

Lena was fortunate not to get burnt, not so the other waitress who, in addition to the food on the tray was also carrying a pot of freshly made coffee. Lena was sacked on the spot! It hadn't been her first accident and she had lost count of all the breakages she had been responsible for in the two weeks she had worked. In any event there was no salary coming to her as all the previous breakages had been deducted from her due wage and these new ones combined with the cost of the wasted food, wiped out any change she had hoped to get.

Her resources had been further depleted by her buying some decent second-hand clothes for a few shillings, food and a few treats - chocolate, crisps and lemonade. She had spent all her free time in the local department store, which was in a shopping com-plex that included a Wimpey bar, a coffee shop and a small pub on the basement floor. She was making her way dejectedly back home wondering how to tell Mrs. Mulcahy, who had turned out to be pretty decent and who had tried to be helpful, when she realised that she was hungry. She knew that she hadn't much money left, and despite the fact that she now had no job, and just enough for a week's rent, she decided to buy herself to a burger and fries lunch at Wimpy's. It was too expensive a treat, but she had no idea about finance let alone survival and before she knew it all her money had 'run out'.

Mr. and Mrs. Mulcahy tried to help her find other work, but her reputation for breaking things had gone before her and it was hard to find. Finally she went to the Social Services who paid her rent for her and gave her a small allowance to live on. They too, expected her to find work soon.

Lena felt that she was in a hopeless situation and as she didn't know any better, was fast becoming easy prey for anyone who wanted to use her.

She had been on the 'dole' for two weeks when one evening, bored with being alone and with nothing to do, she went down to the pub. Although she was meeting Francis, she imagined that she would find her old boyfriend Gary there, and put on her newest jeans which hugged her boyish figure and a shocking pink t-shirt which enhanced her dusky complexion. She would take some make-up to apply in the pub's toilet, as Mrs. Mulcahy didn't 'hold with young girls wearing that muck on their faces'.

Lena was by now a very attractive young woman with a fine bone structure. Her face with its Grecian nose set between deep brown eyes and a naturally smiling mouth was framed by heavy, dark brown hair tumbling down her back. Her natural tan and slim body meant that for many men she would be an instant magnet. These things never occurred to her, for although she rebelled against her upbringing, she believed what the nuns, what everyone seemed to think about her ... that she was evil, and as evil was ugly, she also believed that she was ugly.

She put her coat on and slipped out the house, not realising that she had been observed. With her freedom she never imagined that the watchers would still be there, reporting her every movement back to the nuns.

Francis was waiting for her and took her hand, kissing her briefly on the cheek. Lena smiled at him and they walked into the pub together. It was fairly empty as the local cinema was showing what it called a 'blockbuster' and many people were there. Lena had wanted to see the film too, but hadn't enough money for the ticket. As it was, Francis would be buying all their drinks, as was done in those days. Lena was trying a Guinness, a drink she had found too bitter when she had first tried it a few months earlier, but Francis had ordered a 'Guinness and black' and the blackcurrant juice in it had sweetened it enough for her to enjoy it.

She was on her second Guinness and black and the pub had filled up somewhat, when a shadow drew her eyes to the top of the stairs, and as she looked, a vision in denim appeared at the top of the stairs. His shirt, jeans and jacket were all denim, and he wore cowboy boots that stopped just below his knee. His head glinted blonde and red and Lena felt herself getting flushed.

Who is this foin thing coming down the stairs?' was her first thought, the second being ... and I forgot to *put* my make-*up* on. The warmth filled her then gathered itself and flowed to the place at the top of her legs. She felt her heart thumping and as she stared at him. His eyes, which had been roving round the room as he descended the stairs, stopped their busy tour when they met hers.

His moustache was full and red, as were his thick eyebrows, and his reddish blonde hair was cropped short, very short. Lena couldn't help but notice that his slim form filled his clothing very nicely. Her eyes automatically made a quick trip to the crotch of his jeans which also seemed full of itself. He smiled as though he had not only known her all his life but had also registered her quick look, and started walking to their table.

"Who's that?" She managed to mutter to Francis. He looked round and said, "Och! *Don't* worry about him. That'll just be Jimmy Reagan."

"You know him?" "Aye."

Just then Jimmy Reagan reached their table and without much ado sat himself down.

"Francis." He said.

"Ach Jimmy, but how are youse these days?" Francis replied.

"Middling ... and who is this charming beauty?" Jimmy asked gazing at Lena as though he had never seen such a wonder.

Francis made the introductions, adding that Jimmy was in the army, which explained to Lena why he had such a 'clean' look in these days of rock stars and much hair.

Jimmy took her hand and kissed it and with his mere touch, Lena was infused with such fire that she knew that she was on a fast chariot to trouble, if not hell.

"Lena! That's a lovely name for a lovely woman?" He asked, still holding her hand like it was a precious jewel.

Lena blushed more deeply that she'd thought possible. He thinks I am a lovely woman. How could that *be*? She barely registered the thought as she heard, "Gorgeous!" Jimmy breathed the word out as though he was in awe. "What will you have to drink?"

Before she could answer, Francis said "For heaven's sake man, let go of her hand. You're embarrassing her. Can't you see she's blushing?"

When Jimmy let go to Lena's great disappointment, Francis continued. "It's my round. You're having the usual?"

Jimmy laughed and said, "That's right, m'man."

Francis picked up his empty glass and walked to the bar. Jimmy was still looking at Lena with a slight smile on his lips. It seemed to Lena that they stayed that way for several minutes, just gazing at each other, not speaking. The meaty bits under his eyes crinkled and as the smile grew wider and long, narrow 'dimples' appeared on his cheeks. In the light Lena could see angelic blue-grey eyes twinkling at her.

"Are you embarrassed?" He asked eventually.

"No." She was astonished for her voice sounded cracked and hoarse. They gazed at each other for a few long moments more before he spoke again.

"I didn't think so. Would you come to the filums with me tomorrow night?"

Lena could think of nothing better as she very much wanted to go to the cinema.

"Aye." She whispered, happy that her voice seemed to be coming back to normal.

"Then that's fixed."

"What's fixed?" Francis had returned with their drinks and both men had whiskey tumblers in addition to their Guinness.

"Jimmy and me." Lena's excitement was clear to all. "We're going to see the filum tomorrow night."

"That's so?" Francis sounded like Sr. Clare and Lena suddenly disliked him. She didn't reply.

When he had settled into his chair, there was an awkward silence broken only by Jimmy cheerfully saying, "What do you think of Leinster's chances then?"

The men began a heated discussion about hurling and Leinster's chances against Munster's. Hurling was one of Ireland's national games ... a game that originated in this country and as far as Lena knew was played nowhere else in the world.

Disturbed by the aggression in the air, she excused herself and went to the ladies' room, where after using the facilities, she tidied her hair and applied her make-up, critically appraising her face. She wanted to look her best for this man who took her very breath away and made her heart race like it never had before. She was still turning this way and that ensuring that everything looked good, when she heard the commotion. She rushed back into the bar.

Jimmy and Francis were throwing punches at each other while two of the barmen held them away from each other as best they could.

"She's going nowhere with you, you bloody tom-cat." Francis screamed at Jimmy as both men were being ejected from the bar.

Lena followed, aghast. When it hit her that two men were fighting over her, she was momentarily pleased, for no-one had really cared so much for her before. Then she heard Jimmy saying. "We can settle this right here, right now. Let her choose."

"Alright. Lena choose!" Francis barked. "I don't understand."

"You have to choose one of us. You can't be friend to both of us." Francis replied as aggressive as ever.

"But why ever not?" asked Lena. Francis was a nice man. She liked him. It was good to have friends.

"You can only have one." Jimmy explained gently as he took her elbow. Once more the flames of that bewildering feeling rampaged through her and she made the only choice she could.

Jimmy Reagan was seven and a half years older than Lena, and had a sophistication she had never experienced before. He proved to be enormous fun, always skirting on the edge of danger. He provided an excitement that Lena found addictive and when he took her, she understood why sex was such an obsession for so many people, for she herself became obsessed with it, and with this man.

Soon she found herself a new job in a cafe, but as she spent more time thinking about Jimmy and being in bed with him, it was not a job she would keep for very long. She spent every free moment with him, going home to her digs late at night, and when Jimmy had no money, they used what little she had. They found all manner of places to indulge their passion, and because Jimmy took up so much of her time, and all of her available cash, the Mulcahys threw her out the house. They told her that it was because she was 'always out and about with men', but there was only Jimmy.

For a while, she lived under a bridge in Galway City and made friends with some of the homeless. Jimmy was living at the barracks. After a few weeks he found a bed-sitting room for both of them by which time, she was pregnant and once more without a job.

Feeling confused and unsure of herself, she made her way back to the convent hoping for some advice and possibly help. As she was telling Sr. Clare what had befallen her, she realised that the nun not only knew that she was living with Jimmy, she also knew that Lena was pregnant.

"I knew this would be your downfall. You're a wee divil, just like your mother and her mother before her. The whole lot of you don't know when to keep your legs together. Well, it's nothing to do with me. You chose your freedom and the road straight to hell where you'll burn for an eternity. It's all out of my hands now. Thank the Lord."

Lena returned to Galway feeling rebellious after her conversation with the nun. She convinced herself that the nuns were wrong again and that everything would work out just fine. So she began her new life with Jimmy full of excitement and hope. Their 'honeymoon' lasted exactly one week - a week when Lena was delirious with happiness. Jimmy was with her constantly when he was not at the barracks, and she could not ask for more. After that first week ended, Jimmy went out drinking with his pals, leaving Lena home alone. He didn't return until after three o'clock the next morning. Upset, Lena asked where he'd been. His reply was to smack her in the mouth, and say, "I come and go as I please."

It was the beginning of a roller-coaster life for Lena - one which would be filled with Jimmy's neglect, lies, physical and sexual abuse. Lena discovered that in addition to all night drinking sessions with his buddies, he had a love of pornography, and sleeping in beds other than her own. He gave her £20 per month to live on, a pitiful amount even in those days and she found out that he was a thief – though not from her, as she had nothing worth stealing that he hadn't already taken from a willing young girl. He was arrested many times by the Galway Garda for theft of foodstuff and other items. For Lena, there was no other choice but to stand by her man. She had no place else to go. She had tried once more to get help from the convent, and quickly realised that if she persisted in asking them for help, she would end up having her baby taken from her and be sent to the laundries. She vowed that she would not even consider it again. Her child was not going to the hell of convent life, or any other the nuns could devise for it, and she'd washed enough clothes for strangers!

As her pregnancy progressed, she felt life becoming more hopeless by the day, then one day, the telephone out in the hall rang and someone knocked on the door of her bedsit. The call was for her.

"Hello? Lena?" The man had a light tenor voice and Lena frowned. It sounded familiar yet not.

"Who is this?" She asked. "Daniel."

She screamed, delighted. "Daniel! You sound like a man!"

Daniel laughed. "I am a man." He replied. "And from what I hear, you're a woman."

"What do you mean? What have you heard?" "Are you pregnant?"

"Ach! You heard about that didja? Who told you? Sr. Clare?"

"Mrs. O'Shaunessy. She heard it from her daughter who heard it from some relative of theirs who is a nun."

"Well you know how these things get around the school system. You've always known. How many people did we learn about after they left the school, eh?"

"Aye. You're right. So you're calling to congratulate me?" "Actually, I'm calling to ask you if you'll give up the babby for adoption ..."

"What? How could you even suggest that? Have you forgotten what they did to us? Your life with Mrs. O'Shaunessy is so good that you've forgotten? I'll never let those nuns have my babby. God knows who they'd send it to. I'll never ..."

"I'm not speaking of the nuns. Mrs. O'Shaun ..."

"No, Daniel. No! I'm not letting that auld bitch have my child either. You might be in the lap of the gods in her house, but I'm not having her beat my babby as she beat me, us ... saying the rosary at every turn ..."

"Mrs. O'Shaunessy doesn't want your child either. She's too old!"

"She was too old when she took us and ..."

"We were not babbies and she's even older now. It's her daughter who would adopt the child. You know she can't have children herself."

"Her daughter?" Lena paused, remembering Mary McKinley. She already had two adopted children, and they all lived in a big, comfortable house. Then Lena remembered the prayers, the constant work, the condemnation that she was a slut, 'like her mother before her', and she knew. If her child was a girl, as soon as she was old enough, she would be 'just like her mother' ... a slut to be beaten, worked till she dropped and abused every which way.

".... and they will take really good care of the babby."

Daniel's voice was back in her head.

"No, Daniel. This babby is mine. I am responsible for it, and if I have to die doing it, I will take care of it myself. I am not going to let my child burn in hell."

"What? What are you talking about now?"

"You have forgotten haven't you Daniel? We will all 'burn in hell', remember? Well not my child! You can count on that!"

"Well ... if you change your mind, just give us a ring. Have you my number?"

"I'll take it, but not to give up my babby. You're my brother and it would be nice to have a chat now and again."

The pains had begun and the neighbours took her to the hospital. When Jimmy finally visited, she begged him to stay with her, she needed him there to hold her hand but he'd said giving birth was a woman's business and he went on his way. The girl was worried not just by the impending birth ... after all she had never done this before, but she was worried about what the baby would wear. Except for the two tiny dresses she had managed to buy, there was nothing else.

Jimmy had simply ignored her pleas to get things that the babby needed ... like clothes, nappies, a cot, a buggy, even feeding bottles.

She'd been put in a small cubicle on a narrow bed, and the nuns (it was a hospital run by nuns), looked at her like she was a bad smell on their top lips. The pain hit her hard and she cried out before she could bite it back. Within minutes, a couple of nuns were there.

"Spread your legs. Heels together!" The older one ordered and moved Lena legs roughly even as the younger listened to her abdomen. After a few moments she joined the older nun at the end of the bed. Despite the pain which was now coming at regular intervals, Lena sighed. Here she was with more strangers looking up her gee. Tonight of all nights ... the last night she would be fifteen years old.

"You're not ready yet." The old nun said. She threw a sheet over her and both of them walked out of the cubicle.

Moments later, a nurse walked into the room. "You're O'Leary? Right?" She said as she checked a chart at the bottom of the bed. She glanced at Lena and did a double take. "I know you. You are one of Jimmy Reagan's bits of fluff. Well I never! It will be like he's having twins!"

"What do you mean?" Lena was frowning with puzzlement.

"Oh, there's another woman down the ward having a babby for him. Hers will come today too. See? Twins for him from different mothers." The nurse was highly amused, especially when Lena began to howl.

"Pull yourself together, girl. Jimmy Reagan's got little redheaded kids all over Ireland!"

Six hours later, at 05:17 am, an exhausted Lena looked at the tiny 7lb 8oz. bundle feebly sucking at her nipple. All at once, it seemed to recognise what was in it's mouth and it began to suck harder, feeding. The tightly closed eyes opened briefly, and stared directly at Lena before closing and opening again. The young woman stared back and her heart thudded loudly, 'LUP! DUP!'. It was then that the emotion, unlike anything she had ever experienced before, similar to what she'd felt for Jimmy when she first saw him, yet very different, simply swamped her and she knew that she would die for this child. "My baby. My beautiful baby." she whispered to the child.

The baby had closed its eyes again, but the jaws moved rhythmically as she sucked. Lena took the tiny hand and counted the fingers, then she did the same for the other hand ... and the feet. There was a label on the ankle that read 'Baby O'Leary'. Lena smiled. Baby O'Leary. She had not even discussed a name for the child with Jimmy. Baby O'Leary would simply not do. She needed her own name, and she needed her father's name. Lena had never had her father's name. Perhaps if she had, life would have been better.

She considered what she had learned about the man she thought of as 'her man' no matter what he had done. He was with her now and he would give his child his name. It never occurred to her that if it was true that another woman give birth to his child on the same day that she did, he may have had sex with one of them, still warm from the other. She also never considered any claims the other woman might have on him. She simply didn't think that way.

Several hours later, Jimmy walked into the ward. "Dawn! Her name is Dawn Reagan." Jimmy said when Lena broached the subject. He looked at his tiny daughter and seemed instantly besotted. "She's beautiful!"

Lena frowned. She had been thinking of names but Dawn hadn't been one of them. "Why Dawn?" She asked, suddenly jealous that Jimmy might have been naming her child after one of his 'fancy women'.

"That's when she was born. This morning at dawn." Relieved and happy, Lena immediately said to the baby nestling in her arms, "Dawn Reagan. Welcome to the world."

Jimmy laid the parcel he'd been holding behind his back on the bed beside her. "Happy birthday." He said.

It was then Lena realised that with Dawn's birth, she had forgotten. It was 1979. She was in the hospital in Galway and it was the 17th of May ... her birthday too. She ignored the parcel and looked at the best birthday present she had ever received. Dawn Reagan. Today was the first day of her life, and the first day in the rest of her sixteen-year old mother's life.

"The key doesn't work." Lena held her baby in one hand whilst working the key with the other. Jimmy, behind her, had her small bag.

"That's right." The landlord came down the stairs and looked at the young couple. "Youse haven't paid the rent for the last three months. Youse out!"

"Jimmy!" Lena looked at her man aghast.

"Come on." Jimmy said as he turned to the door. Lena followed him stunned. He hadn't even tried to argue, plead, nothing. Where were they going? It was the second time in eight months that they were being evicted. It was an adventure when they were alone but now they have the baby to think of.

"Jimmy! Where are we going?"

Jimmy didn't speak until they were at the bus stop. "My mother's."

Lena immediately became fearful. She had visited Mrs. Reagan once before for a long weekend. She had seemed nice, but Lena was unsure how she would react to a longer visit. What she knew of older women was not very promising. She worried about what was in store, not simply for her, but also for her baby.

When they arrived, Jimmy's mother asked where the baby's cot was and it was only then that Jimmy seemed to realise that not only did the baby need a place to sleep, but clothing, a pram and a lot of other paraphernalia. He walked out of the house and Lena lay on her bed beside the baby who was wrapped in a blanket the hospital had given to her. Granny Reagan visited. So did two new aunts and an uncle. That night, Lena slept alone with just the newborn for company.

The next morning Jimmy arrived, put his hand in his pocket and dropped the money he'd pulled out onto the bed. Lena's mouth was wide open first in amazement, then with laughter as the money rained down. When she had counted it all, she had £500 in her hands.

"Come! We're going shopping!" Jimmy pulled her to her feet.

Leaving *Dawn* in her grandmother's care, the two went to the town when Lena had a fine old time buying a buggy, a cot, baby clothing and toiletries. She suspected that the money had been stolen and Jimmy laughingly admitted that he had 'liberated' it from one of the pubs he'd visited the night before. He wandered off briefly, returning with baby formula and a couple of feeding bottles. "I don't want that babby stretching your tits." He'd said. With a start she'd remembered that as her baby grew within her, he'd rejected her, making various comments about 'big bellies'. Lena truthfully didn't care as in her head, she happily dressed and re-dressed the baby in the clothes she'd just bought.

The young mother was deeply depressed. She had become moody, often crying for no reason she could find. Three months had passed and she was still living at Maggie Reagan's Mayo house with Jimmy's mother, brothers and sisters. He verbally abused her regularly despite his mother's intervention whenever she was there. The place was loud, overcrowded and the baby cried a lot. Believing that it was the constant noise that disturbed the child, Lena made a decision. Two months earlier, when baby *Dawn* was a month old, she took her to see Sr. Clare, depressed and desperate.

"Please Sr. Clare. I don't know who to turn to. Can't you help me?"

The nun appeared sympathetic, encouraging ... and Lena told her everything. She spoke about the abuse that had begun almost as soon as she had settled in, about the overcrowding at Mrs. Reagan's house, about Jimmy always getting into trouble for stealing, about the constant lack of money. She poured her heart out as the nun listened silently.

"Please, Sr. Clare. Can you help me? I just need a place to stay and little money to tide me over until I can find a job and a child-minder for *Dawn*."

"I'm sorry Miss O'Leary, but we are a convent. We are not rich. We can barely make ends meet."

Lena took a deep breath. She hated what she was going to say next but she was desperate. "Can we stay here then? At St. Joseph's? I'll work hard, keep out of trouble. I'll earn our keep. I swear."

The nun smiled the terrible smile Lena remembered, throwing her back into childhood. "Miss O'Leary. You have made your bed. Now you must lie in it with the divil of your choice. Thank you for updating me with your news, but there is nothing I can do for you or this spawn of yours ... and mark my words, she is just another of your line that will burn in hell."

With that the nun got up from her chair and showed Lena the door.

Even so, a few days later an envelope arrived with a cheque for £50 and a note saying that she had a total of £500 pounds in a savings account that had been taken out for her some time ago. Excited, she told Jimmy who took charge of the savings account and that was the last she saw of that.

Lena returned to Mrs. Reagan's to find that the woman, worried about her being missing, had called her son. Jimmy was not pleased with her. He demanded to know where she had been and when Lena told him, he grabbed the baby and handed her to his mother. His anger was such that he grabbed Lena by the shoulders, slammed her against a wall and proceeded to give her a tongue-lashing she would not forget in a hurry.

So life went on with Jimmy. His army life and his continued drinking binges when he was off-duty meant that he did not return home for days, sometimes weeks. When he did, the disgusting pornography he brought back, lack of trust, incessant lies, physical, emotional and sexual abuse created a home environment that pushed Lena into a surreal existence. Now, finally, unable to cope any longer, she packed her few items, kissed her baby, knowing that her grandmother loved her and would take care of her, and did the only thing that ever gave her peace for a time. She ran away with her 'mother-in law's' permission..

She found a room in Galway sharing with four other girls she had known from her street days. They all shared the one room to reduce their costs, and as three of them worked the street at nights, the sleeping arrangements turned out just fine. Lena found a job and worked as diligently as she could during the week, to earn what she needed to support her child. At the weekends, she would hitch a ride back to Mayo to be with her baby. Jimmy's mother had proved to be a friend and caring person and she'd refused to tell Jimmy where Lena was staying, or that she visited at the weekends. Then Lena's luck changed. It was Sunday evening and she had just returned to Galway from Mayo. She turned the key in the outer door of the house when she heard his voice. "Hey! Lena."

Startled, she looked around to see Jimmy running across the road towards her. She slipped into the house quickly, slammed the door turned the key in the lock, and seeing his shadow in the sliver of frosted glass in the door, she quickly removed the key and backed away.

Jimmy who was drunk as usual, became quickly enraged, and as she scampered up the stairs to her first floor room, she could hear him banging on the door screaming 'Lena! Open the focking door!"

A woman came out of her room and was walking to the door when Lena screamed, "Don't open the door. He's a madman. He'll kill us all!"

There was the sound of breaking glass and Lena hurried to the top of the stairs just as the woman below ran back into her room. From the bend at the top of the stairs, Lena could see Jimmy's arm and hand as he scrabbled round for the doorknob. It was pure luck that in order to lock or unlock the old door, a key was required to be turned in the keyhole, and it was with clear frustration that Jimmy removed his arm. The hole was too narrow for anything more than an arm to get through so Jimmy ran back into the street where he apparently found a few stones. He systematically smashed several windows of the house, before climbing into one of them and finding Lena's room after a terrified woman pointed it out to him. He slapped her into submission, ordered her to get her belongings and returned her to his mother's house where he forced her to have sex with him.

Lena never had a chance to run away again. Indeed despite the abuse she suffered from Jimmy, life was getting better. The brothers and one of the sisters had left home so there was more room, and

Mrs. Reagan was slowly becoming the mother Lena never had. Jimmy behaved badly towards her but Lena found that she couldn't really hate the father of her beautiful daughter. When *Dawn* was 18 months old, she became pregnant again. She gave birth at Castlebar hospital, to another beautiful girl, who she named *Danielle*, after her brother *Daniel*. They had recently met up again for the first time since Lena left Mrs. O'Shaunessy's house, and Lena was finally beginning to feel like she had a family ... flawed, but a family no less ... and unknown to her, she had broken both her mother's and grandmother's records. Her two children had arrived before she was eighteen and a half years old.

Maggie Reagan was upset. Her son had ended his stint in the army and was now working for her in the coal merchant's business his father had left her. After her man died, she had worked her fingers to the bone and had expanded the business. She now had a shop too, in which she sold groceries and 'brickettes' as well as a small amount of 'bagged' coal. It was all getting too much for her and when Jimmy demobbed, she was happy to offer him the coal 'side', delivering coal to customers by the half ton or ton. Unfortunately, Jimmy turned out to be highly unreliable. He held back monies paid, didn't deliver when he could be in the pub and generally was a nuisance.

In a way she didn't blame him for the drinking. It was in his genes. Even she liked a tipple now and then, but Jimmy was like his father. All of her sons were heavy drinkers but Jimmy just didn't know when to stop. When he was only fourteen, he would drive to *Dublin* with his father to collect coal supplies. She often thought that God must have especially liked them for often they would return, both rip- roaring drunk, but safe and sound. A year later, Jimmy Snr. died.

When her son first brought Lena to her house she wasn't at all pleased. She was a middle-aged woman, who had struggled to raise and educate her brood of six children after Jimmy Snr. had died and she was looking forward to them leaving and making their own way in life ... not bringing more problems to her. Her son's girlfriend was a beautiful, exotic looking woman to be sure, and the babby was a dream, but she'd had enough.

It took a while for her to get used to Lena, but she'd asked about the orphanage she'd come from and learned enough to know that the girl would have had a hard life - a very hard life. She thanked her lucky stars that she had been able to raise her six without them being taken from her ... but it was touch and go at times. She managed to make time to help out in the church after Sunday Mass and she gave as generously as she could, so she, a single woman who was, albeit discreetly, seeing a man at the time, kept her children.

Lena was like a wounded bird, and her son didn't treat her right, and Maggie soon found her heart opening to the kid. When her own children began to leave, she found herself feeling relieved that she still had someone to care for. When the girl left, even though she hadn't taken her baby daughter, she felt there was a hole in her heart that would never be re-filled. She missed her children! If that didn't beat it all, the thought flashed through her head ... Then Lena came back, there was a second babby now on the way and Jimmy was still not doing right by her. If she's not careful, she thought, she would lose her daughter-in-law and her grandchildren too. If they are not careful, they'll lose their children to the State and the Church ... she'd heard the rumours that were beginning to circulate in some quarters.

Some young people were beginning to make strange allegations about the religious, especially about the priests. She wasn't sure she believed what she'd heard, but it had been enough to unsettle her. She decided that she didn't want to lose her grandchildren to the system. Jimmy had to do the right thing to save them all.

"Lena how do you feel about marrying my son?" "He hasn't asked me. I don't think he ever will." Lena replied as she made faces at Dawn who was on her lap. "You haven't answered my question. Would you marry him?"

"I don't know if marrying him would make life better." "Lena, believe me. It would. I know that children are sometimes taken from their parents and given to the Church to be taken care of."

"Is that what happened to me and Daniel?" Lena looked hard at her mother-in-law.

"I don't know exactly what happened in your case but it is possible. If you are not married, they could take them away from you. Is that what you want?"

"No! No, of course not!"

"Marrying my son would keep them safe!"

Maggie was relieved when after a few moments Lena said, "Alright. Aye. If he asks me, I'll marry him."

Then she went to work on her son who was tougher, but she'd read about Chinese water torture and she dripped the word, marriage, marriage, marriage, until fed-up with her badgering, he finally capitulated.

The wedding was a mundane little affair attended by, in addition to the bride, groom and the priest, Maggie herself, one of the groom's sisters (the other was baby-sitting the children), and the groom's best friend who acted as his best man. There was no-one there for the bride, except the groom's mother, of course. After the service Maggie and her new daughter-in-law went back home to look after the children and continue the usual domestic routine, whilst the groom went to the pub with his best man.

The bride was in tears. She had hoped for something special. She didn't even have a wedding dress having married in an old frock Maggie had altered to fit her. To Maggie's distress, Lena soon decided that the time had come for her and Jimmy to find their own place. It was a mistake, Maggie knew, but the girl was adamant, and Maggie imagined that Lena blamed her for chaining her to her abusive son.

Jimmy rented a caravan in Salthill, for Lena and the children to live in. He would mostly stay elsewhere.

"Here we are. Home sweet home."

Lena looked around surprised at the bleak place she had been brought to. The caravan was in a farmer's field some distance out of the town. It would require a trip of at least two miles there and back with the groceries. She looked at the caravan and was surprised at how small it was, but this was the best Jimmy could do and she vowed to make the best of it.

She stepped inside the caravan and her gasp was audible. It was awful! The walls were black with some sort of fungus and it was clear that the place was damp. Lena aghast.

"We can't live here! This place isn't fit for pigs even." "Then set yourself up in the field, because here is where you'll stay!" Jimmy looked at her, his gaze cold and hard. "Now get your stuff in here. I'm off to work."

Lena had no option but to clean the place up as best she could and make a life for her two children. Except for the occasional visit to demand his conjugal rights and leave scarcely enough money for his wife to provide for the children, Jimmy was never there. He had rejoined the army after his mother sacked him for stealing. There was precious little money, precious little food and virtually no warmth.

Lena was still breast-feeding *Danielle* but she and *Dawn* were always hungry. Sometimes *Danielle* too as the breast milk could not always be depended on to flow. The caravan was not only damp, it was appallingly cold and both children became ill, bronchitis and chilblains being the main culprits.

When Lena had some money, she would bundle the children into the buggy, a tight squeeze as it was a buggy for one, walk to the town, do the shopping for the few things she could afford, then walk all the way back. Sometimes the children cried the whole time and often on the way back Lena would find a rock by the roadside where she too, would sit and cry.

One afternoon feeling cold and desperate, she went outside thinking of getting some food, leaving the children in the caravan. The wind had been howling all day. It was a cold, wild day and the waves were crashing into Galway Bay with a great deal of force. She did not want them out in this weather, and anyway she had only the 'single' buggy. There was no way that she could have gone shopping with a babe in arms, another in the buggy, and a wind threatening to fly them to Scotland. In addition, both children had been crying non-stop and were driving her nuts. She, crying herself, had wrapped them both firmly in their blankets, as she had often seen the baby Jesus wrapped, and put them to bed. Dawn kept wriggling free, so she wrapped her more tightly, pinned the ends of the blanket together and tucked her back into the bed. Still crying and she ran outside. She waited around for a while, listening and the children's cries became whimpers, but despite this, she felt a growing sense of evil around her. She didn't want this life for them. She didn't want this life for herself. She considered taking them to the town, leaving them on a doorstep of a big house, but she knew in her heart that she could never do that.

"Better they are dead." The sound of the devil came to her.

"No!" She shrieked as she ran round the caravan circling it.

"Set them free. Send them to me! KILL THEM!" "No! Noooo!"

It went on this way for a few minutes and if there had been any onlookers, they would have seen Lena howling her anguish as she ran round and round the caravan. They would have thought the young woman completely mad, which she probably was for this these few long minutes.

"They are mine!" The devil in her head said. "Let them come to ME. KILL THEM!"

Lena wheeled round and began to run. She didn't know exactly where she was headed, only that she was heading in the direction of the town. She ran trying to escape the demons that drove her ... ran to escape their cries of 'kill them, kill them, kill ...'

She slowed to a walk as the building loomed before her. A pub. There would be groceries there. The plight of her children returned to her. They were hungry! She walked into the pub and found it unbearably hot even though she'd forgotten to put on her coat.

"Dear God! I'm in hell." She thought.

The barman came over. "What're you drinking?" He asked.

"I just want some milk, bread, spuds and ..." Lena checked the coins she had in her pocket. "... and that's it."

The heat diminished and she felt more comfortable as she was served. Change came to exactly five pence.

Lena walked to the door and as she opened it, the wind howled ominously. She shrank back realising that it was stronger than before.

There was no way she could venture out into that. She'd have to wait a few minutes. See if it dropped. She went to a long seat in the corner, and sank into it, worrying about the children. Surely they were safe.

The barman sauntered over. "What're you drinking?" He asked again.

Panic hit her briefly. She had no money. He'll throw her out. Her voice surprised her with the calmness of the reply it gave.

"I'm waiting for a friend. He'll order the drinks when he comes in."

Slowly her heartbeat readjusted to normal and her body temperature matched the ambient warmth. She sat with her thoughts about what she was, what her life was and where she was headed. None of it made sense to her, for despite her womanly looks she was still an immature little girl looking for someone to love her.

She was in the pub for about an hour having pointedly ignored the looks the barman was giving her when he moved as though to come over to her table once more. The pub door opened and a man came in.

"Ach! But it's bitter. Bitter, bitter cold. I wouldn't leave a dog out in this weather." He walked to the bar as he said this and Lena vaguely heard him asking for a Guinness with a whiskey chaser.

"Oh God! My babies!" The thought flashed through her head. She had forgotten them! How could she do that? For almost an hour she had forgotten them!

She got up and quickly left the pub.

Back in the caravan, she looked at the now sleeping children and sighed. Her first thought was that they had died, for they seemed so pale, but they were just asleep, and after loosening the blankets round them, she crawled into the bed with them giving them what warmth she could and was grateful for the small warmth they gave in return. After a while, she too fell asleep. This is how they were when the door of the caravan opened and Maggie Reagan walked in.

Within the month, Maggie had begged, badgered and persuaded the officer she knew at the barracks to speed up the process for her son's family to get an army home. It had been a trying time for her. She was appalled at her son's neglect of his family. She hadn't realised just how bad it was until Susie Doyle had told her Jimmy must have left his wife 'for hasn't he been living with Carol Hegarty these last few weeks, and just down the road too?'

She had found Jimmy within the hour, and gotten him to tell her where her grandchildren were. Surprised that they were in a caravan, she had driven straight to the farm mentioned, and then to the caravan the farmer had pointed out. There was no lock on the door and having no reply to her calls, she opened it and looked inside, to see Lena and the babies looking like marble statues in the freezing caravan.

Anguished, she managed to waken Lena and persuade her to return to Mayo with her. The girl agreed readily much to her relief. The army officer came through and told her that Jimmy had been allocated a third floor flat in the block they had for married soldiers.

"It's nothing special." He'd said. "In fact we want to be moving people out of those flats, not in. They are due for some major repairs."

"Anything is better than that caravan. I swear if I'd gotten there a day later, I'd have been looking at corpses."

Jimmy had been trying very hard to be a good husband. His mother had a way of prodding him that meant he had to try. He had joined Alcoholic's Anonymous and seemed to be a different person, though he could be moody. Lena was content. She had a place that she could call her own for herself and her children, and although the two-bedroom flat was in sore need of re-decoration, with its under-floor heating, it was warm and dry. Her man would also be there as the army expected him to live in the 'married' quarters they provided and despite everything, in her heart and mind, he was the first for her - the first real love, the first real lover, the father of her children and this was their first real home. He would not be with Lena for too long though as he was due to be shipped to the Lebanon with his regiment.

She set about making the flat as comfortable as she could, aided by her most capable mother-in-law - a woman for whom Lena was developing a deep respect and love. Soon the flat was spick and span and Lena settled down to her new life. Jimmy still slept away often. He still read pornographic magazines, and he still 'forced' her when she wasn't in the mood but it was generally over in seconds 'he was like greased lightening, without romance or foreplay' as she would say. Jimmy ejaculated prematurely as far as his wife was concerned, but Lena accepted these privations for the sake of her children who were fast becoming healthy, sturdy little girls.

The day came for Jimmy to be shipped out and Lena was experiencing mixed emotions. She wanted him gone, but she wanted him here too. He didn't seem bothered one way or another. Several hours after he'd left the house, he returned banging on the door. He was paralytic ... and had been thrown off the plane for being drunk and disorderly. His regiment left without him.

It was seven in the morning. Lena got Dawn up, put her on the potty and put baby Dani, who was still asleep in the buggy which Lena had pushed into the living room. Dawn pleased with her performance in the bathroom, received her mother's praises and was sent into the living room. She was playing before the television which had been turned on with the sound low, so as to entertain the toddler without disturbing the baby.

Lena smiled briefly at the sight of her daughters as she went to the front door to pick up the milk. Leaving the front door open as was the norm so that the neighbouring children and indeed neighbouring friends could 'drop in' if they so wished, Lena put the milk in the fridge and went to use the toilet herself.

She had just begun to take her pants down when ... BOOM!

The explosion threw her to the ground and she looked around to find its source. Black smoke was pouring out of the living room. Shocked, she stood up and without stopping to think, Lena rushed into the eerie silence of the room.

The thick smoke was everywhere. It bit at her throat even though she was trying not to breathe. It burned her eyes and she could taste its acridness. Lena stumbled, fell and got up again. Everything was as silent as the grave. All was black.

"*Dawn!*" She tried to scream, but instead felt the burning in her lungs. She reached out to the flames even as she was falling ... falling into the darkness. Even as she fell, she felt one of the demons grab her foot, and she heard clearly a cruel voice saying, "Fire, fire. Burn in hell."

Voices. "She's coming round."

Lena emerged from the darkness into the bright white of a hospital room. There was no confusion for her. She knew exactly where she was. If the room had been painted red, and flames and shadows danced around her, she would have known where that was too.

"You're a lucky woman." The doctor was saying, "Billy Sweeney from next door covered himself up with a blanket and got in to save you. He found your foot by pure accident and dragged you out. You had already passed out on the floor."

Lena pulled the oxygen mask off her face.

"My babbies!" She thought she had spoken but nothing appeared to have come out her mouth as she heard nothing. She tried to get up and was forced back to the bed.

Someone put the oxygen mask back on her face.

"My babbies!" This time she heard a strangled croak.

She felt the stinging in her arm and after a moment or so, a strange calmness came over her, then as she fell into the abyss once more she heard the voices.

"They're okay. The babbies are okay."

The doctor watched the young man before him wondering how to break the shocking news. Two ambulances had arrived at the Accident and Emergency department - one bearing his unconscious young wife and one carrying his two dead babies who had finally been brought out the flat by firemen. The paramedics had tried to resuscitate them but failed. Jimmy Reagan had apparently walked up to the flat from his stint of night-duty and saw the ambulances. When a neighbour told him what had happened, he had immediately rushed to the ambulance in which he'd spotted his wife's long dark hair.

Having been told that the children were alright, he jumped into the ambulance and travelled to the hospital with his wife. Even as Lena was being re-oxygenated, the doctor was told what Jimmy had not been told. Now he must correct the falsehoods and tell the young man that while his wife had been rescued and would survive, the neighbour who saved her couldn't get any further into the flat because of the heat and smoke and neither child made it.

Jimmy Reagan sat by his wife's bedside, not knowing what to say. Lena was still wearing an oxygen mark and had trouble speaking clearly, but he knew she was asking about the children. As yet no-one had broken the news to her.

"Jimmy? Where are *Dawn* and *Dani*? I am so afraid. I thought I saw fire near them, but all anyone will say is 'they're fine, get some rest'. Were they hurt bad?"

"No ..." Jimmy's voice cracked. "They are not hurt. They're in a place where they will never be hurt." His eyes filled with tears as he looked helplessly at his wife.

"Jimmy?" Lena's mouth trembled and huge tears fell down her cheeks. She pulled the oxygen mask off and with her hospital gown failing to do its job, got to her knees in the bed and began hitting her husband with her fists while shouting, "Jimmy? Jimmy?"

Jimmy grabbed her fists and held them tight. "They're gone, Lena. They're gone." He spoke in a hoarse whisper and his eyes opened wide as Lena threw her head back and screamed, "No! No! Noo! Noooo!"

There was a flurry behind him and a nurse rushed in and slid the needle into Lena's butt. Seconds later she was calm but trembling. Shortly after that she was asleep.

They had delayed the funeral at Lena's wish, and despite the doctors advising a few more days rest, Lena left the hospital three days later, shortly after a couple of nuns from St. Joseph's paid her a visit. If Lena had craved some comfort there, she didn't expect what she got.

"It was God's wish." Sr. Concello had said. "Clearly you are not meant to have these two children, so He has taken them from you. I understand that they were baptised. Be thankful that they were seen as worthy of His love, for if they had stayed with you, they would have ended up as worthless as you are."

She and Jimmy had returned to Maggie's house and today, her children, in their two tiny white coffins, were laid to rest in consecrated ground beside other tiny graves in the churchyard.

"Did you leave the chip pan on? They're saying it was the chip pan." Jimmy's face was in hers the moment they returned to the house.

"No ... no ... we'd just gotten up. They didn't even have breakfast yet." Jimmy's fist smashed into the wall. She didn't blame him. She wanted to smash things up too. She too had heard the whispers ... It was the chip pan. The stupid bitch left the chip pan on ... but she didn't have the strength to set them right. Anyway she blamed herself. How could she let her babies die? Why couldn't she save them?

The words of those she thought of as the 'hypocrites' continued to batter her. There was nothing you could do. They'd said to her face. It was not your fault. But behind her back they'd also been saying, What kind of mother leaves a chip pan unattended? Somehow it hadn't mattered what they'd thought. Her babbies were taken from her. This for her had been the crux of the matter. How could I have been given the life I have? What did I do to deserve it? My hell began when I was a babe in arms and it seems like there is no end to it. How could God do this to any person? He's supposed to be a benevolent deity. Why was he acting like one of the evil gods of old? And why did he reserve so much of his evil for me ... and others like me? Why did he let his servants and favoured ones damage me so?

Her thoughts returned to the tiny coffins. I should have found a way to save them. I should have done it! They were my babbies.

They depended on me to keep them safe. I was negligent! What kind of mother am I?

Jimmy's friends took him down to the pub to help him drown his sorrows. Maggie took the girl-woman to her room where she did what she could to make her comfortable, but even as she did so, it was clear from her awkwardness that she knew that she would never be able to comfort this grieving child.

Finally alone, Lena got on her knees beside her bed. "These were my children. You gave them to me for some reason. You sent these children! I truly adored them. They were all I had in the world. Why did You take them from me?"

She paused as though waiting for an answer, but there was nothing. A vision of fire surrounding Dani's buggy, writhing flames on the ground came to her, bright and unbidden. She could see Dawn clearly, the darkness of the body moving in the bright, bright flames that consumed her. It was a dream she'd had last night ... the night before the funeral. The hallucination faded.

"They did nothing! Nothing! Why did You punish them so? They had no sin!" Lena got up and began to walk in agitation round the room, trying to dispel the visions before her eyes. She stumbled into the furniture, gathered herself, and walked round some more. All the while she was croaking, then screaming, "Why? Why? Why?"

"Lena! Lena! Oh baby!" Maggie Reagan was in the room. She grabbed Lena and held her close. At first the girl-woman struggled against her mother-in-law, then she suddenly gave up, and Maggie held her close, crooning at her for some time.

After a while, as though both knew that a threshold had been crossed, Maggie released her, and Lena turned away to sit on the bed. She looked at Maggie who, like Lena, had tears pouring down her face.

"Why Maggie? Why?"

"I don't know, luv. Sometimes life is just too cruel. I wish I could bring them back ..."

"They told me it was God's will."

"Who?" Maggie looked shocked.

"The nuns. They visited me at the hospital yesterday. They said that it was God's will, so my children would not turn out like me."

Maggie exploded. "Those nuns know nothing of life! Nothing! If they'd take their heads out of their own backsides, they would know that. How can they call themselves 'Sisters of Mercy'? Where is the mercy in what they told you? They know nothing, you hear me? Nothing!"

"Maybe it was because they loved me."

Maggie looked puzzled. "Eh? Who? The nuns? Love you?"

"*Dawn* and *Dani*. They loved me. They were the first ones to show me unconditional love. They never asked for anything except that I love them back, and that was exactly what I needed ... to love and be truly loved in return. I thought I knew, but before they came into my life, I had never, ever known such love. They would look at me as though I was the only one in the world. I was their heart, and they were mine ... and now it's all gone ... all gone ... and it's His will."

Maggie didn't know what to say. She took a package of tissues out the pocket of her voluminous skirt, took one out and tossed the packet on the bed beside Lena. She blew her nose loudly, several times and sat on the stuffed chair in the bedroom. Lena also took a tissue and blew her nose, tucking her legs under her as she sat cross-legged on the bed.

The gloom of evening descended slowly as the two women sat, each deep in her own thoughts.

It was weeks before the investigation was completed ... a trial Lena waited for fearfully, partly because Jimmy was insisting that she had killed his children - he clearly didn't believe that there was no chip pan, partly because she blamed herself. She had let her babies down, like she'd let down everyone she had ever known. She couldn't get to them through the smoke and flames ... and that was their end. The inquest ruled an accident, but she knew it. She had killed her babbies ... the only love she had ... she let them burn ... they burned!

The results of the inquest were being read out and it was a long time before the import of the words hit her, in vague snatches of memory. She spent the entire session reliving what she dreamed had happened in the burning room with the tears blinding her vision of the people in the room. From the judge's first words when he mentioned what the case was about, she was lost in her visions, only half hearing what was being said. Instead it was Jimmy who told her later what the judge said. A match had ignited in the lounge, possibly under a couch. The men of the court had debated briefly, speculating as to how this had happened. Perhaps the child lit a match which fell under the couch. Perhaps the source of the fire was simply near the couch. They were not sure what happened.

Jimmy pulled her into his arms roughly. "Well it wasn't the chip pan," was all he said, before he turned away and walked off with a couple of his friends.

Lena returned home. Although *Dawn* was not seen as culpable, for if she did have matches she was too young to understand what lighting one might mean, there were those who seemed happy to lay the blame at the child's feet, which appalled Lena for these self same people had once hypocritically blamed her.

Then she heard them whispering, What kind of mother lets her child *play* with matches? She found she hated that even more, for now they were saying that at least some of the blame lay with her child. Even so, the whole affair puzzled her as she continued to put the blame where she thought it was due ... on herself.

Where did Dawn get matches from? She hardly smoked and certainly left none of them around. Perhaps Jimmy had left them somewhere, *but* I should have seen them! I should have seen them! I should have found them and moved them. What kind of mother am I anyway?

The thoughts whirled round and round her head, changing almost completely from the numb grief that engulfed her before to the grievous and deep shame she felt at having let down the two little girls. She was responsible for the hell she gave her children before they died. *They burned! My babies burned!* Round and round went the thoughts as she paced up and down her room. If she escaped the room and went outside for some fresh air, she could be found walking round some object, a tree, the large flower bed at the front of the house, even the house itself. Round and round and round.

They burned! It was my fault! They took my hell and burned! Lena suddenly stopped her perambulations. She considered the house for a brief moment then ran to it. Maggie was at work. She was alone. She went into Maggie's bedroom and found the drugs she had been taking since her grandchildren died. Lena looked at them. There was Valium, paracetamol and some other pills with long names that Lena didn't recognise. She got a glass of water from the kitchen and as she was swallowing the last pill, the phone began to ring. Lena ignored it, walked to her room and lay down on her bed. She had not yet reached her twentieth birthday.

"Why? Lena, why?" A woman psychologist was sitting beside Lena's hospital bed. This was her third visit to Lena in as many days as she lay in Castlebar's general hospital. They were still running tests to see if her drug cocktail had done any damage to some of her internal organs. Maggie Reagan had struck again. When she got no answer to her telephone calls after an hour of trying, she drove home to find Lena unconscious on the bed.

"This grief is so hard to live with day in and day out. I loved my babbies so much." Her voice cracked and she struggled to regain her composure. "It was the only time I understood complete love. If you really want to understand why, you have to put yourself in my shoes and think ... I killed them ... could you carry on living through all this pain? How could I ever learn to accept my loss? My shame? I had to try and find peace ... a place where I have no feelings or emotions. I did not ... do not want to live! What am I to do now? How can I stay sane? I let down my babbies! I didn't protect them! I feel so trapped and I miss my girls so much ... so very, very much. I am alone again in the world. It would make no difference to anyone if I live or die. Why didn't they let me die with my children?"

It was a beautiful house - nothing fancy, but exactly what Lena had always dreamed of having. It had two storeys and the outside was painted cream and green. Inside it was all white ... every room, so that if the young couple wished to change the colours, they could. After Lena had left the hospital with a clean bill of health, the army gave them the house near the barracks. Even as she looked through the three-bedroom house, Lena's heart was heavy. There was nothing in it. Everything she had ever owned had burned ...

including her photographs of the children and the medals and plaques that had given her own childhood some meaning. The house came too late, way too late, but she was a married woman and had responsibilities to her husband. Her children were gone, but as everyone kept telling her, 'Life must go on. You're young. Other children will come'. She felt like she had no other options so decided to give life another chance.

Jimmy Reagan sat in the pub alone. Since the kids died it was like he had some nasty disease. Not many seemed to want to drink with him now. He didn't know why. It wasn't his fault! The wife should never have left that focking chip pan on or left matches lying around or whatever the fock caused the fire. He felt a vague unease. The inquest had ruled out the chip pan as the source of the fire. He couldn't remember if he'd left his matches lying around. He always had several packs as he was constantly losing them. It wasn't his fault.

She should have found whatever danger there was and took better care of his kids. That's what a focking wife was for. He became aware of Jonjo Flynn approaching his table.

"Jimmy," he said, "How are youse holding up?"

"How the fock do you think? Pull up and have a drink." "Er ... sorry Jimmy. I can't. I just came over to say how sorry we ... me and Una ... are. It's a terrible thing ... burning up like that. We pray for them, for all youse."

"Bugger off Jonjo. We don't need nothing from youse." Jimmy returned to his glass, and Jonjo returned to the bar, shaking his head. Several hours later, the bartender gently helped Jimmy to his feet and showed him the door. As Jimmy walked unsteadily out he heard the barman say 'Poor bugger'. Jimmy tried to turn around to show him the finger, but instead, he fell. When he woke up with a spitting headache, lying in his urine, he found that someone, probably the barman, had pulled him into the shelter of the door's niche, and had thrown an old sleeping-bag round him.

Embarrassed that he'd peed himself, he staggered up and returned to the house, expecting to find his wife there. He felt like thumping someone and she was always convenient. Not finding her, he showered in the bath, using the rubber hose she'd bought to wash her hair and clean again, looked in the cupboards for a bottle. Finding none, he was about to leave the house when he saw her note which simply said, 'At your mother's'. He sucked his teeth loudly, and returned to the pub.

He'd just sat down with the first pint when Lt. Gillespie walked in.

"I thought I'd find you here." The lieutenant said as he approached.

"Drink?" Jimmy responded.

"Not for me. I'm on duty in an hour. I just brought the rest of your cash." He handed an envelope to Jimmy, who opened it and began flicking through the thin wad of notes.

"Wait!" Jimmy said. "Where's the rest?"

"There's no more. You had the rest. Spent it on the funeral and on the wake … both before and after the funeral. Remember?"

"There was more! There was enough to start over. Where is my money?" Jimmy was belligerent.

"Down your gullet where money always is. I pity your wife being stuck with you, you sorry little man!"

"Aaaargh!" Jimmy threw the punch with all the energy in his 5'9" frame, catching the six-footer squarely under the chin. The man's head snapped back and as he fell, Jimmy saw it bounce off the edge of the chair, which fortunately for Jimmy as it happened, was uphol-stered. Lt. Gillispie lay as though pole-axed and Jimmy ran.

A week later, he sidled up to his mother in the supermarket.

"Jimmy! Where the hell have you been? The army are looking for you. You've truly burnt your boats now."

"Is he dead? I heard he was dead."

"He's in hospital. You broke his skull. If that chair wasn't soft, they said he would have bashed his brains out. They came to the house looking for you, and Lena's going mad with the worry of it."

"I didn't think she'd care."

"She's your wife ... a good woman. Anyway that's the least of your problems. They are going to court-martial you. If you don't get out of this country now, you'll face a long stretch in prison."

"I'm not going to prison. Could I have some money?" The woman sighed. "Aye, but I only have a few pounds here. I have to go to the bank."

Maggie Reagan hurried to the bank and took out almost one thousand Irish punts from her account. It was all she could spare. Her son was waiting across the street.

"Tell Lena to stay home tonight. I want to see her." Late that night he sneaked into the house. Despite the hour, Lena was waiting up for him.

"Pack a bag. We're going to London. Those bastards are not going to court-martial me."

"London? London? But that's in England. That's in another country. This is my home!" Lena protested. She had few enough friends here, in her own country, let alone some foreign place she had never been to.

"That's enough!" He had been packing his own bag as she protested. "You can come with me now, or you can stop in the bed next to Lt. Gillespie." The danger was clear. "Now hurry!"

Lena grabbed her day backpack, not imagining for one minute that she would be away long. Somehow she would escape and return home. She stuffed a pair of jeans, a blouse and a change of underwear in the backpack, and followed her husband out into the darkness.

Ten

A Near, Far Land

LONDON 1983 - aged 20

The trip across the Irish Sea from Dun Laoghaire to Holyhead was uneventful and morning was dawning when Lena and Jimmy arrived at Euston Station after a four hour long journey in the packed mail train. She had never left Ireland before and the few journeys she'd made there were to peaceful little towns. The one time she had visited a quiet section of Dublin, she was amazed at the 'overcrowding'. Now she was in London. She had never seen so many people in one place before and all of them were strangers, even the man hurrying her from the station to the bus-stop.

Despite the large number of people around her, she felt the loneliness of the hour. She gazed at the huge buildings from her seat on the bus that was taking them to their final destination, and for a few moments was petrified for she had no idea where she was going in this strange and bewildering place, with the strange and bewildering man that was her husband. As the bus drove on, eventually the curiosity of the young enveloped her and she looked at her new surroundings with fascination.

When they got off the bus, Lena noticed the street sign which indicated that they were in Old Street, E1. Soon they were marching up the stairs to a flat. Jimmy rang the bell, the door opened and to her surprise, Jimmy and another man began slapping each other on the back and laughing.

"So this is the good lady wife is it?" The man said. He leered at Lena as he wiped the back of his hand across his mouth.

"Yeah! Lena, this is Patrick. We're staying here for a while."

Patrick made a deep bow, moving his hand as though he was swirling an imaginary hat, but his eyes never left Lena's face and she could see a pink tongue in a mouth that it seemed he never quite closed when he was looking at a woman.

"Call me Patsy." He said. "Patsy O'Brien."

Lena smiled nervously. This man gave her the creeps and she wanted to go somewhere else, but Patsy O'Brien had already begun to move away and as Jimmy took her elbow, Patsy said, "Let me show you to your room."

Lena was amazed at the size of the flat and could not quite believe that Patsy O'Brien lived here alone. Why the place was big enough for a family! Two even! Feeling some relief, for surely she could manage to avoid her new 'landlord' in all this space, Lena settled down, making the room homely for herself and Jimmy. Despite this, she never really 'unpacked' her backpack, keeping the single change of clothes she had in it when they were not being washed.

A week later, and alone in the flat, she settled down in front of the small television in her room, feeling aggrieved and desperate at the same time. Since they had arrived in London, Jimmy had spent every waking hour 'out' somewhere with Patsy O'Brien. Both men came back late each night roaring drunk. If Jimmy was sometimes a mean drunk, Patsy was worse and sometimes Lena would awaken to the sounds of their fighting. Yet every morning, they were again the best of friends ... they probably never even remembered the fights from the night before.

More disturbingly for Lena, Patsy never seemed to eat much, and often he would take to the whisky bottle like he was a baby, and this was for breakfast, lunch and dinner! She feared for Jimmy who was beginning to emulate his friend, though he was still pouring his drink in discreet amounts in a glass and he ate the regular meals his wife prepared for him.

So once again she was alone and she wondered how she could escape this flat with its two drunks. As she sat there she heard the front door open. It was only just past seven- thirty on a pleasant summer's evening, too early for them to have returned and Lena looked to the door of the bedroom as that too opened. Patsy O'Brien walked in. His trousers were hooked at the waist, but his zipper was down and Lena could see that his 'thinking organ' had been released and was ready for action. She also saw the large knife he held in his hand.

"Yoush been in my house a long time, dearie. Time to pay yoush rent." His words were slurred and he was unsteady but the thing sticking out his trousers suggested that he was not so drunk as all that.

Quick as a flash, the girl grabbed a heavy ashtray from the occasional table nearby and threw it. It struck Patsy on the side of the head and he fell, momentarily stunned. When Lena heard him shout, 'You focking bitch!', she knew it was time to run. She grabbed her backpack and reached the front door just as Patsy came charging out of the room, his knife retrieved.

Lena bolted down the stairs to the front of the building and was relieved to see her husband approaching, albeit unsteadily.

"Jimmy! Thank God you're here. Don't go upstairs. He's got a knife and he's mad. He tried to rape me! Let's get out of here."

"You're a lying bitch! Patsy would never do such a thing to me."

"You! You! It wasn't you he was trying to fock!"

"Come on up, bitch!" Jimmy grabbed her arm. "There's Patsy. He don't look mad to me. Come!"

Lena looked up to see Patsy O'Brien standing by the door to the flat. He had one hand to his head and the other was folded across his waist. There was no sign of the knife, but his habitual leer was back on his face. She began to wrest her arm from Jimmy's grasp, shouting that he was a bastard. Although Jimmy held on, he was inebriated and Lena was a strong, young, athletic woman. She twisted her arm out of his grasp and ran.

She had no idea where she was going, but she continued to run as fast as she could. She wanted to be as far away as possible from the two men and she wasn't sure whether they would be coming after her. When she stopped running, she looked in her backpack to see what she had by way of change. She had been allowed out to do some grocery shopping a couple of days earlier, and she'd hidden some change in one of the pack's pockets. There was just her spare clothes. The money was gone.

Frightened, but determined not to go back, she continued walking, hardly aware of her surroundings as her thoughts assailed her.

"You've been raped before ... no big deal ... why didn't you let him? Then you'd be safe and warm in your room watching the tv."

"Are you nuts? Why should I let that slimy toad rape me? I am not some hole in a mattress. I am a human being. I have dignity. I have worth."

"Yeah, yeah, yeah. You are picking up some strange ideas in this strange land. Just who do you think you are?"

"I am Lena O'Leary. Human being. Person. Individual. I am me. I am good. I am a child of God."

"God? You? Have you forgotten your upbringing already? You are the child of the divil!"

"No! Not the divil ... maybe not God either for He's never ever done anything for me ... but I exist. I am. I must have had a mother ... I am the child of the ... of the ..."

"Yes?"

"I am a child of the Creator! That's what! The Church says that I was made in the image and likeness of the Creator. That means that the Creator is a woman like me. That's what I know!"

"You are the child of the divil!"

"No!" From the startled looks of passers-by, Lena realised that she had shouted the last word. A woman scuttled by her like she thought she was a crab, and Lena though she saw the fear in her eyes.

"She thinks I'm mad! Am I mad?" "You're hearing my voice, aren't you?"

"Voice? No I don't hear a voice, I simply know my thoughts. I don't hear you. I know you. You are me, not someone else. I am not mad. I am simply thinking ..."

Lena stopped in amazement. Where was she? The buildings looked familiar but she had been in London for just one week and could not possibly know where she was. The tears came to her eyes and she almost began to wish that she had stayed behind and struggled with Patsy ... force him to kill her with his knife.

She leaned against the walls of a large building on the corner and the tears flowed more freely. Someone stopped and said, "Are you alright?" and he hurried off when Lena nodded. But mostly people either ignored her completely or they stared as they hurried past. She dried her tears and began to look around again. Once more a sense of familiarity struck her and she realised that the bus had come along this road. However she could not think where it had come from.

She looked at the street names - she was at a five-point junction. She was on City Road. When she crossed the road, she'd be on Pentonville Road. She followed her feet. Soon she was standing in front of a huge railway station, not the one she had arrived at, but it made her dearly wish she was on a train back home. She walked on, found herself once more staring at another huge railway building and this time she recognised it! Her feet had brought her back here. They must have followed the bus route and they brought her here. Her feet wanted to go home too. But there was no money and no hope of finding any so she made herself walk on.

Eventually she came to a large park and found a quiet place to sit down with her thoughts. Before she knew it, darkness was beginning to fall, but she found she could not leave this place, which was the closest thing she seen so far to her homeland, with its big empty spaces. She realised that people were hurrying out of the park and noticed a police officer speaking to a man who got up from the bench he was sitting on and hurried away. Fearful that the policeman would tell her to leave, she placed a large tree between him and her, and quickly climbed up it.

That tree in Regent's Park was her home for the next three nights. She managed to feed herself by begging ... and tourists often threw out large amounts of fast food. There was a literal army of people who lived off what they could find, so Lena always stood near a tourist group with bags of chips and hamburgers. Sometimes, they left their bags on the benches and Lena would 'clear' them away, 'for a small fee', if they were gullible enough. Whether they paid or not, she would explore their left overs. There were always plenty of chips.

Realising she couldn't stay in the park for much longer, partly because she had no plans to become a street person and partly because she had attracted the attention of some of the men who frequented the area, Lena set out again, continuing to wander westwards along the Marylebone Road. She wasn't sure why she looked back towards the park, but in doing so she noticed two middle-aged black men staring at her. She continued walking but at the next traffic lights, looked back to see that the same two men were behind her. Panic struck her and she turned south onto Baker Street. She hurried along, keeping an eye on her back trail. She found another great park and hurried through it, dismayed to see that the men were right there behind her. She kept tracking west and south eventually ended up in the borough of Hammersmith. The two men were still there. Terrified, she ran into a nearby Indian Restaurant and asked the couple for help.

It was the best thing she could have done, and later when she'd thought of it, she silently thanked the men who had followed her, for if they hadn't, she might have remained on the streets for much longer. As it was, the Indian couple called the police who immediately arranged for her to stay at Centre Point in Soho, a refuge for the homeless. There she was given a bed, some vouchers for food and was told to look for a job during the day times. She had to be in the refuge by 7 p.m. and out at 7 a.m. She met all kinds of people staying at Centre Point - including drug addicts, alcoholics, homeless teenagers, glue sniffers and prostitutes and they terrified her. She stayed in Soho for four days and was then transferred to another hostel in Kensington where she remained for a month.

With the poor education she'd had and minimal qualifications, the only work she could find in London was pub, kitchen or cleaning work. She got a job as a barmaid near Baker Street, which she soon lost. She found many of the accents she heard incomprehensible, as London was a place with a huge cosmopolitan population. She found it hard to communicate or concentrate. This was made worse by the nightmares she was beginning to suffer, as lonely nights led her to think of home and her dead babies. The people she worked for thought she was 'thick', just like those at home in Ireland, and soon asked her to leave.

She bumbled along like this for some time, losing one job after another. She told no-one of her past and asked for nothing but to be a normal child of the Creator.

One day, about five weeks after she had run away from her husband, the police turned up at the hostel she was in and told her that Jimmy was looking for her. When she explained why she had run, they asked if she wanted to press charges against Patsy O'Brien. Fearful of what Jimmy would do, and not quite understanding how the police could protect her, she declined. Instead, she gave the police permission to arrange for Jimmy to see her.

They met at a McDonald's restaurant, about six blocks away from the hostel. As they sat with their meal, Jimmy reached out and took Lena's hand.

"Come home. I miss you."

"No. I'm not coming back. I can't. Please understand Jimmy."

Jimmy bit into his burger looking at her with his bright eyes and mischievous smile. "I remember when we first met. You're as beautiful as ever, only this time you're my wife."

The old magic began to work on Lena and she felt herself softening.

"At least come to the cinema with me." Jimmy continued. "It will be just like starting over."

Lena was tempted but instead she said, "I can't. I have to be back in the hostel by 10 p.m."

"No Lena. You're not going there. You're my wife and you're coming to the cinema then home with me. Remember how we used to be?" Jimmy was still persuasive, though his voice had hardened.

Lena remembered but she said, "I'll not come back to Patsy O'Brien's."

"Patsy and I had a long talk about that night. He said that he was pissed and walked into the bedroom, mistaking it for his own, forgetting that we were staying with him. Then you threw that focking ashtray at him and ran like a bat outta hell. It won't happen again."

"He had a dirty great big knife in his hand and his thing was saluting the world like a bloody soldier." Lena hissed back at him, not quite believing how stupid drunks could be.

Jimmy's anger leapt out at her. "He didn't, you little bitch. You just imagined that. You see cocks everywhere just waiting to visit your c**t. Youse just a little whore always gagging for it, and you know what? Youse not even a good fock! You have no idea how to please a man and you'll never find another daft enough to want to marry you. They'll take a little taste to see if you can cut it and when they find you can't, they'll dump you like youse hot shit!"

Lena spat in his face and did what, in her childhood, she did best. She ran. This time however, Jimmy wasn't drunk and he was ready for her. He ran after her, surprised at her speed. Neither of them saw the police watching from their panda car. Jimmy was soon winded and Lena having lost sight of him, slowed to a walk. She hurried back to the hostel when wham! The blow struck her and she fell forwards hitting her jaw on a stair. She managed to roll on her back just before Jimmy fell on her with a barrage of blows. Just as suddenly, Jimmy was flying backwards off her and through a bloody eye, Lena saw the 'boys in blue' force Jimmy to the ground and put handcuffs on him. They got him into the back of their car and one of them came over to Lena who was struggling to stand straight.

"Miss? Are you alright?"

"Yes, thanks." Lena found it hard to speak for a moment. "*Do you want to press charges?*"

Dazed, Lena said "What?" as she felt her sore jaw and peered through the blood at the officer. He stared back at her offering a handkerchief. When she wiped the blood away, he seemed satisfied and responded.

"We can arrest him and you can press charges." "What's that mean?" She mumbled.

"It means we can toss him in jail long enough for you to find a new hiding place."

"Jail? He'd die in jail. In Ireland he once told me what it is like for attractive men in jail. He said they were just fresh meat for the old timers. I don't want that on my conscience. Anyway, he's the father of my children. I just can't do it ... and there is no place I would be able to hide from him if I did that. He would always try to find me and that would surely be something to be afraid of."

"Are you sure Miss?"

"Yes." Lena's voice fell to a whisper. "What will happen now?"

"We'll take him to the station for a few questions and we'll put the fear of God in him. That will give us time enough to arrange a new hostel for you."

"Thanks." She hesitated for a moment and as the officer still peered at her with some concern asked, "Why are you so nice?"

"I'm just doing my job Miss ... plus I have two daughters, and if any of them married a man like him ..." He stopped speaking and walked into the hostel to speak to the woman in charge.

Before the night was out, Lena had been moved to another hostel in Camden Town. She was delighted, happy to be safe. It was like all her Christmases put together and she stayed there for a year. In many ways it was a chaotic year. She continued to have arguments with herself about herself and who she was but the nightmares that plagued her had receded somewhat. She also learned to hold down a job for more than five minutes.

A few weeks before she left this hostel, she and Jimmy were reconciled and were able to live there for a while as a married couple. Although Lena was pleased to have someone from 'home' with her, and truthfully, despite everything she still loved her husband, their relationship was a strained one. Jimmy continued to drink and Lena soon found out that he was a regular at London's many strip bars.

Whenever they talked to each other, Jimmy generally ran her down, as an individual, as a woman, as a sexual being.

This gave Lena more to think about as she continued to auto argue, often using Jimmy's comments as her counter- arguments. She had also bought herself a small cassette- player and some cassettes and when Jimmy was asleep, she would listen to them, learning lessons from the lyrics, continuing to find herself in them even as she lost herself in the music.

Occasionally, Jimmy took her out to a pub or a nightclub where he would flirt with every woman he saw, intending to further destroy Lena's confidence. Instead she watched him and the women assiduously, learning the tricks of flirting to put into practice on the occasions when he was not with her.

Soon, the Greater London Council made them an offer they couldn't refuse. It was something they did every year, when three council flats would be provided for the hostel's long term tenants. They were given a one-bedroom council flat in Peckham, South East London, on the 11th floor of a tower block. It was not salubrious. There was abject poverty all around her. The flats were in a block where the ambience of the stone stairway and the lifts was of stale beer and human waste but to Lena, once she was in her flat, it was paradise. She had panoramic views across London and could even see Big Ben and the GPO tower. Lena managed to furnish the flat using her Social Security money carefully to buy some good second-hand furniture. She felt like she had finally found herself. She was *22*.

To Lena's relief, Jimmy who clearly missed the army life decided to join the Territorial Army, which required his attendance one evening per week and one weekend per month. This gave his young wife some time away from his constant bitching at her. He always returned from his weekends away drunk and boasting of his exploits 'in the field'.

This interested Lena not a whit. She had found out from flirting with this man or that man as she served them in the pub, that she was considered by many to be an attractive woman. She began to spend time gazing in the mirror, trying to find the beauty others saw in her face. She compared her features with the millions of women she saw everyday as she hurried about her business, with the photographs she saw of models and actresses in magazines, and came to the inescapable conclusion that yes, she was a beautiful woman.

She began to experiment with make-up which hitherto she had used inexpertly, and she brushed her hair constantly to make it shine, critically examining the best way to present herself. Jimmy soon noticed her careful attention to her appearance, the time spent licking her lips as she stared in the mirror.

"Oh fock it! She's in love with herself now. Just look at the focking eejit!" He laughed uproariously.

Lena ignored him, but Jimmy had found a new thing to taunt her about and he upbraided her every chance he got. It bothered Lena, but only slightly. She turned his words over in her mind. 'She's in love with herself now'.

"He's right! I do love me, and it's high time someone did! I am going to make something of my life. I want better things for me."

One Friday night, Lena returned home from work and found the flat empty as usual. Jimmy was clearly out somewhere enjoying himself. When he had still not returned on the Saturday she was still not too bothered. By Monday, when he'd still not made an appearance she went to his workplace to make sure that he was safe, and find out why he'd not come home.

"Who are you?" The man asked her. "I'm his wife." She replied.

"You can't be or you'd know he's gone on holiday in Israel."

The look on Lena's face must have immediately told the man that she was indeed his wife, because he continued more gently. "He's in Elat."

"Thanks." Lena could barely speak as she turned away. She couldn't help the tears that had filled her eyes and were fast running down her face. She hurried back to the flat where she howled her pain. She called in sick at the pub and spent the next several days crying her rage, disappointment and every feeling she had for Jimmy out of her system. Then she looked for Elat on a map, just so she could have some connection to him, for as she'd discovered in her days of crying, she still loved the louse. It was from this point that the loneliness grew daily, threatening to swamp her. Crying became an integral part of her private life.

She returned to work and life went on without him. She had no idea when, if he would return. In another attempt to feel closer to her missing husband, she too joined the Territorial Army and began training in the Nursing Corps. It was a whole new world for her as she met new and interesting people. She also realised that she didn't like the pub she was working in, catering as it did for the poorer elements of society, so she found a job at a more up-market pub in Fleet Street, which catered to the journalists and office workers in the area.

"Hallo Lena. Whisky and water four times, two ploughman's, one shepherd's and a cottage pie." Charles Davis was an older man who had taken an interest in the attractive barmaid. He was the manager of a local building society and often arrived at midday with three of his colleagues for lunch and drinks. Lena liked that he, like most of her new clientele, never seemed to leave the pub inebriated.

"Sure. Coming up." Lena quickly gave the food order to the kitchen and poured the drinks.

"What do you do after you leave work?" Charles asked as he waited for the drinks.

"Other than the TA, I don't do much."

"You look pretty fit. Don't you play any sport?"

"No. I just cycle to work. When I was a kid I used to be in athletics."

"We have a couple of teams that play football and hockey. You interested?"

Lena jumped at the chance and found that Charles coached both teams. His continued interest in her was evident and when he offered her a job as a clerical assistant, she opened up a little to him, telling him some of the less disturbing aspects of her childhood. He in turn encouraged her development, advising her to go back to school and study various subjects at the Ordinary Level for the General Certificate of Education. She did as she was told and passed several subjects with flying colours. Life was beginning to fall on a track that Lena loved.

In this time of obvious light, Lena found herself wallowing in the dark every time she went home. Despite all the positive developments in her life, she missed her wayward husband and without him she felt very alone. She'd begun dating but was resentful of her dates, becoming jealous if they looked at another woman. As a result, she was always being dumped, so that even as her sense of worth grew on one front, it diminished on another.

Her lost children were always somewhere in the back of her mind and dreams of them returned again with a vengeance to fill the empty place in the bed with her. Her studies both as an 'O' Level chemistry/biology student and for her role in the TA's Nursing Corps, began to work on her subconscious especially in her sleeping moments.

Nine month old Dani had been very drowsy that day. Dawn had been watching the television as she waited for her breakfast.

Lena hugged her before sending her into the lounge with her favourite Teddy. "The underfloor heating is superb. It is warm enough to dry nappies on. Too warm and I've already got the thermostat on its lowest point. I must ask someone to come in and check the boiler." She thought as she rushed to the toilet. She was taking her pants down when she heard the explosion.

I can't remember. I can't remember. Lena mumbled even as she slept. She was writhing constantly in the bed and the sheets wound their way round her like a shroud. The pictures flickering below her closed eyelids continued.

Was it gas? Why don't I know that? Was there a fatal build-up of gas? Why did the lounge explode? The baby was sleepy. Was that gas too? Wait a minute! Could there have been a hot spot under the couch that caused it to ignite? The boiler! Where was that? Could that have been in a room under the lounge?

Jimmy's voice boomed loud in her head. "They said that Dawn was playing with matches."

Suddenly, through her streaming eyes, she saw the fire. It encircled the buggy which was already burning and as she struggled towards it she saw a section of the fire writhing, silently.

There are no matches! I don't see any matches!

Dark acrid smoke rose up and swirled round her. In its centre was a bright light. *Dawn!* She could see her clearly! *Dawn* was dancing in front of the flames. She reached out for her. Come quick! Instead *Dawn* ignited.

No *baby*! No! Come to Mammy! Dawn! Dani!

She was choking, suffocating in the smoke. Even as she did so, Lena woke up and immediately panicked. They'd wrapped her up like a corpse. I'm not dead! I'm not dead! Her brain shrieked. She struggled her way free from the sheets, her heart galloping like horses on a racetrack, and saw that she was alone in her bed. As her heart quietened, she considered the dream. Was the army at fault? Why didn't this come out at the inquest? There were no matches. Dawn was not the cause. It wasn't a chip pan. Lena was not the cause. The explosion and the seat of the fire ... both were in the lounge. Was the underfloor heating at fault? There was a boiler somewhere below the lounge. Was the boiler at fault? Was the army at fault? Why couldn't I pay more attention? And why don't I have a copy of the inquest's report?

Lena got up, zombie-like and walked to the bathroom. After using the toilet, she gazed at her reflection in the mirror. Dawn, fair like her father was sitting on her left shoulder. Dani was dark like her, and now Lena could see for the first time that her second daughter looked remarkably like her ... she sat on her right shoulder. They stared at their mother in the mirror. She stared back at them, and slowly they faded. Lena shook herself moments later, seemingly coming out of a trance. She was alone in the world, and her loneliness overwhelmed her. She opened the medicine cabinet and took out some pills. There weren't many there, but perhaps they would be enough. She swallowed the lot and went back to bed.

Two days later, she woke up to a loud banging on her door. Feeling like death warmed over, and sore on the spots where she had lain, she struggled into her dressing gown and opened the door to Martina Clarke, her boss.

"Lena! Are you alright? We were worried ... it's not like you to miss work ..." Her voice tailed off as Lena swayed alarmingly.

"Got the 'flu, I think." Lena's voice was a mere croak.

"Better get back to bed then. You need anything?"

"No thanks. I'll be better tomorrow, I'll come in tomorrow."

"No you won't. Take a couple of days. Rest. Come in when you're better."

"Will I not lose my job?"

"No of course not! You're a good worker. You just get well. Will you be alright getting back to bed?"

"Yes. I will. Thanks."

Lena went back to work, but her demeanour had changed. She was desperate for a child and went to bed with anyone she thought would provide her with viable sperm. There was one man called Neil that seemed special to her, but she found herself comparing him to Jimmy and was unable to trust him, or indeed anyone else. She began to drink heavily which made her jealousy and unpredictability even worse. And so Neil left her too.

Even in the TA, she became known as game for a laugh and the drinking sessions, which still not at 'Jimmy' proportions, continued unabated. It was in one such session, that a colleague suggested that she should study to be something he called an 'operating department practitioner', and Lena, as always ready to please, made the application for training.

Her acceptance letter came and thrilled, she gave her notice at the pub, informed Charles Davis of her plans and began to pack her property.

Knock, knock, knock.

Lena opened the door and almost fainted with shock. "Youse gonna let me in?" Jimmy stood before her. "Sure." Lena stood back and without much ado Jimmy said.

"I need some money. Have you got any?"

"Sure." Lena said again and she took the £60 she had in her purse and gave it to him.

"I'm away, but I'll be back."

"I won't be here. I'm moving to Kent."

"You have an address? So I'll know where to come?" "Sure." Lena scribbled her new address and telephone number on the back of an envelope and gave it to him. "I'll be back." He said.

"Right." Lena replied.

Two weeks later, she moved out of her apartment in Peckham and into hospital accommodation in Ashford to do her training. The hardest part of her leaving was not she'd had no word from Jimmy since he got his £60, but saying goodbye to her friends in Fleet Street, and especially leaving Charles *Davis* who had continued to provide her support as a father figure, often giving her sound advice.

In Kent she made a new bunch of friends, mixing with doctors and nurses and finding a healthier lifestyle, she spent much of her free-time on sporting activities. Dating was easy too, and for a couple of years she dated a South African Orthopaedic Surgeon, and having met his family in Africa was considering settling down with him when he cheated on her with another doctor and she left him.

Undeterred, she worked hard, studied well and got her ODP qualification. She would later top this off by successfully studying at university for a BSc in biochemistry. Throughout her educational journey, she supported herself and her studies.

During this period, Lena met a woman, a student nurse called *Deana* Godwin and for some reason, the two women hit it off and became fast friends. For Lena it was a wonderful friendship for *Deana* soon became the sister she'd previously before found only with her good friend Crumbs.

Since she and Crumbs had parted company years earlier, there had been no such friendship for her. She was probably the only person that Lena truly loved at that time, and their friendship continued for a few years. As far as Lena was concerned, *Deana* was her family now. Unfortunately, this lay a heavy burden on *Deana* for Lena's demons ensured that her friend had a lot to cope with.

Although Lena loved her friend deeply, she didn't understand friendship, just the laws of survival. She found herself unable to fully able to appreciate that people who were not used to a certain kind of behaviour would not tolerate it forever. She competed with *Deana* over everything, and Lena short-changed her friend whenever she could. When they moved into a flat together, Lena selfishly took the larger bedroom, a matter which caused some friction between them. On every level she competed with *Deana*. Needless-to-say, despite *Deana's* patience, they would part company acrimoniously.

This proved to be a distressing episode to Lena, as words were exchanged which made her realise how badly she had treated *Deana*. In her heart, she realised that she'd become the friend from hell! She was left deeply disturbed by the split, and felt disgusted with herself for the pain she caused someone who truly tried to understand her and be a good friend. The damage between them was never repaired, although Lena wanted that desperately. She missed *Deana's* caring, her humour and the fact that she was a loyal person. Indeed, if she ever got the chance to, she would humbly apologise to the one woman she'd known in her adult life, other than Maggie Reagan, who treated her as someone truly worthy.

One day, Jimmy telephoned her 'out of the blue' ... and it was literally out of the blue as he was back in sunny Israel. He begged her to join him and as she had just celebrated gaining her ODP qualification, just split from her doctor boyfriend and completely at a loose end, she agreed ... who better to share her successes with than the man she still loved ... the man who always told her she'd amount to nothing.

The heat felt almost like it was sand-blasting her face as Lena stepped out of the airport building. Jimmy was at her side as they hurried to a bus stop.

"Have you any shekels?"

"Yes, I got some from the bank." Lena frowned. Surely he wouldn't take her 'holiday' money.

"Pay the driver. We're heading into town."

Lena, relieved, did as she was told. However her relief didn't last long as Jimmy took her to his flat, where he continued to use her as his personal bank over the next few days. Lena had refused to hand over the lot when she realised that Jimmy had no intention of letting her stay at one of the nicer hotels complete with swimming pool, as he'd promised the second day of her visit. His flat wasn't air- conditioned and she was formulating a plan to move out, with or without him.

The door was open as were all the windows as Lena tried to encourage a draft through the flat when a woman appeared in the doorway. She was tall, slim, blonde, blue- eyed and had a huge grin.

"Hallo." She said, "You must be Jimmy's sister. Is he around?"

Surprised, Lena said, "No. He went out about half an hour ago. Who are you?"

"I'm Rebecca. I live next door." She smiled brightly. "Well Rebecca, come in. I am Lena. His wife." "What?"

"Really. So what are you to my husband? His girlfriend?" "You are making a bad joke, aren't you?" Rebecca said as she walked into the room. "I wish I were. I truly do."

"Well I'm not his girlfriend. That's Misha ... um ... I really live next door. Jimmy borrowed some money and I just came to get it back."

"I doubt you'll see that again."

Lena hurried round the flat packing her things as Rebecca followed taking in the sleeping arrangements. She was sick at heart, sick of Jimmy and sick of this woman, her silly grin and her busy eyes.

"Who's this Misha person you were about to say was Jimmy's girlfriend?" She asked trying to hold her temper which threatened to overspill onto the stranger who was now trying to back pedal though not very successfully.

"Oh ... no-one. I mean I don't really know. I can't believe this. Are you really his wife?"

"Not any more." Lena replied as she walked out the door.

She walked to the bus stop, found her purse and looked in it. Most of her money had gone. So too was her passport. Frustrated and angry, she looked back at the flat. Rebecca was watching her, so she began walking, where to she didn't know, but she hadn't enough money now for a hotel. She wandered down to the beach and sat for some time watching the holiday makers. As evening began to fall, she realised that the temperature was quite pleasant, and determined to find a place to sleep, right there on the beach. It took Jimmy two days to find her.

His first words to her were, "You're coming back with me." "Who is Misha?" Lena countered.

"Jeez! You heard about her? That was focking quick. What do you know?"

"Everything ... except who it actually is."

"Okay, okay. She's a German bird and I didn't mean to make her pregnant."

"She's what?" Lena was aghast. Here she was desperate to have a child and her husband had made another woman carry the sibling of her dead daughters.

"Oh fock! I thought you said you knew everything!" Jimmy was angry.

"Apparently not!"

"Michaela was a mistake. She's history now. You are my wife, before man and God. And you're coming back with me."

Lena considered her options. She could spend another night out here on the beach and possible danger, for the night before she had been forced to hide when she saw some men looking around the nooks and crannies on the beach. What they were looking for she didn't know, but she had been scared silly. Alternatively she could return to Jimmy's flat, and no matter what else he was, he was right, she was still his wife. Anyway, she'd not find out about this 'German bird' Misha Ella, sitting on the beach. She picked up her bag, allowed him to take her hand and lead her away.

The next evening, he took her to a local 'watering hole' where they met up with some English holiday makers. The two women were accompanied by their brother, a man who introduced himself as Simon *Darwin*. As Jimmy was busy entertaining Sharon and Tracey, Lena decided to flirt with Simon. It was not something she normally did in front of Jimmy, but he was happy sorting himself out and frankly didn't seem to care what Lena was doing.

"I've seen you around you know." Simon said. "What do you mean?" Lena asked.

"We've been here about a week. We're staying with a relative who owns the flat above the one Jimmy's renting. She seems to know a lot about him."

"Is she sleeping with him too?"

Simon laughed. "If she was, I would say more power to her elbow. She's seventy-two. I don't think even my uncle gets to have a go!"

Lena laughed and buried herself with her drink for a moment. Resurfacing she said, "So, what's your point?"

"He treats you badly, doesn't he?" When Lena didn't answer, Simon continued. "I saw you go off a couple of days ago when one of his neighbours showed up. My aunt is a bit of a snoop and gossips with everyone in the building. She knew you were his wife. Jimmy told her you were coming to stay for a while. She thought it odd, because she also knew about his girlfriend. She couldn't figure out the menage a trois. When we saw you leave, Rebecca warned us that you knew nothing of the girlfriend. Then when we saw him bring you back yesterday, we wondered at the power of your love."

Lena frowned. She didn't know what to say to this stranger, even if he was kind of cute. Before she could decide on a comment, he murmured. "I could love a woman like you. You're too good for him."

Lena's heart thudded.

"Let's dance!" Jimmy shouted as he led the two sisters to the small dance floor in the middle of the room.

"I don't love him. Not any more. I only came back because I was scared sleeping on the beach. He took my money and passport." She skidded to a halt.

Simon took her hand. "We're on our way to Tel Aviv in the morning with some friends. Come with us. I'll take care of you. You won't need money."

"I do need my passport."

"I'll sort that out." Simon replied.

Jimmy was having a lot of fun dancing with the sisters and drinking up a storm and it was in the early hours of the morning when the party returned to the building that housed their flats. Sharon and Tracey went up to theirs and Simon spoke with Jimmy.

"We're leaving for Tel Aviv in the morning." Simon said. "Yeah! I know. The girls told me." Jimmy was slurring his words.

"Lena is coming with us and needs her passport."

"The hell she is! You, get in the flat!" He said this last to Lena.

Lena sidled by him and ran to the bedroom to pack, even as she heard Jimmy scream, "And youse! Get the fuck out of my face!"

The sounds of fighting reached her as she hunted desperately for her passport. Finally as the sounds ceased and footsteps came towards the bedroom, she found the document in a file folder in Jimmy's wardrobe. Terrified she spun around to see Simon walking into the room.

"Thank God, it's you. If it was Jimmy he'd have ..." "Come. You can stay with us tonight."

As they hurried through the flat, Lena saw Jimmy struggling to get up off the sofa where Simon had eventually dumped him. She stepped out of the flat and out of his life.

The next morning she travelled to Tel Aviv with Simon's party and devoted herself to fully enjoying the ten days she had left of her holiday in Israel. When they parted Simon and his sisters went to spend some time on a kibbutz and Lena returned to England. They kept in touch, and through him, Lena learned that Jimmy and his German had a daughter followed by a second child, after which she abandoned him for an Israeli doctor, taking their children with her.

Life moved on. Jimmy somehow found out that Lena had moved back to London to continue her studies and having been kicked out by his girlfriend, decided to return to his wife. He turned up uninvited and unannounced, and seemed shocked to realise that Lena was involved with someone else. There was no room for him at the inn.

Lena's new love was Jack Christie, a fellow student. Lena thought that Jack was a true gentleman, everything a man should be. He looked after her well and this surprised her. She could not believe that any man would be good to her as she had learned not to trust them. They remained close for two years during which time Jack had to put up with Lena's jealous and unpredictable behaviour. She measured him, and indeed all men by the only yardstick she knew and the relationship was destined to be doomed. Eventually Jack walked out on her. Two years or so seemed to be the maximum time she could hang on to a decent man.

Lena had just completed her studies and qualified as a biochemist. She was now thirty-two years old, and couldn't find any work. She was considered too old in a market where newly-qualified people were earning less than £10,000 per annum. She simply couldn't live on that amount and pay off her student loans too. She had no experience, no money, no family and no friends as the students all went their separate ways. She had spent all her life moving hither and yon, never really belonging anywhere, but she was happy ... looking forward to a bright future without the demons that had plagued her life.

She had proved them all wrong. She was not 'thick' ... not destined to live a life of washing other people's clothes. She was somebody. She had proven it and had the papers to show. She only wished she could have been given a chance to be a biochemist. She would have worked hard and been the best!

She hired a car and drove herself to Holyhead in Wales where she spent most of the day watching the ships coming and leaving. At least one had headed off to Dun Laoghaire, Ireland. As that ship left, she spoke to it sending a message over the water to her homeland.

"I had to come to this near, far land, to find myself and it was a good thing to do. It is good. I never had anywhere to call my own, and I will never leave my new homeland ... this place where I was born. Here I found hope, a belief in myself and studying was a great way to keep my mind sidetracked from my hell of a life. I really enjoyed the buzz of learning and I did not have any problems doing the exams. So I was not thick at all, would you say? Send that message to the nuns, especially Srs. Clare and Bridgette! Send it to Mrs. O'Shaunessy! Send it to all those who thought I was nothing! And please, let Fr. Finnegan know, for he alone believed in me. Let him know that I was determined to use the brains God gave me. I am sad that I'm not a biochemist now, but hey! It's not the end of the world, eh!"

Eleven

Storm Clouds, Storms and Treasure at The End of The Rainbow

It was 1993 and Lena decided to buy a house. She was fed-up of constantly having to move from place to place and wanted some-place she could call her own. She had her new degree and high hopes of finding a good job soon - one that didn't start her off at the most basic level.

She rolled a cigarette in which she had added a few bits of 'leaf' to the tobacco, lit it and inhaled deeply. She hated herself for doing it, but it was something she had picked up at university and she needed a 'smoke' now. She had wanted to think of what she would do about work, but the reefer soon relaxed her to the point where she could allow her mind to wander. She missed her student friends with whom she had tried everything, coke, heroin, speed, ecstasy ... she found that she didn't really like any, though a bit of grass was fine. She briefly allowed herself to wallow in her memories. She had worked in the student's bar and as all of her friends frequented the place, she had a great social life, even when she was working.

The reefer finished, she shook herself out of her reverie and focused on what to do about finding an appropriate job. Feeling that she had no option, she continued to do 'agency' work as an operating department practitioner, a job for which she had some experience. This combined with her qualifications ensured that she was better paid and allowed her to pay off the debts she incurred as a mature student. Armed with her degree and relative job security, she managed to get a full mortgage on a house in Walthamstow, N.E. London. This marked a new stage of her life which coincided with many events, some of which she could control, others not.

And Jack came back! They developed an on-again, off- again relationship which Lena's lack of trust, jealousy, moodiness and bad humour would eventually derail completely.

Now equipped with a home of her own, but alone, she began to miss her 'co-orphans' and other friends in Ireland. Most of her English friends had been students who moved back to their own homes or got jobs far away. She spent all her time working on her house and making friends with the many Irish nurses she met at work to assuage the need she had for Jack.

It was at this point that Claire and Angie came into her life, and Claire moved into the spare room for which she paid a small rent. Lena now had both companionship, and a source of extra income which helped pay the mortgage. With her new-found friends, she began to make trips home to Ireland - trips in which she re-made contact with various orphans, as and when she found them.

She was on just such a trip when the telephone rang. "Hallo?"

"Lena! Thank God I got you!" It had been a few years, but with a shock Lena recognised Maggie Reagan's voice in her ear. Before she could say anything Maggie continued as though they had seen each other just hours ago.

"It's Jimmy! He's in hospital!"

"What? What's the matter with him?" Lena felt concern for this man who had been husband to her flooding her senses.

"He's taken bad. I think he's dying!" Maggie's distress was clear.

"I'm on my way. I'll be there in an hour or so!"

"No! No. *Don't* come to Mayo. He's in *Donegal* Town - at the hospital. You must go there."

Lena didn't pause to ask why he was in Donegal, but as she grabbed her handbag on the way out, it crossed her mind to wonder.

A little over two hours later she walked into intensive care. Jimmy lay in bed, his eyes closed and tubes entered various parts of him. She could see a bag under the bed collecting urine. Two drips were going into his arms - one on each side. One provided a clear fluid, the other blood. More tubes round his nose provided oxygen and wires from his chest ran to a small machine which beeped, blipped and hurried with his heartbeat.

As she gazed at the face of the man she once loved to distraction, she thought she was too late, so grey and haggard he looked. Involuntarily a sound escaped her. What exactly it was she didn't know, but it could have been a gasp ... a sob ... for wasn't this her husband? And he heard her!

The blue eyes flashed open, as blue as ever, but no longer set in the clear whites she knew. Now they were blue on red.

"Me mam called. She said you were coming."

Lena's lips tightened as she fought back the tears. He sounded so weak, so tired. As she walked closer to him he spoke again. His voice was stronger.

"Lena, I'm so sorry for all I've done. Please forgive me. Find it in your heart to forgive me."

"Jimmy." She said then faltered. She looked at him, saw the child that was returning to the man's face, but she saw the old man too. He had aged! Yet something about him seemed young ... at peace ... accepting.

And of course she forgave him. How could she not? He was her husband. Her first love. The father of her dead children. And now he too was dying. She took his hand in hers and kissed it gently, surprised that it shook like a old man's. She sat with him for hours, holding his hand, waiting for death to steal him away.

A few days later he left the hospital, having surprised everyone with his recovery. Lena stayed with him as much as she could helping him to recover, keeping him away from the booze, for she had learnt that his friend Pasty had died from liver failure when Jimmy was in Israel.

"You love me still don't you?" He asked her.

"You were my husband. How could I not have tender feelings for you? But please don't mistake it for love. I haven't been able to feel that for years."

"Sleep with me. I'll make you remember. You will love me again. I never forgot you and despite all I did, I love you still."

"I'm sorry Jimmy. I'm not going to bed with you. I am not going there. There is so much in my life that I have to straighten out and I cannot take on the added responsibility you are asking from me. I care for you. I guess I know now that I always will, but I haven't been your wife since the day you walked out of my life, and you are not going to be allowed to walk back in again ... not as my husband."

Several days later, she returned to her life in England, and he promptly fell off the wagon.

She kept in touch. He was another piece of her past she had knitted back into the tapestry of her life. Then two months later there was another telephone call. This time he had a mild stroke. Lena managed a brief visit and once more Jimmy recovered, and although his speech improved and he regained some mobility in the side affected, he would never be the same man again. He moved back to Mayo to live with his brother, and Lena went back to work in the country she now thought of as 'home' whenever she was in Ireland.

During this brief visit, Jimmy tried again to woo his wife back unsuccessfully. One evening she went out for a drink with a mutual and platonic friend and when Jimmy heard of it he went ballistic. That convinced Lena that there was no going back and she returned to England refusing to see him again. Her own baggage was so heavy she could carry no more. Since then she has lived with her guilt, for she never saw him alive again. Jimmy's liver failed and in addition he suffered a massive heart attack and, as Lena thinks of it, he went home ... to be with their children.

Shaken more than she'd realised by Jimmy's death, Lena's old demons came back to haunt her with a new vengeance. She began

to compete with Claire over men, and there were so many other dis-
agreements, so much hurt given and received both, that it was not
long before she and Claire parted company.

Alone once more, Lena began to miss having someone around
and it wasn't long before she met Mark. An auxiliary nurse, he was
both funny and caring, and soon Lena rented out her house and
moved into a room at the hospital. She and Mark became a regular
item and they dated each other for a year before moving in together
in Ongar, a quiet town in Essex. She and Mark were the same age,
which was surprising as she had always been with older men. They
got on well together and Lena loved his family.

One day, she found some pornographic magazines amongst
Mark's things, but although it set off alarm bells, she decided to do
nothing about it. Perhaps she reasoned, it was a male thing, and I
can't keep losing my rag over everything. Then she began to notice
other things like his flirting with every attractive woman he met and
even though she tried to think of it all as innocent, the demons within
her drove her until there was an explosion. That was the beginning
of the end. For the next eighteen months or so, they had a turbulent
relationship interspersed with his leaving her and returning to his
parents.

Their reunions were always joyously consummated and soon
after one such reunion, Lena felt unwell. She had been bringing her
meals back up and had the general feeling of nausea all day. She
visited her doctor.

"... But you're pregnant, Mrs. Reagan. That's why you are nauseous. The doctor smiled as he gave Lena the good news. His smile
grew even wider as he read the stunned delight in her face. Then she
frowned and said, "But this wasn't morning sickness. I'm nauseous all
day!" "It sometimes happens that way and I'll give you some tablets
to take it away. If you find that it doesn't help, come straight back
and we'll try something else. You have to be able to eat properly not
just for your sake, but for the baby's too."

"Yes doctor! Thank you doctor!" Lena took the prescription he
offered and almost ran out of the surgery. Wait till I tell Mark!

On the way home, she felt the nausea returning so she had the prescription filled and took one of the tablets right there at the pharmacy.

"Mark! Mark!" She called excitedly as she walked into the house. "I have great news!"

Mark came running down the stairs. He had been taking a shower and wore a towel round his nether regions. His hair was dark with moisture.

"What is it? Are you alright?" He asked looking both mystified and concerned.

"Yes! I feel great. Listen! We're pregnant!" She blurted out.

"We're what?" His posture changed. Instead of leaning towards Lena as he did before, he was ramrod straight. His expression also changed, from warm concern to cold disapproval. And his voice was like ice.

"Um ... pregnant? I'm ... I'm pregnant." Lena stuttered to a halt. She had never before seen this reaction to the news of a pregnancy. Everybody loves babies ... don't they? Even as she thought that, she realised that everybody doesn't. My man doesn't.

Mark's eyes narrowed as he stared at her and without another word, he turned and bounded up the stairs. Lena didn't know what to do, so she sat and waited for him to come back downstairs so they could discuss the matter. She knew she would be calm and rational. I have a tiny baby growing inside me and I have to stay calm for its sake.

Soon after, Mark was downstairs again. He didn't come into the lounge where Lena was and curious she went to the window. He was putting a suitcase in his car. He returned to the house and walked into the lounge. He took his house key off the key-ring and laid it on the telephone table.

"I'm off. It's not my kid. I'll not be back." He turned on his heel and walked out, and Lena slumped into the sofa, her mouth open, her eyebrows working as she tried to figure the steamroller that had left her house. Then as she fully understood what had happened, she began to cry.

Why doesn't he believe this is his child? I have never been unfaithful to him and he knows it. And I want this baby so badly. Why couldn't he want it too?

Thoughts too swirled round her head as she snuffled. *I need a father for my child. That is the safest way. If anything should happen to me, there is still a father. My child won't be so vulnerable. And I need my man for me. How can I manage as a lone parent? I'm no longer a crazy child. I know more about motherhood now and I don't want to do it alone.* She spent a difficult night and rose exhausted the next morning to go to work. There she found herself unable to concentrate and her ready tearfulness began to drive her initially concerned co-workers, completely nuts! She plodded on for seven weeks, then a show of blood sent her rushing back to the doctor's surgery. She was stabilised and she returned to work.

However, in addition to the tearfulness, came severe anxiety. She was worried about her baby. *What can I do to keep it safe?* Eventually she worked herself into such a state, that one of her remaining friends, took her back to the doctor who referred her to a counsellor.

When Lena arrived for her appointment, a mix-up with the paper-work meant that she was not expected and Lena did what she had never before done in public. She went magnificently ballistic! That night, she began to feel pain and as she had some painkillers, she took a couple. When it seemed not to ease, she telephoned her brother who now lived in Brazil with his wife and children, as though somehow hoping that his voice might help ... that he would have answers to fix her problems. Instead she found that he had problems of his own and anyway from that distance could not do anything constructive.

Then Mark returned. His parents had been driving him nuts, not believing that he could walk out on his pregnant girlfriend. Lena was in two minds regarding whether to take him back but eventually decided she could not reject the father of her child.

A few nights later, Lena feeling unwell, decided to have an early night. Hours later, whatever dreams she'd been having changed in quality.

"Mammy, help me! Help me!" Dawn was ablaze as she stretched her hands out towards her mother. As Lena reached over and grabbed her child, Dawn showed surprising strength. She pushed her mother over, pulled open her legs and returned to the womb.

The pictures behind her eyelids flickered and changed, but not by much. She was once more in the burning flat. Dawn had taken baby Dani out of her buggy and was moving with her, almost dancing, towards her mother as the flames licked and crackled round both children. Even as Lena struggled towards them she could see their skins blistering, their flesh peeling away, the skeletons blackening and still the children moved towards her. Lena rushed to them and realising that she had a blanket in her hands, threw it over her babies. As soon as she snuffed out the flames around their legs, their heads burst into flames again. When she switched to their heads, their legs were once more in flames Suddenly Mary Noonan was there. She pointed a finger at Lena and said, 'Lick it'. Immediately ghostly voices took up the refrain. 'Lick it! Lick it' As Lena frowned at Noonan, Dawn and Dani once more a united pillar of fire, ran away from Lena. As she started in anguish toward them, Lena saw what looked like the double shadow of a small creature approaching the girls. She recognised it as a foetus trailing a double placenta. It jumped into the children's arms and it too begin to burn. The two children and the small creature in their arms turned back to Lena and they too began chanting 'Lick it. Lick it.'

Noonan smashed them with an arm saying. 'Get away ye divils. She's mine!' The children disintegrated into ashes and as Lena screamed, Noonan's right arm, which had made contact with them burst into flames. She advanced on Lena, struck at her throat with her left elbow, knocking her down to the floor. With that arm across Lena's throat, she shoved her fiery hand between Lena's legs.

Lena felt the burning and pain high up and realised that her womb was on fire. "You wee divil. You'll burn in hell." The cold cruel voice echoed in her brain.

Lena screamed - a deep guttural, strangling scream.

"Lena wake up! Wake up!" Mark was shaking her. Lena knew immediately that something was wrong. She looked between her legs as she imagined that she was on fire and saw the blood. At the hospital, her baby spontaneously aborted.

She fell into a depression so severe that Mark couldn't cope and once more he packed his bags. Alone, Lena knew that she would take her own life if she didn't get help. She heard the nuns voices often these days. You'll amount to nothing. Your mother was nothing. I can see that you will lie in an unconsecrated grave. You have no moral fibre, why don't you just start digging your grave. You're not one that will last. The voices went on and on and on.

Eventually she crawled out of her bed and went to her GP.

"I want you to commit me into a mental institution for the rest of my life. I hate myself. I want to die. If you don't commit me, I'll take my own life."

"Mrs. Reagan. You have just been through a terrible experience. It's natural to be depressed ... but commit you? No that is not necessary. You are still young and you have your whole life ahead of you. Here, take this prescription. It's for anti-depressants, and I'll arrange some counselling for you. In the meantime, have you thought of getting away for a while? A nice holiday somewhere can be a great restorative."

The anti-depressants would stay with her for the next two years.

Despite losing the baby, Lena had what she thought was some residual pain. She continued to have nightmares and was always exhausted, something that affected her work and her relationship with her colleagues who felt that she wasn't doing her fair share.

The pain retreated to a dull ache for which Lena was grateful. She was tired of going to the doctor and didn't wish to go back if it wasn't necessary. A girlfriend, Rachel suggested that she needed a holiday, and bearing in mind the doctor's own advice, Lena readily agreed. A break away in some sunny place was exactly what she needed to bring her back on an even keel, and Rachel, her friend, was a happy-go-lucky, fun loving sort who loved nothing better than a girl's night out.

She and Lena booked their holiday for Corfu, one of the Greek islands, and determined to make the holiday worthwhile, Lena packed some tapes by a hypnotist in her bag. They were meant to help her control her temper and build her self-esteem. She lay on the beach each day, trying to listen to her tapes but instead promptly fell asleep every time.

Once awake, the feeling of tiredness persisted and the fun seeker that Rachel needed was non-existent. Lena also developed severe pain much worse that what she'd felt before leaving home for this holiday. Rachel was none too pleased because Lena was so listless and as she left their flat every night to party alone, Lena decided to cut short her holiday and return home.

Back home, as the pain waxed and waned, she took a couple of painkillers, made a routine appointment to see her doctor three days later and went to bed. The next morning she felt well enough to go to work. A couple of hours later, the pain hit her with such ferocity that she collapsed. It was clear from the blood on her clothing that she had suffered a massive haemorrhage, and she was rushed to the hospital. There an ectopic pregnancy was diagnosed, she had been carrying twins and the second baby was growing undetected, in her tube. In the resulting surgery Lena lost her remaining child, her right Fallopian tube and right ovary. The left tube was also damaged, leaving her with a severely diminished ability to be naturally impregnated. She was devastated!

She survived by eating anti-depressants and avoiding work, but at home, every room had memories that added to the pool that she saw in her nightmares.

Ongar was now a place she didn't want to be in. It had too many painful memories for her and Lena decided to do what she did best. Run! She found a new home in Chelmsford and was packing up her belongings in Ongar when Mark arrived. He'd heard that she'd lost the second baby, and wanted to reconcile. Lena told him to go and mentioned a place 'where the sun don't shine'.

Then a letter arrived from the hospital she worked at. Unless she was back at work soon, she would lose her job. Lena realised that if she had no work, she would also lose her house. She found another job in Chelmsford.

Years later she would say to Becky in one of their chatting sessions of this and other relationships and friendships, "It was a horrible time, just after I lost both twins, my right ovary and tube. I thought I'd never be able to have children, I was 37 at the time. I could not look after myself anymore.

For a long time from about 21 years old and onwards, I was a very suspicious, jealous, angry and sometimes very aggressive individual ... in any relationship I had, platonic or not. Lovers learned to stay out of my way whenever I seemed a bit moody. They always dumped me eventually. My friendships were very much the same. I destroyed them all. I could not get close to anyone. But I had always managed to take care of myself. With that depression I had, I simply didn't care. Nothing mattered!

You wouldn't think that I'm a very out-going person, always reaching out for new adventures. For despite this, I do not have many friends. I cannot get close because I cannot trust, and this is all due to the people who contributed to my life's experiences, from babyhood to now.

I let myself be abused in one way or another by most of the men that I got involved with ... perhaps it was a learning process from the past. For I have to recognise too that I may have contributed more than my fair share to garnering that abuse because of the demons within me.

I went for counselling so many times. If you ask me, it was wasted money! They didn't help me in any way, perhaps because I never trusted them. I would sit with a therapist for an hour going on about my life and when the hour was up I had to leave. I was left with a bunch of emotions, feelings and fears as I walked out of their offices with no words of support, advice, reassurance or whatever it was I was seeing them for. I simply spoke while they sat, sometimes scribbling on a notepad, sometimes gazing at me or even into the distance ... maybe they were in a daydream somewhere while I prattled about something they had nothing to contribute to. Maybe they were counting the money they earned for doing sessions like these. Maybe they were counting the minutes left in my hour. Maybe they were trying not to count sheep. Anyway, they never said a word and then my time would be up. They might, at this point, tell me when my next appointment would be, or ask me to check with their secretary. Many times after a session, I would go outside or in the toilet and cry my frustration away until I felt strong enough to go home.

There was just this one time when I went for hypnotherapy. That was great but too expensive for me to have many sessions. However, I felt this was the only method that was going to help me. When I was in session I talked freely and felt very comfortable. The therapist told me that I talked about it like it all happened to someone else and I was still avoiding my trauma, which gave me some insights about myself. Unfortunately I could not afford to continue this treatment which I think might have been the best way for me. Then I bought some tapes to help me and often they did. They really did!

So there I was, knowing what could help me but not being able to afford it. When I was with Mark, I was having all manner of emotional swings. Almost like I was a manic- depressive, but not as extreme. There would be times when I was what I think of as my 'normal' self, that is as happy as a bee in clover, then I would be sluggish, not wanting to do much. All this in addition to being jealous and all the rest of it. Then came the depression after I lost the twins.

I must admit that I am terrified of depression because if I go down that road again, there would be no-one there to support me emotionally, even though Scott and others might try. I've seen co-orphans affected by it, and although I understood exactly what they were going through, even though I tried everything I could think of, there was no lifting them out of it. Sometimes they seemed to snap out of it by themselves, but most of the time, they lived in that dark, lonely place. So I try constantly to be ahead of my emotions. I tell myself to keep my nose ahead. It's like a race at the Grand National and I always try to have my nose ahead of the rest of my body, for if my body catches up with my nose, it means I've fallen."

The house in Chelmsford belonged to her. She had sold the Walthamstow house which she had previously rented out and used the money she got as a down payment on this one. She spent her time nest-making after work, spending time alone and not wanting to go out or meet friends. She had made the decision that she was through with men and would somehow manage the rest of her life without any input from them. All they ever did *was wreck my life*, though when she thought that over she decided that she couldn't really blame them. *I am to blame. It is my fault I'm so screwed up.* Then she thought of that again and decided that no, *it wasn't my fault that I'm screwed up. That blame belonged to those sisters who thought they had the right to the title of 'Mercy'.*

In Chelmsford, she continued to work as an operating department practitioner for six months, then decided that as the stress was too great and the availability of the means to kill herself too convenient, she would work for herself. She raised the money by selling her house to start a soft furnishing and lighting business.

The weeks and months passed slowly and although Lena was finding a new peace within herself, she was also beginning to find the loneliness and lack of social contact unbearable. She was not cut out to be a hermit. So she rolled herself a reefer, smoked it then strolled down to her local pub where it was nice enough out for her to choose to sit at one of the outdoors tables. She was enjoying a glass of lager and a 'normal' cigarette, when a young man approached her.

"Excuse me." He said, "but do you remember me?" Lena stared into blue eyes that crinkled when the man smiled and felt the stirring of something she had been working on for weeks to repress.

"No. Should I?" She asked.

He brushed the blond hair from his eyes and pointed to a chair. "May I?" He asked.

"Help yourself." Came the reply. As he folded his athletic looking 5' 10" frame into the chair, he grinned at Lena as he said.

"My name is Scott. I rather hoped you would remember me. I once asked you out and you refused me."

"I don't remember that. I'm Lena." She was sceptical having heard many chat-up lines before.

He sighed as the bartender brought what looked like a pint of bitter. "You're breaking my heart. I admit it was a while back. I was still in school and you laughed and told me to come back when I had grown up! Well I'm all grown up so I'm back. I'm ten years older and a full grown man."

Lena frowned. She vaguely remembered a schoolboy who had tried to chat her up a long time ago - a skinny, wee, cheeky fella he was. She looked at the man sitting beside her and the years rolled back.

"Yes. I do remember you so your heart can be patched. You've matured nicely, but you must remember, I too am ten years older."

"And you look just as beautiful as ever, if I may say so." Lena blushed. She was also embarrassed. He is just a kid! Then she thought, boy is he gorgeous.

He spoke again. "Nothing to say? Perhaps you're waiting for me. I asked you then what I'll ask you now, will you go to the pictures with me?"

Lena laughed as memory flooded back. "Are you kidding me? Is Rocky still showing? Or was it Rambo?"

He laughed too. "My tastes have changed and I can promise you will be able to enjoy the film."

Lena smiled and finished her lager.

"Will you have another?" He asked. And so the evening sped by as Lena enjoyed the company of a younger man.

This man called Scott. The man who would learn to become the rock she needed.

As the evening drew to a close, a car pulled up. It was Scott's father! Lena nearly laughed. His daddy has come to take him home? But Scott offered Lena a lift and daddy dropped them both off at her house. Scott accompanied her indoors. He walked into her house and into her life.

That first night they spoke, or rather Lena spoke and Scott mostly listened.

"I'm not the lovely woman you think I am ..."

Scott began to interrupt but she stopped him saying, "If you want to be a part of my life as you said earlier tonight, you have to listen to me."

He nodded and sat back and Lena spoke some more. She told him of her moods, told him that they would place a lot of stress on their relationship and in response to his interested questions she gave him brief glimpses of her childhood, her marriage and her struggles to educate herself. She told him what she could give in the relationship and what she wanted ... needed from it. Then she said that if all he wanted after all she'd said was friendship, that was fine by her, and as it was late, he should go. But if he believed that he was really a man who could give her what she needed, that would be fine too. He stayed. He was twenty-seven. She was ten years older.

Scott was a gym manager and fitness trainer and the couple decided to open a small gymnasium for the over fifties and people with disabilities in addition to Lena's business. Having settled down to life together Lena was desperate to have a baby. They paid for two cycles of IVF treatment, but both of these attempts failed.

Lena was by then hunting for her past and Scott was often by her side as they travelled backwards and forwards to Ireland. Although she still had nightmares, she found that smoking a bit of weed before bedtime helped her to sleep better. She worried that her planned trip to the orphanage would derail her, but managed to visit her old friends Bryan and Gaby, before she met with Sr. Clare, now an old woman, From Sr. Clare she learned that the nuns no longer had any orphans and that her old friend Ann, the musician, was suing the nuns personally, for her childhood abuse, and for the abuse she'd received from one of the families. That's when she first heard of the Redress Board, and that Ann was facing a lot of opposition to her suit.

After leaving the nun, she found out that Ann had become a singer in pubs and bars. She managed to track her down and the two old friends spent hours talking.

"You have to put in your claim at the Redress Board." Ann said after the old memories had been dug through.

"What claim? Sr. Clare mentioned the Redress Board but I didn't know what that was and didn't feel inclined to ask her."

"Your claim for compensation. Time is running out. Of course you mightn't have heard of it over in England, but a few years ago, all Ireland woke up to the fact that the religious orders in Ireland were a sadistic, raping and buggering bunch. The Government was shocked into setting up the Redress Board, to compensate us for the crap we had to live through. The stink of it finally got up their noses." Armed with this new knowledge Lena and Scott returned to England. It was an emotionally difficult time for the couple, for in addition to everything else Lena was still desperate to become pregnant. Her body's clock was ticking away and she chased down any method she'd read of that could help her have a child. They also found out at this time that Scott too had to work at improving his chances of fathering a child. Lena tried herbal treatments, acupuncture and a number of other not so well known and probably 'quack' remedies so desperate was she to become pregnant. She seemed to spend all her time checking her temperature when she was not swallowing something horrible tasting.

Despite these tremendous pressures, the couple finally and naturally became pregnant, which Lena credited to the herbal regime she had adhered to. Jubilant, but now anxious, Lena moved around like she was walking on eggshells that she didn't want pulverised. She had a small haemorrhage at six weeks, and a scan showed that once more she was carrying twins.

She was deliriously happy that finally everything was going her way, for her business also ticked along merrily. Then a scan at twelve weeks showed that one baby had died. Now terrified and exceedingly anxious about the surviving twin, Lena stopped working, employing someone to do her job in the business. However this was unsuccessful and to add salt to her wounds, Lena's business failed leaving her with a major financial loss. The stress of these times had clearly affected Scott too as the gym also failed and he became a declared bankrupt for the next couple of years.

Scott was as anxious as Lena over his unborn child and sometimes Lena wondered who was supporting whom as he changed from being her rock to being a jelly of nerves.

Her waters broke one month early and seventy-two hours later after a difficult time, Maisy was born by Caesarean section, in 2004, less than two months before Lena's forty- first birthday. For Lena it was the happiest day of her life when they placed the small bundle in her arms, and Scott, who had been with her the whole time, tried to keep the tears from his eyes and assume the air of one who had done the entire job all by himself!

Lena sat with Becky enjoying a cuppa and a biscuit.

"It has been a hard slog these last years even with Scott by my side." She said. "I am terrified of becoming depressed again and I sometimes smoke a reefer at night before going to bed just to help me sleep without nightmares. It seems to calm my mind which is constantly thinking about something or other. It just won't stop! I don't use any other drugs apart from alcohol but after being married to an alcoholic, I tried not to follow suit even though I had my fair share. I think too much alcohol would have sent me into a depression from which I would never be free.

I have to admit that a lot of my healing is done between God and me. He has kept me alive all this time. Even when I was severely depressed, I stopped trying to commit suicide. First because He found a way to remove me from my job as an anaesthetic technician just at the time when my life was at its lowest. I had access to drugs like paralysing agents, morphine and other heavy narcotics and sleeping agents. It would have been too easy for me to help myself, so He had them send that letter. After that in Chelmsford, I always felt under pressure and didn't stay there long.

Then He made me understand that suicide would harm me in other ways. I want to be with my kids again when I pass over. If I take my life, I believe I will be stuck between worlds.

As I think about God and look back over my life I go through periods of agonies. How will I be judged? After Jimmy but before Scott, that is between the ages of *26-37*, I was constantly searching for love, and always with the wrong people. I was promiscuous and when I look back upon those years, I feel only shame and guilt."

And Becky spoke for the first time. "Your trials are known to Him. He sees you and protects you according to your own words. He forgives you. Believe me. He does."

Twelve

The Quest Begins

I first started to look for my mother when I was 21 years old. By this time Jimmy was in and out of my life and I was regularly 'seeing' Dawn and Dani every time I fell asleep, but sometimes these horrible nightmares transmogrified into dreams about my mother. Then it began happening the other way round. I would have dreams of my always faceless mother who was lost and searching for her babbies - me and Daniel. Then we would burst into flames just as she found us and somehow I would be back in our Irish flat fighting black smoke, trying to find my children.

My initial journey took me to Birmingham after my brother had found information in the local library and on the electoral roll. The address on my brother's birth certificate did not exist anymore, so he decided to talk to the neighbours. He met the family Mammy stayed with when she'd first arrived in the area - the Simmons ... but they didn't tell him much. We had a brief conference, he and I, and we decided that I, as a woman, might get more information out of them.

It was a gloomy looking afternoon when I turned up on the Simmons doorstep and introduced myself. I found out that they had not forgotten the 'strange' young woman that Frances O'Leary had become after her Dublin accident. I'm not sure if they knew about the accident, but at that time, I had no idea of it or indeed of anything about her.

The Simmons family was huge. I cannot be sure but I thought I saw at least 15 children. Mammy had been friendly with the family matriarch and with one of her daughters whose name was Sheila. I was introduced to Sheila and sensing that she was roughly my mother's age, aimed my questions largely to her. However, Sheila had nothing much to say to me and her mother was even less forthcoming. It was like meeting a wall ... not what I had imagined would happen.

"I have longed all my life to find my mother and you and your family are the first real lead I have that could point me in her direction. Is there any thing you could tell me that would help me in my search?" I beseeched them.

"It was a long time ago. When she left, she left and that was it. I have no idea where she could be now." There was bitterness in Sheila's tone and I wondered about it. I immediately sensed that there was ... had been discord between her and my mother. I glanced at the older woman. Her mouth was downcast and her expression was sour. So my mother had upset *both* of them. Still they were my only chance to move forward.

"What was she like? Did she have any special interests that could probably point me in a direction she would have been likely to go in?" I asked hopeful that one of them would give me some clue.

"I'm sorry kid. I would like to tell you something to help you, but the fact is that your mother was not a nice person. She is someone my family tries to forget." Sheila responded. Her mother left the room.

"But ... but why?" I was staggered. Somehow in my dreams, I had imagined a mother universally liked. In my mind's eye, she was a woman of beauty, had few faults and it was only some terrible circumstance that forced her to abandon her children in the sure knowledge that a benevolent Church would take us in.

"She caused a lot of pain. I won't go into it with you, for it would open wounds ... some things are better left in the past." After a few awkward moments she spoke again. There was a sad smile on her face. "I do remember you and your brother too. Cute as buttons you were. I even have a small photograph of you. It was taken on the day after you were born."

She went into another room and came back with a key ring holder. I peered at the old photograph in awe. There I was, just a day old. The tears came to my eyes, and her voice was gentle when she spoke again.

"Take it. It's yours by right. I'm not sure why I kept it all these years. I destroyed everything I had of her, but somehow couldn't ... well, you were just a tiny baby and ... and he liked you."

"He?" I asked curious, but she just smiled and I saw a glint in her eyes that spoke suspiciously of tears. However she turned away quickly and when she turned back there were no tears to be seen.

She gave me the photo. I was overwhelmed and delighted. I thought it was weird that she had kept it, but I found out later that despite the large number of children running around, she and her husband did not have any of their own. I assumed at that point that the 'he' who liked me was her husband, but even later still realised that her husband had never met me and surmised that the most likely 'he' was the brother who died after my mother turned down his proposal of marriage.

In any event, although Sheila would say no more, she gave me the address of her older brother who she said might be able to shed some light on what happened to Mammy.

As he lived nearby, I went over to his house immediately. Bill's house was one I will never forget. His garden was full of what I could only describe as scrap. It reminded me of a tinker's yard back home. It also appeared to be a menagerie, as I could hear several dogs barking within the house. I was petrified but I knocked anyway. This was about Mammy, not about me being scared of dogs.

Inside the house was similar to the garden. There were old machines and bits of metal everywhere. In addition to the unortho-dox 'furnishings' in his house and the numerous dogs, were a crowd of people. A few more of the extended and extensive Simmons fam-ily were waiting. They had been warned that I was going to be at

Bill's and as they all lived in neighbouring houses to his, they had managed to get there before me.

They seemed to me to be a strange bunch, probably largely because they spoke with such broad Brummie (Birmingham) accents that I could not understand a word they were saying. I just basically agreed with everything they said, hoping that I was not getting myself into trouble. To this day, I do not know if they'd said anything that could have been useful to my quest to find my past.

After that abject failure to communicate, I tried to speak with Sheila several times more but she refused to add anything to what she'd already told me. It was time to send in the reserve, so *Daniel* went back to see if he could do any better. He had as much luck as I did.

The Simmons family filled my every thought, even as I worked in the pub chatting with the punters. After work one evening, I wandered down to the chippie on my way home. The aroma of my cod and chips was so tantalising that I opened the package and began to eat as I walked back to my flat. Even the pleasure of eating didn't stop the thoughts swirling round my head. Why did the Simmonses react the way they did to my questions? What happened between them and my mother?

"Your mother was not a nice person ... she caused a lot of pain. ... some things are better left in the past." Sheila's voice echoed in my head. My mother was 'not nice'.

This gave me pause for thought. Until now, my thoughts and dreams about Frances O'Leary were the starry-eyed dreams of a small child looking for her mother. Now I began to wonder about her as a woman. Who was she? This ancestress of mine? By the time she was twenty-one, she too had a couple of small children. Mine died. I couldn't save them. She abandoned hers. She couldn't keep them. But why?

I began to wonder too about my father. Who was he? Was he like Jimmy? *Did* he abandon her? Was that why she abandoned us? If I were in her place, what would I have done? I shied away from the thought that I could abandon my children. My thoughts shrieked,

"Never!" And almost immediately the picture of me begging Sr. Clare for help soon after *Dawn's* birth rose unbidden. It was that easy. When your world was in chaos, it was that easy.

"There but for the grace of God go I." The old saying popped into my head easily, but I did not throw it out again. Instead I began to see the woman that was Frances O'Leary. The tears rolled down my cheeks and I cried for her. I cried for her small children, and then for me and mine. Luckily, the street was dark and virtually deserted. I dumped the last of my fish dinner in a nearby bin and hurried the last few yards to my flat, shutting and locking the door after I'd entered. I threw myself onto the sofa, and before I realised what was happening I was moaning my pain, my mother's pain until somehow, I fell asleep exhausted.

The morning sun shining cheerfully on my face woke me next day. I recalled the painful rite of passage the night before, realising that I had finally grown up. I was no longer a child looking for her mother, but a woman searching for her history. I spent the morning doing what researches I could and was getting nowhere when *Daniel* called. He had found another birth certificate issued to my mother. It was for a Mark O'Leary born to Frances O'Leary at the same hospital where *Daniel* and I were born. He had been born in June 1964, which means that if he was full-term, she was busily getting pregnant again in the days around the time when *Daniel* and I were being sentenced to a life with the Church. And there the trail ended. We found nothing else to help us in our search for Mammy.

For me life went on. I was slowly pulling myself out of the trap I was in and was studying for the academic subjects that would later give me access to a university education. It was another four years before I was ready and able to make the next move in my search for Mammy.

I wrote to Sister Clare and An Garda Siochana asking for information and/or help in finding any information that could lead me to her. All they needed to do was point me in the right direction.

The letter from the Garda referred me back to Sr. Clare and they forwarded my letter to the Department of Education.

The Dept. of Education official told me which hotel my mother was staying in, at the time of our sentencing back in 1963, which was unhelpful, my father's name, which I already knew from our birth certificates, and then gave me a seven line history of my own life which simply included the date of my committal to the industrial school system and the dates of my time and my brother's time with Mrs O'Shaunessy, as if I wasn't there and aware.

I heard nothing constructive from Sr. Clare. When she responded to my letter, she simply said that she had no information in relation to my mother or her family.

In 1998 the Freedom of Information (FOI) Act became law and we were able to get our documentation from the Education and Health boards. I simply couldn't believe my eyes. It was all there in black and white - the family address in Dublin, an address where my mother could possibly have been reached. I was raging! "Wankers!" I thought, "they denied me knowledge of my mother and family for years!"

By this time Daniel, who had married a Brazilian woman and lived with her and their two children in Sao Paulo, had returned with them to Ireland. As he was there in Ireland, and I in England, we decided that he would investigate the O'Leary Dublin address. Then he got cold feet. He was worried about being rejected by the family who had apparently rejected our mother. So he left it. Finally he thought it would be better if he went with Fr. John O'Shaunessy, Mrs O'Shaunessy's eldest son who is a priest. I, still untrusting of that family and of the Church generally, and not knowing anything of the kind, told him that if he took a priest with him the O'Leary's would likely shut the door in his face. I recommended caution and suggested that he should be as informal as possible when he went. I also urged him to visit quickly as we had already been waiting so long and impatience was upon me. Still he didn't go.

Time went by and I met and fell in love with the man who is now my partner. Scott and I were too busy dealing with the intricacies of our life together for me to just swan off to Ireland, so it was another two years before an opportunity to meet the O'Learys would fall to me. In 2004, I had a meeting with my solicitors in *Dublin* as by then the scandal about inappropriate behaviours of the some of Church's religious servants, which had been simmering quietly under the surface, had erupted in a blaze of publicity, investigations, arrests and even suicides. It had been decided that those of us who suffered abuse would be offered compensation via a Redress Board, that was largely funded by tax-payers, and we all had Board approved lawyers. Scott and our still rather new baby Maisy, were with me. I decided I would just show up at the O'Leary address and told no-one of my plan, not even Scott. I feared that I would be persuaded to let things lie and I was too agitated for that. Although my nightmares had lessened over the years, I still had them ... still had the need to understand, to find my roots. So I told no-one of my plans.

When I had finished my business with the solicitor, I told Scott that I was curious about an address I saw in the FOI documentation. I didn't say which or why as I didn't want him to talk me out of it. If I wasn't going to be accepted then so be it.

It was a freezing, cold October day and to my astonishment a light snow was falling. We were grateful for the warmth of the taxi. The driver dropped us off right outside the door of the terraced house. Feeling a great deal of trepidation, but determined to press on, I knocked hard on the door but got no reply.

"Who are you looking for?" The voice surprised me and I turned to see the woman next door on her doorstep.

"The O'Learys." I replied and Scott, who was carrying Maisy, glanced at me sharply.

"There are no O'Learys there. Not anymore. The old folk died long ago. There are still some of the kids around. Some of them live on the next road up. Would they be any use to you?" I listened to the accent of my youth and immediately felt comfortable and at home.

"Yes, I think so. Where exactly can I find them?"

I listened to the woman's directions and Scott said nothing. We walked along the street to the address indicated and I looked around me appreciatively. It was a lovely neighbourhood. The people we saw all nodded or greeted us in some way. They were friendly in a way that I hadn't seen anywhere else but in Ireland. A few even stopped and complemented us on our baby. Maisy was just a couple of months old and slept through most of it.

Walking beside me, Scott looked somewhat bemused. He'd still not said a word about my seeking the O'Learys when it must have come as a shock to him. As we reached the next road along, we saw a woman getting in her car which was parked in front of the house we were seeking. I ran up to her.

"Excuse me. Are you Ms. O'Leary?" I asked, surprised to realise that I was trembling.

"No. I'm not. But there she is. That there is Theresa O'Leary standing in her garden." The woman nodded over at where a fair haired woman was looking over at us.

"Thanks." I said as I turned to face Theresa. I approached her carefully.

"Hallo." I said. "I am Lena O'Leary."

She looked at me, clearly surprised. "O'Leary?" She responded, her eyes searching my face. She was a plump woman in her early fifties. Clear blue eyes looked out of a friendly, happy face.

"Yes, that's right … Lena. Have you heard of me?"

"Not a word. Who are you? Where do you come from? How come you are an O'Leary?"

I ignored her questions suddenly feeling fearful that if I said too much she would clam up and refuse to help me. After all, I still didn't know why my mother had abandoned us.

"Actually, I'm looking for Frances O'Leary." I countered. She seemed startled as she stared at me. "Oh! You're too late! Frances is my … was my sister. She's dead. Passed on some months ago."

I felt the shockwave hit me and I swayed. I think I would have fallen but Scott was right behind me and he held me secure.

"Oh dear! You'd better come in and sit down!" She took one arm ... Scott had the other and we walked into her house where I sank onto her sofa. Scott sat close. She bustled round me for a moment before hurrying off. I buried my face into Scott's shirt and felt the hot tears well up and over. My head was buzzing. I could hardly think. Then Theresa O'Leary returned with a tray and taking one of the mugs filled with hot sweet tea, pressed it into my hands. I took a sip and got a mule kick from tea heavily laced with whiskey. I glanced at Scott and saw from the look of surprise on his face that he was getting the 'treatment' too.

I sniffed, dried my eyes and looked at Theresa who was sitting looking concerned in a chair opposite me.

"I'm sorry." I said. "You need an explanation. Frances O'Leary is ... my mother. I am her daughter Lena. I've been looking for her for so long ..." At this point I broke down and cried. Scott, still cradling a sleeping Maisy on one arm, slid the other round me again and held me close. It was from Scott that I later learned that Theresa started to shake. She apparently open and closed her mouth several times reminding him of a fish lacking oxygen. She sat there seeming in shock as she stared at me and eventually I regained control of myself.

Finally it seemed that she too had recovered enough to speak.

"Frances died. I'm so sorry, but she had cancer you know ... from the amputation." She was speaking rapidly but stopped when she saw the look on my face. "You didn't know?" She continued and I shook my head dumbfounded she added, "clearly not."

She began to heave herself out of her chair. "I have to phone my sisters. I ... they have to know this." She left the room again and we could hear her on the phone, asking someone called Bridie to come over immediately and to bring Rita with her. She returned to the room and we sat quietly finishing our tea. The only thing she said in that time was, "They won't be long. They just live round the corner."

Then Bridie and Rita came. Bridie whose blonde hair was impeccably groomed was an exceedingly good looking woman. One could see that she must have been pretty special when she was younger.

Rita was also fair, and she was the smallest of the three. Both she and Bridie had similar blue/green eyes.

Finally, here before me were just three of the twenty-one brothers and sisters my mother had and to whom I had yet to be introduced. At first the two sisters were agog wondering why they had been summoned. When they heard what I had to say, they were at first disbelieving. Shock followed when I showed them by birth certificate and they began to put two and two together. They accepted that I was who I claimed to be and sank into chair visibly shaking when. The sisters began talking ... both to us and among themselves, remembering unexplained absences, problems with their father and my mother, other details that for them suddenly made sense. I learned of my mother's accident as a teenager and of her flight to England. After that, her contact with the family had been sporadic ... patchy.

The sisters had known nothing about any of Frances's children. They had heard only of ill-health, problems with her leg which eventually had to be amputated, of the cancer that developed in the stump and her eventual death on April 30th. So close ... so close. Why didn't we make contact earlier? Finally the sisters looked at me, still shocked but no longer shaking.

"So where is this Daniel?" Theresa asked.

"He lives in Dublin with his wife and two kids." "How come he's never contacted us?"

"We didn't know about you until a couple of years ago. I was in England, but he tried to visit. In the end he didn't. You see we didn't know why Mammy had given us away and he thought it might just be causing trouble for someone if he just turned up. He thought maybe Mammy had a family that didn't know about us and them finding out might have caused her problems."

"So why did you come then? Weren't you worried?" Bridie asked.

"Yes I was, but this need to know my family has been eating at me like a rat in my entrails for so long. Ever since I can remember, I've been wanting to know my mother. I wouldn't have done anything to hurt her or any family she might have had. I would have told her who I was when we were alone and abided with any decision she'd made. I just had to meet her ... to understand why? Why did none of you want to know us?" My voice broke as the anguish welled up once more. I felt like my heart was breaking. If we had come to this address when we first saw it, we could have had a couple of years with Mammy. Why didn't we? Why? Always why? Suddenly clearly, I heard Sr. Clare's voice. "It was God's will."

Before I could respond to that, and if I had it would probably have been to scream abuse at my tormentor, I heard another voice, which brought me back to reality. It was Rita who had not said much to me before that point.

"None of us knew you existed. Our father never spoke of Frances after she left. We remember when he left for England to bring her back but that never happened. When he came back home and we asked where she was he just told us never to mention her name in the house again. We had no idea what happened. As we grew older, we used to speculate. We suspected she was with someone ... a man, but she never contacted us and we had no way of knowing. It wasn't until after Daddy died, that Frances made contact.

Even then she never said anything about her private life though we talked about her health as that was the starting point of our initial conversation. Then Mammy died and we just had contact with Frances once in a while."

I told them about myself and my brother, about our lives with the nuns and the adoptive parents. I told them about the hardships and the constant aching for my mother. About the sexual abuse, I said nothing, and I also saved the news about the deaths of Dawn and Dani for another time. After all, I really didn't know them. I wondered if they were lying when they said they knew nothing. It didn't seem possible to me at the time, though I know now that I was being harsh because I was blaming myself.

Why didn't I get here sooner? Why did I fail the people I loved? I'd failed my children now I've failed my mother. Surely if we'd met we would have become friends.

Eventually of course I came to my senses. My mother lived the way she did because of the circumstances that led her ... just as I did.

Perhaps the nuns were right and some things are simply not meant to be. But I had met some of my family, and there was more to come. I was finding my roots ... and the branches and one day soon, I would be a whole tree, like I always wanted to be.

In due course, following the trail which was becoming easier with every new discovery, I learned that after Mammy left us on the steps of Dublin castle, she returned to England with her compensation and got together with the man who would be Mark's father. From all accounts, this relationship didn't last though we never found out why. Daniel, intrigued by the idea of a younger brother, managed to track him down but Mark would not speak with him. Once he found out that Mammy had died he just didn't want to know. I managed to make contact with his wife Mandy, and she told me that Mark was brought up by his father's family in Asia, pushed from one aunt to another. All his life he searched for his mother and when he couldn't find her, he apparently took to drinking. She was concerned that now he knew mammy had died, his drinking would get worse.

Mark himself had been married more than once and his wives, between them, had five children for him. He would not even speak with me and to my sadness, there has never been any contact between us. Finally we discovered that our mother had yet another son whom she called Eddie but we were as yet unable to find him, or anything about him. Later we did and were delighted to find our gorgeous half-brother whose father is English, and who is now a good friend.

Maisy was baptised in May 2005 and in response to my invitation, my new-found Irish relatives said that they would love to come over to England for a visit. I thought it was great that they accepted us without any problems at all. My heart was full. All of my 21 uncles and aunts were invited to the christening and 14 of them attended. It was great crack for they are big drinkers and they drank our local pub dry.

They sang and danced to their heart's content and without a doubt, they left their mark here in Tiptree, Essex.

Thirteen

The Gathering

The Journey home

Connemara; Co. Galway

It's been a long time since I was here in my childhood home of Connemara, Co. Galway, on the west coast of Ireland. I drove along the narrow roads in startled amazement that they still had grass growing down the middle. I had long run off to the urbanity of an English city and such sights were rare there. Scott sat beside me, admiring the wild beauty of my homeland, exclaiming from to time at some sight or other. Restriction, before unfelt, slipped away and I basked briefly in the sense of beauty and freedom of it all. Home! I was home.

As usual for this part of the world, it was raining, the skies dark and foreboding. It was truly a dirty day! The wipers alternately screeched and shuddered, or swept furiously from side to side with a rusch, rusch as the rain also alternated its tempo. Right now, it beat furiously down ⌐ raindrops as big as peas pelting the car with great ferocity ... and defeated the wipers in their attempts to clear the windscreen. I pulled over into a 'lay-by' just big enough to hold one car and waited for a few moments. Sure enough the pounding stopped and visibility improved.

In the distance I could see the peaks of Benna Beola, their dark shapes like ghostly sentinels in the haze, and suddenly feeling the cold, I slipped the car into gear, turned up the heater and drove on. September was perhaps not the best month to come home . but it suited my mood and the darkness of my memories.

The boggy land that lay on either side of the road had lost its green and all looked grey and forlorn, except for the whitewashed cottages with their dark slate roofs that dotted the landscape here and there. Swirls of mist played with my imagination and I could almost see the leprechauns and banshees, kobolds and 'ghoulies' that I heard of, when some adult wished to frighten a wee child into silent contemplation.

I shook myself, resolving to find some cheer somewhere. After all, I had come home. Moments later, as though sensing the change in my mood, the rain stopped and the land began to 'green up'. Animals grazed in the nearby fields. I saw sheep. Scott saw a stew! The road became even narrower and I could feel the grass brushing the underside of the car. I began to laugh but quickly choked it off when a bus appeared over the brow in front of me. Sighing, I began to reverse to another lay-by I had passed about 20 metres behind me. Even though I squeezed my little car into the hedge, there was barely enough room for the bus to get by. As the driver inched his way along, I realised there was only one passenger on the bus. At least only one was curious enough to peer out of the windows at us.

Finally the road was free and the sun staggered through the clouds to light up the newly washed day. I was delighted to see one field glittering with the diamonds some raindrops had become. Close to me in the hedge, a mini rainbow danced about the droplets in a spider's web. I reluctantly tore myself away from this sight and drove on and it was with some uplifting of my heart that I finally arrived at the village, perched so close to the cliffs of Moher.

Parking the car, we made our way with a group of tourists along familiar paths that had not changed in the intervening twenty-five years since I was last there. As the tourists strolled along the 'official' walkways, I cut away to the right to use a path known to the locals. Scott and I climbed slowly and eventually walked up near the end of the land. Getting on my knees and hands, I crawled the final inches to the edge and lay flat looking down. Scott, nervous of the height and the fierce wind that was blowing, elected to stand safely away from the edge and operate our *DVD* camera.

To my right, the cliffs of Moher rose majestically and implacably from the shoreline. A dark spot marked a cave that the banshees were known to frequent - tales of whom we were told, to deter the fool-hardy from venturing there. The powerful wind swirled and howled, turning my long hair into a twisting flying rope, which whipped and scoured my face. I pulled up the hood of my anorak, tucking my hair into it even as another sound, louder than the wind, again drew my eyes downwards.

As a child, I always enjoyed the beauty of the 'white- horses' as we called the white crested waves, and now I watched enthralled as they chased each other, crashing onto the rocks below and into the cliff walls, disappearing into holes here and there. A couple of black-headed gulls screamed for my attention, as they fought over some scrap they'd found.

I would have lain there indefinitely as I had done so many times during my childhood - escaping my life into a brief, exhilarating free-dom. Scott however only had so much patience and filming me lying there for hours did not much appeal to him, especially when he had lamb stew on his mind.

"Come on then. This wind is getting cold and I'm hungry!" His voice pulled me out of the reverie I was about to slip into.

"I'm coming." I returned as I eased back from the edge and stood up. I blinked the sudden unbidden tears from my eyes before turning to face him. I'd had no idea that returning to this spot would induce in me so much emotion that tears would be near the surface.

"Where's a good spot to eat?" He asked, his fair hair flying around reminding me that he needed a haircut.

I thought for a moment wondering if all my old haunts were still there. "Let's head on into the town and we'll see." I replied.

I got behind the wheel and drove cautiously down the narrow roads to Clifden, feeling more trepidation than I expected. The place looked just the same. A couple of businesses seemed to have changed hands, or at least were given a new coat of paint, but most of the names were familiar and when there was a clear change, for example of an old Irish restaurant, it was still a restaurant, though it might now be serving Chinese food.

We quickly found a likely looking pub to satisfy Scott's hunger. Mine would only be sated when I'd returned to the house where I was brought up. After lunch we visited the buildings and made a video of them (described towards the end of chapter 5).

Returning to the compound of buildings was exciting, depressing and yet somehow fulfilling. I was excited to be showing Scott something of my history. At the same time I was depressed because I was once more the abused child and I realised that depression must have been a deeply embedded feature of my life here. And yet, this was where I belonged for a long time. This was where I identified myself. I am an Irish woman from Connemara. This pain filled, depressing place set in such exquisitely beautiful surroundings was home, and somehow I was full of something that seemed to define me ... all of me. I was Lena, the child that I was, the rebel that I was, the woman that I am. It could have been better in so many ways, but I am who I am. For good and bad, better and worse, this is who I am and it all started here.

Part of the reason I returned to Ireland both then and subsequently was to find my history via any official documents I could find. This trip was just the beginning of many more that would culminate with my re-living my past with my co-orphans. It was all about re-energising old friendships and 'relationships' that throughout my years in England I had never really let go of. Somehow we clung together, via letters, telephone calls and visits to each other when they could be managed. Several of my 'sisters' and 'brothers' had holidayed in England and had visited me. Now I was back home for the first of many trips, I was determined to see as many of them as I could, not simply because of our deeply bound friendships, but because the time had come for me to explore the bonds of suffering we shared.

With my increasing number of visits, after I'd made the decision to write my history, I hoped to persuade some of them to contribute to this book too and some have in small but important ways, yet I was not surprised that so many simply did not want to think of the past. It was too painful for them. Others have shared thoughts but didn't wish to be named and indeed as I mentioned in the foreword to this book, I finally decided to change all names except for those of my immediate family who agreed to be named.

One thing that would surprise me, was how very differently many of us would speak of the past. We shared our lives, experienced the same things and yet each experience was qualitatively different. Often our memories coincided closely but never completely. Sometimes our perspectives were quite different though the basic details were there. There would be arguments and counter- arguments. Sometimes a memory of mine would be nudged away from its original place. Other times a co-orphan would exclaim, "Yes! You're right! I'd forgotten that."

On one recent trip, I met with my old pal, Crumbs and another friend I shall call Ann Sheehan, and as I watched them, I realised that they were enacting something that afflicted many of us. Ann was carefully decanting vodka from a two litre bottle into a number of plastic water bottles. That way, even if we were in a pub, we could add additional alcohol to our glasses and others, bar staff in particular, would think we were getting high on what they sold us. I recognised then that we all had some sort of crutch which we used rather excessively too often, either alcohol or nicotine or both. Some of us succumbed to more illicit needs. Armed with our extra supplies, we then set off to meet a group of co-orphans at Paddy O'Neill's house. We chose his house because his wife and two boys were on a weekend visit to her parents. There would be no 'outsiders' to have to think about.

"I remember," Crumbs was saying as she waved her glass around, "that she was a lovely nun."

There was a general chorus of "Neh!", "You must be joking!" and "You're outta yer head, woman."

Crumbs looked around at the group of about a dozen of us and insisted, "No. She was really lovely. Not like her sister!"

"What's her sister got to do with anything?" Paddy asked already beginning to look red-faced as the drink worked on him. The receding hairline was busily pushing his wispy blonde hair to the back of his head, but I could still see the child who was one of the 'big boys' when I was a 'small girl'. I recalled that he was always in trouble with the nuns and tended to keep to himself. It was only later, after he left St. Joseph's that he began to 'flower'.

"Sr. Emmanuel was Sr. Bridgette's sister. Her real sister. At least that's what I heard. And we all know that Sr. Bridgette was a bastard."

"So what yer saying? He did the right by their mother and married her in time for Sr. Emmanuel?" Barry asked to shouts of laughter.

Crumbs grinned but continued her story. "Anyway, Sr. Emmanuel used to get cast-offs from another sister of theirs who had three or four children. They were quite nice clothes too. She used to let us wear them to school and would always take them back after school. It meant that we had something nice to wear. She was really nice."

"Well she wasn't nice to me!" Barry interjected. "She was just another of them auld bitches."

"That's right," Paddy added. "She was a right auld bitch. I remember one time when she slugged me in the mouth. I had been practising a new swear word I'd heard, not realising she was nearby and she heard me. Next thing I knew 'Wham!'" He demonstrated by striking his left palm with his right fist. His mouth turned down at the memory and long buried anger smouldered in his eyes.

I was relaxed and happy to be with my 'family' again. I had hoped to have some kind of ordered discussion with them, but most people joined in the conversation as they wished, went off on tangents of their own diverting us willy- nilly, or even had their own private discussions within different small groupings. I moved from seat to seat in order to get a better flavour of what was being said.

"... apparently there was some kind of court ruling in 1963 which is why we were together. The ruling said that children from the same family must be kept together. That's how both my brother and me ended up together in the system. We had an older cousin who wanted to help but could only take in one of us, and the ruling prevented that ... If he could have been allowed to take Patsy then we needn't both have suffered ..." Aiden was tearful, remembering the younger brother who suffered such appalling abuse at the hands of the Brothers on whose farms they worked that he committed suicide.

There was an awkward pause as we were all pulled into the horrors of our past. Finally Declan broke the silence.

"Well I had twin brothers, not much younger than me. They were separated. Connor looked like me and we ended up together, but Jimmy was sent somewhere else. Recently Connor and I decided to look for Jimmy. We haven't found him yet, but we did find something else in the records. Something that shocked us to the core."

"What was that?" I asked, my attention perking up. I too had found things in my records that distressed me.

"We had a sister ... just a baby. The records said she'd died but that as she had no birth certificate, they couldn't give her a death certificate, and there was no record of where she was buried."

"But that's rubbish!" My brother Daniel looked shocked. "I know." Declan responded. "We spent ages trying to figure out what happened. We remembered the rumours we used to hear about children being sold, particularly to rich Americans. We reckon that's what happened to her. There were a lot of records missing."

"And that's a fact." Aiden replied. "You know I went back years later to find Patsy's grave ... just to pay my respects, like. And I couldn't ... I couldn't. I tried to find the papers that would lead me to him, but there weren't any. It was like he never existed.

The conversation turned towards the gaps in the records and I moved on. I knew all about missing records.

Ann Sheehan was saying, "I was eleven years old when I got my first period and I thought I was dying, she pronounced it doiying, when I saw the blood all over the sheets. I began to cry 'I'm doiying ... I'm doiying ... I'm doiying' and I offered myself up to God."

"Say what?" Finbar asked in disbelief.

"I offered myself up to God. I thought I was doiying." Ann responded emphatically, pushing back the dark hair which was flopping into her eyes with every shake of her head.

"And what did God say to you?" Finbar's watermelon grin split his features as he too brushed his hair cut fashionably long, out of his smiling blue eyes.

"He said 'It's all right daughter ... just your period starting'." Came the response to shouts of laughter. "Anyway someone must have told Sr. Bridgette because she turned up and said. 'Come here.' I followed her to her office and she showed me a packet of pads saying, 'Take one of them. Put it on you. Put it in your knickers'."

As the conversation descended to the ribald, I returned to the group where Crumbs was listening to Paddy.

"She looked like a proper witch." He was saying. "She was bad. She was focking vermin. She was so bad she needed exterminating. I sat beside her on the bus and tried to talk with her but she didn't want to know who I was."

"What do you mean she didn't want to know?" Declan asked. He'd been gravitating between two groups as he was sitting on the edge of both.

"Who are you talking about?" I asked simultaneously. "Sr. Patricia. She wouldn't acknowledge me ... wouldn't acknowledge who I was. I asked her, 'shall I refresh your memory?' ... anyway when we got to St. Joseph's she got up and made for the door. I told her 'I don't give a fock where you're going to. If you walk all round the convent, I will follow you until you acknowledge me.' Eventually, seeing that I had indeed followed her off the bus, she spoke. 'Give me time to think.' She said. I told her who I was, that I was a child at St. Joseph's and what it was like ... what they did to me.

Anyway she blamed Sr. Clare and suggested that I speak to her. So I went into the house and waited around until Sr. Clare turned up. By then she knew who I was. She then blamed Sister Philomena. *Do you remember her?*" He asked raising his voice so that all could hear him.

There was a chorus of murmurs. "Yes ... no. No."

243

"I do." A voice a the back shouted. It belonged to Eamonn another of the older orphans.

"Was she there when you were?" "Yes" Eamon shouted back.

"She was all right." Paddy responded. "The only bloody one that was all right, and they had to blame her."

"Sr. Philomena! You liked her? I remember her ... I must have been just about three or so ... but she terrified me!" I exclaimed.

"No! No! She was good to me! Though to be fair to you, I think she was better with us boys!"

Everyone began speaking at once, recalling nuns that they thought were reasonably decent, and as I listened, I realised with horror that despite my memories, it was just a small cadre of nuns who were universally disliked. I had no real love for any and thought that almost all were equally bad. However, I soon realised that just like anyone else, many of the nuns had their favourites and these orphans remembered them favourably, while the children they were cruel to remembered them only as demons.

As the evening went on, we were joined by other orphans and more contributions were added. I noticed that just about everyone managed not to discuss the sexual abuse itself, though it was alluded to clearly at times. I didn't press as I too felt extremely reluctant to discuss my own abuse.

We went down to the pub carrying our bottles of 'water' with us, which had been replenished from another huge flask of vodka. In between all the social activities, which included singers both professional and amateur serenading the customers, our reminiscences continued throughout the night.

We spoke of the neglect that we suffered and the nuns' failure to provide for our basic needs. True, we had shelter, but most of us were starved and unsupervised so that when we were not suffering at the nuns' hands, physical and sexual abuse from older children could occur.

We did have access to reasonable medical care but our psychological health was not protected and indeed I would go so far as to say it was deliberately damaged. Certainly many of us felt this way.

We had no 'love' except for when a child was favoured and that 'love' was not always appropriate. Their treatment of us ensured that they often damaged our sense of worth, of who we are and where we came from. We were described at 'throwaways', the children whose parents didn't want them. The girls were going to grow to be 'loose women' like their sinful mothers - the boys, 'scoundrels', like their fathers before them. We were the dispossessed, whose only hope was to pray, pray, pray and do as we were told by those holy terrors who were our only route to salvation. And even so, no matter how hard some of us tried, we were constantly assured that we would never be saved, so great was the evil from which we sprang.

They failed us in terms of education and we all recalled having to miss school to work either in the convent, the laundry, on the farms or elsewhere, and we were worked harder than many 'free' adults would have had to. Yet, these infractions seemed to many of us to be the minor ones, serious though they were.

We spoke of the physical abuse that was always there. None of us, even the favoured few escaped this, for if a child was favoured by one nun, he or she invariably ran foul of another. We were beaten, punched, hit (with a hand, stick, strap, or other object), pushed violently, kicked, shaken, stabbed (usually with a fork, knitting needle or some such thing), choked, and had our limbs twisted painfully. We were apparently even permitted to be used as experimental 'animals' in vaccine trials! Something I had not realised till I heard my co-orphans reminiscences.

Although we avoided speaking directly of our own experiences of the sexual abuse, enough clues were dropped for me to understand that it included rape, sodomy, inappropriate fondling, indecent exposure, sado-masochism and 'dirty pictures' being taken.

After the pub, a small core of us returned to Paddy's house. Several of my co-orphans had left to go to their homes rather worse for wear, as we'd made serious inroads into our bottles of 'water' while maintaining a steady order at the bar. I worried about a couple of those who'd left, for it seemed that the reminiscences had disturbed them deeply. I couldn't keep them with me or follow them home as they insisted that they were to be left alone. Another co-orphan, Seamus returned with us to the house where an argument quickly broke out.

He said, "Lena why are you writing this book? Why don't you leave well alone? The past is the past and there's no need to dig it all up again."

"I have to do this Seamus. I have to do it. It's like my life is a great big abscess full of pus and the only way I can heal it is to lance it and let all that pus run out."

"It's waking up the past ... disturbing what should be left to lie. It's forcing us to remember and our memories are too painful."

"And that's another reason why I should write this book. It's not just for me. You can hardly think of your past because it damaged you so much. These people are still doing their evil to young children even today! This book is for them too ... I hope it will give others the strength to fight back."

"There have been others who wrote their books too." Paddy joined in. He squinted as he looked at Seamus. "If they hadn't spoken out, none of us here would be in line for the compensation we're going to get ..."

"Money isn't everything!" Seamus interrupted seeming in anguish.

"No it's not, but it will help! All of us here were robbed of our childhood, our education, of the emotional security every individual is entitled to. All of us suffered. Suffered! And we must let the world know about these sanctimonious bastards who preach morality while breaking every moral rule there is themselves! We're going to get peanuts for our suffering. Well we're not monkeys and if Lena can stick it to them with her book, more power to her elbow, say I!" Paddy's voice was loud and angry. He stared at Seamus with undisguised fury before which Seamus shrank but remained defiant.

"Look. It happened. We were just unlucky to be where we were. It was the State that failed to protect us." Seamus insisted.

"What century are you living in, man? Don't you read the papers? It was happening all over Ireland ... in all these safe havens that the Church created for us children, many of whom they stole from our families!" Paddy thundered and as Seamus' mouth fell open, he continued more quietly, "Yes! Stole. We weren't all orphans. Some of us were taken from our families because we played truant, or because the family weren't in the church every five minutes or some other sick reason. We were just cheap fodder for them. We were taken away and made slaves by the Church and you're right, the State helped them! They did nothing for us either!"

"I don't believe that!" Now it was Seamus' turn to get heated. "The Church cannot be blamed for what happened to us. It has no responsibility. It was the Government. Just the Government!"

"When Father Dicklover was up your arse having his pleasure and driving your sins into a far, dark place, who do you think protected him? The Church. You were not the only one you know ... not in the parish and not in the whole of Ireland. The Church moved that bugger round the country so he could show other small boys just what was needed to push their sins so deep inside them that only the divil would be able to find them. And he was not the only one either."

"Who is Father Dicklover?" I asked, astonished at the turn in the conversation.

"Never you mind!" Seamus said sharply to me and as he turned back to Paddy he continued. "There is no need for so much detail, and anyway he was one priest! One!"

"Seamus, there are children all over Ireland, boys and girls who have suffered at the hands of the religious. The Church knew and protected the perpetrators while frightening the shit out of the victims." I tried to speak as gently as I could for Seamus was looking like he would disintegrate.

Paddy also seemed to realise that Seamus was on the edge. "They shut you up with their soft threats and allowed him to continue his activities. The bishops did nothing ... not to any of the religious - male or female. I remember being in the confessional ... being told that it would be a big sin to talk about what had happened to me ... to anyone. I was told that it would grant me such grace and favour with God to forgive and forget what happened. I asked how could I forgive ... or forget. I said what had happened to me was the 'big sin' and I could only stop it if I spoke out. The priest told me that to speak out would cost me my mortal soul ... that it would be a bigger sin to speak out ... that I would burn in hellfire if I spoke out of turn and that that would be worse than anything I had ever experienced. I learned to keep my mouth shut, and I learned to fight! I was a strong lad and they soon learned to avoid me! Soon after that I was freed."

Seamus began to cry and we gathered round him, all touching him and trying to give him whatever solace we could. "I don't want to remember. I don't want to remember." He moaned.

Paddy held him close, fighting back the tears. After a while he said, "I know you still go to Mass regular like, and you know that I never go near a church. I also don't let my kids go even though my wife is always at me to let them. I never told her what happened to me ... I couldn't ..." His voice faltered then strengthened. "She wants Patrick and Leo to be altar boys. Now listen to me Seamus, do you think I should let my sons be altar boys? *Do you think I could?*"

Seamus shook his head silently, and Paddy continued gently. "Now what about other boys and girls whose parents trust the Church, should they allow their children to serve? Not knowing what we know. If you'd married and had children, would you allow them to serve?"

Once more Seamus shook his head.

"And why Seamus? Is it that deep down inside you know that the Church destroyed your life and you don't want to see it happen to any other kids?"

Seamus looked at Paddy and although his mouth trembled, the tears stayed away. Still he said nothing.

"That's why I must write my book Seamus." I spoke quietly choking back my own tears. "If the world knew about how much evil there was amongst the ranks of the religious, many of us might have been spared what happened to us. Our parents might have fought harder to keep us away from these demons."

Seamus sniffed. "I still say that it wasn't the Church's fault. It was a few individuals and the Government."

Paddy sighed and sat back as though spent. At least there was some progress, for Seamus had said 'a few individuals'. Not 'just one priest.'

"This hasn't just happened in Ireland." I spoke again. "It's been happening all over the world. Bishops have been protecting paedophile priests moving them from parish to parish instead of having them arrested or at least removed from the sources where they could find victims. They abused all manner of children. Even as we speak, in many countries children are being abused. When the shit hit the fan in places like America, they managed to throw some of the priests in prison. Even here they are beginning to prosecute some and as in the U.S., there are those who either commit suicide or die mysteriously just before their cases come to court."

"It wasn't the Church." Seamus almost sighed these words but I continued. I didn't want to hurt him but when I thought of all the damage that was done, it felt like there was a juggernaut inside me battling to get out.

"Did you see that Panorama programme?" I asked. "No." Seamus replied briefly.

"I have a tape and will send you a copy. The programme showed clear evidence that the Church knew what had been going on for something upwards of forty years. Forty years! How many children could they have saved by being tough on the handful of priests they said committed these crimes? The programme featured a man who I can only describe as a priest-lawyer. When he spoke out, he lost his job at the Vatican. He talked about something called Crimen, a Vatican law, which showed that bishops were instructed to cover-up all abuse claims, paying off victims where necessary and putting the fear of God in the rest, simply so the Church wouldn't get a bad name. It turns out that Vatican law or canon law as they call it, was more important to them than civil law, which is the law of the land. As far as the bishops of Rome were concerned, canon law took precedence over civil law. Therefore when a religious broke civil law, he or she apparently didn't break canon law even when the offense included the sexual abuse of a child! Now what kind of thing is that? These people could even confess to murder and that would not break canon law if they confessed and said that they won't do it again."

"You're joking!" Paddy interjected.

"I'm not you know. As I understood Crimens and what they said about confession, I realised that if you are a 'good' Catholic, you could murder someone, confess it all to your priest and unless he is particularly unusual, he doesn't have to tell anyone because he is bound by the 'seal of the confessional'. For him to break this seal would be for him to break canon law which could see him excommunicated from the Church!"

"No shit!" Paddy was astounded as were the others.

"So are you then saying that it wasn't the confessor's fault for not speaking out because he was bound by the Church not to break the seal of the confessional?" Seamus was staring at me.

"No. I'm not saying that, for isn't the confessor a moral being? Didn't the Bible lay down certain commandments for all of us to follow? What kind of human being can hear of children and women, even of nuns being sexually abused and hide behind the words of a Church law? Are the clergy not also bound by the laws of God? They might think canon law is above civil law, but which of them is going to come out and say that canon law is also above God's own laws as handed down to us by Moses, Jesus and various other prophets?"

The discussion went on the whole night through. A couple had fallen asleep ... Perhaps the drink had crept up on them, but Paddy, Seamus and I talked long, discussing the ins and outs as we saw them, and although Seamus had been a good sounding board, being the Devil's advocate, by dawn he too was begging for a copy of the Panorama video. He too vowed to take his head out of the sand and do some research. And Paddy had the last word making us laugh before we ambled into the kitchen to make breakfast.

"Yes Seamus. Be like me. I stopped playing ostrich and took my head out of the sand when I realised that this position left my arse high and dry in the air!"

In the days that followed this discussion, I managed to speak with other co-orphans in quiet meetings, just the two of us together. Many believed as Seamus did, that the Church was innocent, the Pope infallible and the State guilty. I tried to inform those who were fairly receptive, of what I'd learned about our situation but did not even attempt to in a couple of cases, as I did not wish to lose the friendship of those with whom I had endured so much. It was incredible to me. They had suffered so much yet they couldn't see where the blame lay. Others accepted that the Church was not entirely innocent, but their faith allowed them to forgive. That led me to question my own faith ... yet again. And I found that although I have to believe in the Creator, I did not have to believe what is after all, only man's account of how things came into being. I especially couldn't believe these accounts when I realised that they had placed themselves beside and even above God, instead of below where they belonged with all God's creations, and that included women. Belief in the Church is an act of faith that is no longer with me.

In these years of re-visiting Ireland, I not only re- enervated my relationships with my childhood pals, I was also searching for any documents I could that would shed light on my past. I not only found my mother's family but was also able to access records kept of my childhood. On reading information from the Health Board and other organisations, I was disgusted and very distressed to find out how the social workers and others depicted me in their case reports. I was clearly the child from hell in their opinion, and the reports tended to have a sameness of description which I suspected, rightly or wrongly, came from the nuns. When I first read what they wrote I was so dumbfounded that it actually destroyed some of the confidence I had fought so hard over the years, to build in myself. I became clearly hypersensitive once more and it is something I am still struggling with. The unpredictable rages that I had fought to control returned with a vengeance and there were times when I thought my behaviour would drive Scott away.

Slowly, I began to force myself to be analytic when I read and re-read these reports. I showed them to Becky and as we discussed them it struck me that there were clear signs, clear patterns of pain and disruption.

My instability was shown most clearly in my school reports. When life was coasting along, I was viewed as hard working and eager to please. As I looked at the school reports that sometimes showed a difficult, disruptive child, those times correlated exactly with periods of severe abuse. I am not a social worker or a psychologist, and I know that I have the benefit of experience and hindsight, but the pattern was so clear. Why didn't the professionals see it? This is what they were trained to do. Why didn't they? Why couldn't they help?

Then I remembered that they too, would all have been good' Catholics. They had not heard any confessions but they too were somehow bound up in the business of protecting their Church. Perhaps some of them did see something and spoke with the priests about it. Perhaps they too were threatened with excommunication if they spoke out.

I don't know. It all seems so outlandish. Yet ... they should have seen something - recognised the signs.

As I ponder all of these things, I realise that I am immensely happy to now be living in a country where religion and state are kept entirely separate. It doesn't matter what the religion is. When it has grown too great to accept that God's will supercedes whatever laws its leaders proscribe, it has lifted itself above God and likens itself to fascism, pure and simple.

Fourteen

Seeking the Truth

Becky Armstrong sighed as she sat back from the sheaf of papers on the table, removed her reading glasses and rubbed her eyes. She was sitting with Lena in her bright yellow lounge examining the massive mound of paper that their several months long trawl of libraries, newspapers, the Internet and other sources had brought them. Her apparent tiredness was as much to do with the long hours they had spent in research and her grave disappointment in the Church which had always meant so much to her, despite her fixed belief in the scientific.

Becky too had suffered abuse as a child. She had what she, as a child, always described as a 'wicked grandmother' with whom she spent her early years after the old woman interfered so much in her youngest son's marriage that it disintegrated. She then encouraged Becky's father Bryan to fight her mother for custody of the four year old and her older brother and having won, gained control of the two children. The boy was older and could defend himself, but Becky was a small, spindly, ill child who was easy to manipulate … and terrify.

When Bryan re-married, her brother quickly moved in with the new pair as he was too much of a 'handful' for the old monster, but Becky had to endure fully two years with her grandmother until one day, alerted by a neighbour alarmed by the terrified screams of the child, Bryan returned home to witness for himself the horrors his small daughter faced. He immediately moved the girl to his home where his unprepared and unwilling wife Lizzie, suddenly found herself with a second child that was not hers - and one who closely resembled her mother, a long time rival for Bryan's affections. When the marriage had floundered, Lizzie immediately renewed her friendship with Bryan, but somehow hadn't calculated that she would on her marriage to Bryan, have to mother his two children. Once more, Becky's brother Adam was too old to be properly bullied, but the by now six year old Becky was already a cowed and damaged child after two years with her Grandmother and Lizzie immediately went to work to ensure that she stayed that way.

Despite this and the ill-health that plagued her, Becky proved a bright child and she at least had her father's love and support, but it wasn't until she was old enough to be admitted to a rather prestigious convent school for her secondary education, that she began to know the love of others. She too attended a school called St. Joseph's. She too was cared for by Mercy nuns. She too knew and enjoyed the company of priests. She too was encouraged to love God and the Church, but the methods used on her in the South American country where she was born were oh so different. She learned the meaning of love and charity through being granted love and charity, and such was her experience that only the eventual diagnosis of genetically determined ill-health prevented her from becoming a religious herself.

Now she sat rubbing her eyes and feeling that her heart would break as she read the activities of so many religious members of the Church hierarchy. There but for the grace of God go I. If I was in Ireland during these years instead of where I was, I too would have been one of these children. For both her father and step-mother had been excommunicated from the Church when they married as was her mother when she too re-married, and that would have been enough for the children to have been seized.

"Are you alright?" The anxiety of Lena's voice startled her back to the present.

"Yes. Yes. I'm fine. Could do with some more coffee though." She replaced her glasses on her nose and smiled at Lena who immediately got up with the words, "I'm right there withcha."

The two women took a small break, chatting about this and that as they took their refreshment and Becky felt a moment's regret that Scott had taken Maisy to visit her grandparents to allow them this time for their conference. She felt that the innocent chatter of an undamaged child would have been boosting to her flagging spirits. Nevertheless, she finished her coffee, poured another from the pot and as she sipped, looked at Lena over the top of her glasses.

"The BBC's Panorama programme on Sex scandals and the Vatican in which I heard of *Crimen Sollicitationis* for the first time was a good place to start our researches and it led us to many places, even onto the Vatican's website itself. There were also even earlier references to *Crimen* on some of the American websites. The amount of information we found is too vast for all of it to be discussed here but we'll do what we can. As you'll recall, *Crimen* dates back to 1962 and it, combined with its 2001 successor, ensured that the Church was able to act as judge, jury and controller of the fates of everyone concerned in sex crimes perpetrated by priests and other religious groups.

Crimen ensured that the seal of confession was applied to victims, witnesses and abusers, so no-one could publicly speak of what happened under pain of excommunication from the Church. Canon Law states very clearly on the seal of confession that it '... is inviolable ... it is absolutely wrong for a confessor in any way to betray the penitent, for any reason whatsoever, whether by word or in any other fashion ... An interpreter, if there is one, is also obliged to observe this secret, as are all others who in any way whatever have come to a knowledge of sins from a confession ... The confessor is wholly forbidden to use knowledge acquired in confession to the detriment of the penitent, even when all danger of disclosure is excluded ... A person who is in authority may not in any way, for the purpose of external governance, use knowledge about sins which has at any time come to him from the hearing of confession.' That's pretty comprehensive I'd say and senior church members would have no option but to obey this 'commandment' from the Vatican.

It appears that they were instructed to try to help the 'penitent' who might be sent for 'therapy'. Who by, is not clear, and presumably these therapists were also under the threat of Crimen and the confessional seal. The treated priests, apparently miraculously 'cured', were returned to their duty of abusing small children who, playing the role of victim got no therapy whatsoever."

"The whole thing stinks to high heaven ... So how do you think I should tackle this chapter?" Lena asked.

"Just talk to them. Tell them how you feel ... exactly as you did on the video of that meeting with your friends. I was brought up to believe that the Church was my friend, that I could always turn to it in my time of need. If you think of it as a caring parent, how do you let that parent know what you need? You talk. You respectfully speak of your need. You say it the way it is. Sometimes you are calm, sometimes not, sometimes reasonable, sometimes not, but you and that parent have to interact and find solutions, no matter how unreasonable or acrimonious your discussion is. And if that parent is worth his or her salt, (s)he will listen, try to understand and guide you in an open, honest and loving manner."

"Right now I am really ambivalent about the Church. It is so old and has been strong for so long that I feel like I have to respect it. Then I hear about laws like Crimen sollicitationis and that respect is lost."

"You must remember that the Church is run largely by a bunch of old men. They are wise in the way of the politics of the Church or they would not rise to their positions of power, but unlike politicians they are not voted out when they prove inept. Instead we are convinced that the Bishop of Rome is infallible and if we don't like what he says and does, tough!"

"But this Bishop of Rome was the one who policed Crimen, a law that damages rather that protects the Church as they think it does. By keeping these crimes against their members, and especially the innocents secret, and protecting the wrong-doers, they damaged the Church. They further compounded their mistakes by allowing the offenders to continue to have contact with potential groups of victims and by moving them to new parishes when they had saturated the old ones with their filth which was virtually stinking up the place. That is not wisdom, but crass stupidity. How could we allow such stupid men to be our moral guides? They are supposed to organise the rules by which we could develop and grow in the ways of the Lord, becoming more caring individuals. They couldn't organise a piss-up in a brewery, though on second thought, that's all some of them would be good for."

"You are thinking of the Irish Bishop who had a drink problem and may have been coerced by Sean Fortune to ignore his activities?"

"Yes, but Bishop Comiskey wasn't just an alcoholic according to these papers, he took 'first-class holidays in Thailand, a country infamous for its child prostitution'. He also apparently 'refused to cooperate with Gardai enquiries into Sean Fortune's activities.' So what if he was one of them too?" Lena looked up from the newspapers she quoted from.

Playing devil's advocate Becky said, "You cannot accuse him of pederasty or paedophilia himself. He may only be guilty of gross stupidity."

"But isn't this what could be described as circumstantial evidence?"

"Possibly. That the reports have not been contested by the good bishop suggests that perhaps he doesn't want too much of an investigation into his background, but in order to be fair and objective, we must appreciate that newspapers have to sell and sometimes they skate on dangerous ice."

"What about all the other bishops we've read about? Are you going to suggest that they are innocent too?" Lena sounded hurt. She expected more support from her friend.

"Don't get me wrong. I am not saying that these so called 'men of God' are innocent. I'm simply saying that unless something is proven we have always to give the benefit of the doubt. That doesn't necessarily mean that these people would generate any trust in us. They would have an uphill struggle to earn that. It's the nature of the beast I'm afraid."

"So what do you think of all these reports then?" Lena waved at the pile of documents.

"I am convinced that there is too much smoke for there to be no fire or even a little fire. There are major problems in the Church which are being compounded by the apparent inability of the uppermost echelons of the hierarchy to clean up their act. I find their stance disturbing. They squeak ineffectively about a handful of homosexual priests, whether paedophile or not, and what to do about them. However our researches have turned up all sorts of cases, the majority of which do not involve homosexual paedophiles. Although the sodomising of young boys has garnered the most publicity, all things being equal, the majority of victims worldwide will be female. Look here, this article is about nuns being raped by priests. This one here describes lay women who have produced priestly offspring, some after being forced to accommodate the priests' carnal lusts ... and here little girls have been raped just after their first communions. It goes on and on." Becky moved report after report as she made her point.

"So the Church should go after any rapist priest, not just the handful that attack boys, but that is simply not happening. It's like they buried their heads in the sand ..." Lena's voice trailed off as the mental picture of an exposed ostrich's backside came to her. She explained the 'vision' to Becky adding, "maybe that is really their natural position which is why they are unable to act. They are too happy getting shafted themselves!"

Becky tried to look disapproving but, as she had never seen such amusement in Lena's face before, had to be content with giving her a small smile. Lena grinned at her then turned back to the pile of papers which had been set out into various categories. She pulled one out.

"Here this one is a Cafod report." "Cafod?"

"It's that Catholic Charity. It says that in Africa, priests and missionaries wary of catching HIV, have targeted nuns in a bid for safe sex."

"Here's another about the nun abuse." Becky added as she pulled out another report from the pile. This one's from the BBC. She read aloud 'A day after the emergence of a report on the rape of nuns by priests, the Roman Catholic Aid Agency, Cafod, has confirmed that it showed the Vatican the report seven years ago. The leaked report said that priests and missionaries across <u>several continents</u> were forcing nuns to have sex with them. On Tuesday, the Vatican confirmed that such abuse had been taking place, but denied that it was so widespread. The Vatican says it will investigate internally. Among the abuses detailed is the case of a nun being <u>forced to have an abortion by the priest who impregnated her. She later died and he officiated at her requiem mass.</u> Also cited is the case of a mother superior who repeatedly complained to her local bishop that priests in the diocese had made 29 of her nuns pregnant. The bishop, according to the report, subsequently relieved her of her duties'. Horrors and more horrors. And always internal, private investigations which are kept largely secret from the rest of the world, so that we have no option to believe that justice was not done, especially when we hear of the offenders re-offending.

Everything we've read suggests that the Church lied about what it knew of these abuses and when it knew it. They are the theologians. They are supposed to know their Bible. How then can they ignore nuggets like this one. You are of your father the devil, and the desires of your father you will do. He was a murderer from the beginning, and he stood not in the truth; because truth is not in him. When he speaketh a lie, he speaketh of his own: for he is a liar, and the father thereof. John 8:44"

"Gosh! You have read that old book?"

Becky grinned. "It would amaze you even more to hear that far from the days when I wanted to become a nun, I have become an evolutionist. I 'converted' many years ago."

"What do you mean?"

"I believe we evolved from single cellular to the creatures we are today. However, I also know that nothing comes from nothing, so at the moment I can accept a Supreme Being who created the conditions for the Big Bang, possibly knowing that from that, an earth-like planet would develop leading to our eventual evolution. Then I run into problems when I try to figure out where this Supreme Being came from.

Some nights when I cannot sleep from all my wondering and pondering on the cruelties of the world, I imagine that a small girl is playing in her bedroom. She has been given a new chemistry set by her parents and armed with a school project for her homework, gets a ball of mud and sand the size of a small marble. She places this in the middle of a box-like frame on her little desk, in which there is some sort of anti-gravity effect to stop things from falling, so that her marble of mud floats where she put it.

There are no sides to the box. She sticks a tiny but explosive bead into the mud marble and watches it make a bang. Her task is to measure the speed of and distance travelled by different fragments of mud and sand in the box in her bedroom. What she has created is our 'Big Bang' and the earth-like 'planet' in the galaxies in her bedroom is a speck a thousand times smaller than the point of a needle.

She has no idea that highly microscopic life, including Homo not so sapiens, has evolved on this planet. She is too busy wondering if she should measure the movements of such tiny fragments the size of Saturn. She is wondering too if she used too much 'explosive' and whether anything travelled out to the boundaries of the 'box' onto her desk or beyond.

She is the 'Creator', and when she's done her homework, she has to have dinner with her parents before they all go out to a movie with the neighbours.

Of course then I get to wondering how many people are on their planet, what their solar system and their galaxies are like and how they all came about! Even whether they are the creation of some other little girl doing her homework in her bedroom and so on.

And when I have too much a sense of my own importance, I think of myself as a single individual on a planet of six or seven thousand, million people, which is not even large enough for the Creator to see with her naked eye, as I hover somewhere over her little desk and I find my place in the universe."

"You are so funny sometimes." Lena laughed and Becky merely smiled knowingly.

"My methods help me survive both spiritually and intellectually. They might not impress anyone but I'm comfortable with them. We all need something to help us through this constant worrying about why we are here and are we doing any good or just cluttering up the place. We need stories we can relate to, and when you think of it, the Holy books are a collection of stories which help us find our way. The stories of the Bible vary a lot. Sometimes they teach forgiveness and passivity, other times they speak of vengeance and aggressive behaviour. We select what is important to us. Take the information we receive even today. We were talking of the general perception of abuse in the Church. The people who send us our information, mostly men, focus on the problems that they can relate to ... those that affect their own sex so that they inadvertently hide the bigger problems faced by women and girls ... or perhaps I should say, the problems faced by significantly more women and girls."

"You're right! If we hadn't done all this research, even with my own experience and my knowledge of what my co-orphans lived through, I would have thought that the problems of sodomy were greater than anything we experienced." Lena spoke thoughtfully. "I suppose it really does have to do with the level of publicity and attention being paid by the major organisations to these problems. The Church does seem to insist that gay paedophile priests amongst them are responsible for their problems, and the focus of reports and discussions support this. However, the numbers of gay paedophiles would have to be substantial or the offending priests would have no time to do anything else in their lives judging from the numbers of victims. Anyway, if the Church is correct in blaming the gay ones, why doesn't it simply come out, to use a cliched expression, say they have a problem and clean their house out." Lena's hands sketched gracefully in the air as she spoke.

"Think about it kiddo. Who is raping the women and girls? I looked up some statistics which said that homosexuality affected approximately one-fifth of the population. In other words, one in five men and one in five women will prefer to have relationships with members of their own sex. I couldn't find any percentages of what proportion of the population fixate on children, but we can assume that it is a minority and I have no reason to believe that it is different in homosexual populations. Let's assume then that this figure is also twenty percent for both groups and although I have not heard of such a thing, that it affects women equally. That means that one in every five heterosexual men and one in five homosexual men, with the same breakdown for women, would prefer sexual relationships with children.

Now all things being equal, the Church should have one in five clergy who are homosexual. However other factors come into play and it may be that more homosexuals are attracted to a life which gives them an excuse for avoiding heterosexual sex at least, though having taken vows of celibacy ... vows taken before a God they claim to love, mind you ... they shouldn't be having sex at all.

All of this suggests to me that if our statistics hold, one in five of all priests, homosexual or heterosexual have the potential to abuse children, and that eighty percent of this group will be heterosexual ... let's say however that the Church is thirty percent 'gay' and seventy percent 'straight', then it would be reasonable to expect, all things being equal regarding the proportion of abusers, that seventy per-cent of the paedophile clergy who offend, will abuse girls. The fact that women and girls make up the bulk of abuse cases suggest that there is a greater percentage of heterosexual priests in the Church, so it beggars belief that the Church speaks only of clearing out the group who are the minority."

"It's sick! Sick! The Church is going to find itself in terminal decline if it doesn't act fast. Why have they hidden all this away? They have done such a good job that even some of us who were abused believe that the Church is innocent. Still!" Lena then told Becky of the discus-sions and arguments she had with several people who didn't blame the Church, but rather the State for not protecting them.

"It seems to me that the biggest flaw in all this is *Crimen Sollicitationis*. Which clearly states that these heinous crimes must be kept secret to protect the reputation of the Church." Becky pulled out the copy of the translation of *Crimen* as she spoke and pointed at the appropriate section. She read aloud "'The oath of keeping the secret must be given in these cases also by the accusers or those denouncing (the priest) and the witnesses ... The accused however, should be most seriously warned that even he, with all (the others), especially when he observes the secret with his defender, is under the penalty of suspension a divinis in case of a transgression to be incurred ipso facto.' This binds everybody to secrecy ... everybody!

Here this section states '... a secret of the Holy Office in all matters and with all persons under the penalty of excommunication ...'. This is an excellent argument for keeping religion completely separate from the State. In a country where the Church and State are strongly intertwined, excommunication would be a disaster for any individual.

They would become outcast immediately from every activity controlled by the Church/State. There would be no place where they could be welcome except perhaps in the underworld, and even there it would be difficult as underworld members would likely be members of the faith too. This doesn't smell of Godliness at all. An open society is a healthy society, so why this incredibly evil secrecy?

I cannot believe this German Cardinal ... Ratzinger, our present Pope, who according to his own reported comments, in a small way stood up to fascism in his own land over half a century ago, could have policed this law which is clearly fascist. Last January, I listened to a speech made by his compatriot Angela Merkel as she took up the presidency of the European Union for Germany. She was speaking of European Unity when she said and I quote, 'Tolerance becomes a crime if it is geared towards the evil.' This tolerance of the Church for rapists is clearly criminal by all standards. It is a crime of civil law. It is a crime of God's law. It is a crime of morality and it's a crime of common sense! Of course Frau Merkel lived under vastly different circumstances to this Cardinal now Pope who lives the rich life of the exalted. The German chancellor was brought up in what used to be East Germany and must be as attuned to the realities of life as anyone who has had to live with oppression."

"To be fair, the Archbishop of Birmingham, in England, argued that the Panorama programme was 'an unwarranted attack on Pope

Benedict XVI.' He claimed that the Catholic Church dealt 'seriously, carefully and with transparency' the problems of child abuse."

"He must think opaque glass is transparent then. What was your own experience?" Becky asked.

"I wasn't actually abused by a priest, but I still find it in my heart to see how the Church protected my abuser. In a land where so many priests were themselves abusers and where all were bound under the secrecy of the confessional, I can see clearly how my abuser, a prominent church attender could confess his sins, be punished with a couple of Hail Marys and an *Our* Father, and be free to abuse again sure in the knowledge that the Church, via the priest would keep his secrets from the police."

"Forgive my interruption but I must apologise for not being to relocate that article I'd found on the internet about the 90 year old man who was being watched by the police as a known paedophile who preyed on young girls, but who wasn't being arrested because of his age. It wasn't until several weeks later when you told me of your abuse by this man and named him that I realised that he was your abuser.

I have searched and searched but couldn't find the report again. Occasionally when I open files downloaded from the Internet, I find them empty and I suspect that the original item I found was one of them."

"I have friends who still live in that area and who were abused by him. Crumbs who saw what he did also lives there. Why can't the police take this menace off the streets? If he is young enough to still be abusing small girls, he's young enough to be tossed into jail."

Becky shrugged. "Remember as a woman, I'm from Venus. I do not pretend to understand how Martian brain cells function."

She picked up her well worn Bible and thumbed through it. Lena picked through the reports.

"Ah!" Becky said. "Here it is. From the Christ himself ... a thought on secrecy. 'And he said to them: Doth a candle come in to *be put* under a *bushel*, or *under* a *bed*? and not to *be* set on a candlestick? For there is nothing hid, *which* shall not *be* made manifest: neither *was* it made secret, *but* that it may come abroad.' Mark 4:*21-23*

Lena was looking at another report. Picking it up she said, "Here it says that Pope John Paul II spoke in response to the child molestation scandals. Apparently he stated that 'a great work of art may be blemished but its beauty remains'. That really does it! He must have been in cloud cuckoo land! What happened to us was no blemish. The abuse I suffered is not like a pimple hidden away on my butt, or even one on my face for that matter. If we are works of art, then the vandals he called his priests and bishops took a dirty great big pot of black paint and poured it all over us. Or slashed our canvases through several times with a large knife! These are better analogies.

And if he had bloody wanted to see any of the beauty below the paint, he would have had to pay for enormously expensive restorative work. How dare he say that what happened to us was a simple 'blemish'. These old men get less wise to me every second. They are not of the real world, so who are they to be our moral guides?" She paused for a moment and Becky seeing that she was building up a head of steam let her continue without interruption.

"First we are no inanimate objects. Second we cannot be hidden away for restorative work, but must continue to interact with others regardless of whether that is damaging to us or not. If their 'works of art' had deep seated gashes across them as our souls have had, they would be considered to be completely destroyed and many of us were. Some us took their own lives in despair. Others languish in prisons, on the wrong side of civil law because we were broken on the Church's rack. They destroyed our innocence. They damaged our souls. They blamed us for the transgressions of others and twisted our psyches.

I've read of an American priest named Shankley who had venereal disease and taught his victims how to shoot up drugs. And he was protected by one Cardinal Law completely backed by a Canon Law, policed by a Cardinal Rat ... what's it? Oh yeah Ratzinger! In virtually every city we've looked at, there is at least one bishop or archbishop or cardinal who did nothing to protect their young charges.

And if some evil bastard had gone to the Vatican and so damaged one of the works of art there, what do you think those sanctimonious fools would have done? Would they have hidden those damaged works of art away? I don't think so. It would be straight down to the cop shop. Blemishes indeed!

They would most certainly not have turned to the vandal and said, we will protect you. The police will not be able to touch you. What's more, you could visit our other works of art whenever you wish and after you have done so much damage that we can no longer hide what you do, we'll send you to the art gallery down the road! Blemishes! What a load of bull!"

Becky began to laugh. "I love it! The picture you painted of the vandals being lovingly allowed to continue to destroy works of art is good. It does show the value that is placed on the most precious resource the world has ... our people, our children. And while you were speaking, I remembered somewhere in that pile is a report in which an American bishop is trying to get us to understand why paedophile priests behave as they do. He actually had the gall to assert that the priests were making a literal interpretation of our Lord saying 'Suffer little children to come unto me'. What do you think of that?"

"That's strange. Those words were written over one of the doors in the convent. I suppose they played on the word 'suffer' and they made us do just that." Lena responded carefully.

"Perhaps the nuns did, but the priests seem to have taken a different viewpoint and I remember my anger at the bishop using this quote to try to justify their actions. In all my years of dipping into my Bible, which I realise that I do quite often, I have never read anywhere that Jesus said, 'Suffer little children to come unto me so I could rape, bugger and generally cause mayhem amongst them, thus destroying the souls that my heavenly Father created for them'. It just shows the arrogance of the clergy.

Not only do they erroneously interpret the words of God's Son, but they presume to elevate themselves to his position, for if you remember, we are taught of God as being a trinity - the Father, Son and Holy Spirit. So Christ himself is God manifested on Earth at that time and place. In elevating themselves to Christ's place, they are saying that they themselves are God - Lord of us all. Let <u>every</u> soul be subject to higher powers: for there is no power but from God: and those that are, are ordained of God. Therefore he that resisteth the power, resisteth the ordinance of God. And they that resist, <u>purchase to themselves damnation</u>. Romans 13:1-3"

Lena stood and stretched herself saying, "Jesus was no child molester and for these clergymen (abusers and defenders) to suggest that there could be this interpretation of His words shows the total disrespect they have for God who they presumably worship. To try to taint Christ's words in this way, sounds to me like the work of Satan. Either that or the lunatics have truly taken over the asylum."

Lena had never before thought of the Church in this way. She simply believed it had become evil without trying to understand exactly why. She busied herself with a fresh pot of coffee and found some snacks for them to eat. She had planned to cook a meal but the discussion was too interesting for her to stay away from it for too long. Returning to the table, she apologised for not preparing a meal as yet, but Becky assured her that the small cakes and biscuits now sitting amongst the piles of paper were sufficient.

"I never really thought of the Church as an institution before you know. To me it was just the Church ... God's house ... and therefore it always had to be right. It wasn't until I realised the extent of the abuse throughout the world and the Church's role in all of it that I began to think about it. Even so, I had not really considered the individuals that make up the hierarchy, from bottom to top. I thought only of the Pope being in charge." Lena bit into an individual apple pie as Becky sipped her coffee appreciatively.

"The Pope has a tough job to be sure. That's why he needs to have an intuitive grasp about people, norms of behaviour, culture and so on. I don't know what training the religious orders get other than their theological training and that for specific professions such as teaching, nursing and so on. We've see from the Panorama programme that they train as lawyers and enforcers which suggests some kind of police training. They are also scientists, historians and artists but these are specialists doing specific jobs. However the bishops should get extra training if this is not present, in topics like sociology, anthropology and psychology and the closer they get to the Vatican, the more they should be exposed to the norms of human populations all over the world. I'm not suggesting that they live amongst the people, but that they get to know different populations as well as they could in the time they have with them.

It should only be the one who is most amenable to the people, who should then become Pope. This is probably a horrifying thought should the Church hear of it, but perhaps the peoples of the world should be the first tier of the voting process for a new Bishop/Cardinal or Pope via the Cardinals. That Pope would then have to be strong enough to push through those tenets of the Church that are moral and serve the people, allowing them to get closer to their God, and they should be all be flexible enough to accommodate those people."

"I don't think they would ever do that."

"They have certainly shown that they could be inflexible over the centuries, but in some cases they have had to admit that they were wrong as in the cases of scientists like Galileo for example, even though their apology to him came hundreds of years after he died confined as he was by them, to house arrest.

Remember too that the Gospels on which our beliefs are based were written many years after the events surrounding Christ's life had happened. How accurate do you think those memories would have been? You described your and your co-orphans own faulty memories of events that were so powerful to you all, that one could imagine every detail would remain exactly correct! Some bits of the Gospels were even written after the apostles involved were long dead so we're into the realms of hearsay. There were also hundreds if not thousands of Gospels written, but only four were chosen, when the Roman leader, Constantine tired of the warring between the new groups of Christians and others, decided to put an end to it all. He combined the population under the single banner of Christianity, when at the Council of Nicea, upwards of three hundred years after the crucifixion, he sat down with all the groups concerned. They thrashed out what would become the New Testament and the guidelines for the Church. Think of any warring factions today, sitting down together to formulate a plan of peace they could all live by. Would any concessions and compromises have to be made? You bet there would. It doesn't really matter at this stage what compromises were made at Nicea, the result was a book worth having, built as it was on the foundations of the 'Old Testament' which was written by Jews, and focussing particularly on the teachings we know as the 'New Testament', put together by the Nicean mish-mash of politicians and others.

And as you can imagine, all sides had to be satisfied. Elements of paganism were allowed into the Church that had nothing to do with Christ's teachings or indeed the wishes of a single Deity! Goodness knows what other elements were included. Yet today, millions of people accept every word of the Bible as coming directly from God himself, as though God wrote the Good Book, then sent it by thunderbolt direct to Rome.

When we think of the Gospels, what's the betting that the four chosen were those that the politicians of the day thought best suited the needs of all the warring sides. Gospels that might have more accurately reflected Christ's teachings might have been left out altogether as the politician that was king Constantine had to bend according to the pressures of the day. Flexibility was the major consideration to meet the needs of 4th century populations, yet today, in the twenty-first century we are expected to be rigidly force fed the tenets of the New Testament as though we are stuck in a time-warp.

In order to remain healthy and strong, the Church has to have some degree of flexibility too. I don't say that anything in the Bible should be subject to change. It would be like re- writing Shakespeare or Dickens and no re-writing is needed there. The commandments, for example, are timeless in their value to humanity. Rather, comparatively recent laws that were clearly devised by man in reaction to certain stimuli but which are now found to be harmful, should not be clung to as though they come from God. That is just plain stupid. The Church must know this too, but it is led by men who are unbending, even before God. That can be construed as one of the seven deadlies - the sin of Pride. And they commit more of the seven deadly sins from what we already know to be true."

"What do you mean?"

"Apart from the sin of lust, which is in every pore of your story, think of the physical aspects of your own life and that of your co-orphans. Think of the lives of the girls and young women who found themselves in the Magdalene laundries. Think of your own brother and the boys of the orphanage ... what was the dominant feature of your school years?"

"Missing school. We had too much work to do?"

"I asked you this question a long time ago and you responded with something like 'are you nuts?' if I remember rightly, ... but were you ever paid?"

Lena grinned. "Are you nuts? We were slave labour." "So who benefited? You didn't make any money but somebody did. Here, look at this article." Becky reached into the pile. "Read of their worth."

Lena took the paper. "This is about abuse by the Poor Sisters of Nazareth in Glasgow."

"Read out loud."

"Okay. It says, 'The Poor Sisters ... ran homes for disadvantaged children ... could face a bill running into millions of pounds amid allegations of abuse'. They're all the same!"

"Read of their worth."

Lena turned the page over. "Holy Shi ...! According to this, 'the Poor Sisters are worth £154 million in Britain alone'! That's poor? That's over 300 million U.S. dollars! Whatever happened to the vows of poverty their name suggests they took. Man wouldn't I like to be poor like that!" She read some more, "'The Roman Catholic Bishop of Aberdeen, Mario Conti, admitted ... that it was possible, that the nuns may have mistreated the children. We are human beings ...

flawed and fallible and members of religious orders are no different ... There are ... people before whom lawyers have been dangling a pot of gold ...' There he goes. Just concerned about the money!"

"But he does admit that the members of the Church are human and therefore fallible! Are they not all human members of the Church? So why are we told that one of them is infallible? Now do any possibilities come to mind about where they got their money from?"

"Slave labour! We knew that they were earning off our backs, but I never imagined that it could be much."

"Whatever it was, they earned it off your backs as you put it. They gave you nothing in recompense. You weren't paying your way by working, for the State paid them plus they no doubt got generous collections from their congregations. What they made on the farms, in the laundries and so on was very likely pure profit. That makes them guilty of the sin of greed! No servant can serve two masters: for either he will hate the one, and love the other; or he will hold to the one, and despise the other. You cannot serve God and mammon. Luke 16:13.

When you look at their girth, their love of fine food and wine we can think of gluttony. That's at least three of the seven deadlies. Certainly when I see the Pope in designer shoes and so on, I wonder about rich men and the eyes of needles. I don't expect for one moment that the leaders of the church should be in sackcloth and ashes, but living the superstar life albeit quietly, while so many starve is against the teachings of Christ, our Lord. When Christ had his couple of fishes and handful of loaves and he stared out at the hungry before him, did he sit down and enjoy his meal? No! He used what resources he had to feed all of the five thousand. I don't expect the Church to work miracles and in this they will agree that they are no 'gods', but they at least don't have to look so rich! Just that cross alone that Pope Benedict wears would feed a lot of people for a very long time.

The Church is so rich, that it is paying out hundreds of millions to contain the problems of sex and the priesthood, and I am beginning to believe that this is the only reason why the bishops are now finally beginning to take action against those priests that have been clearly exposed for the demons they are. It's beginning to hit the Church's pocket. Why couldn't they have had better quality control guidelines over who they took into their holy orders, and used some of that money to fend off the abject poverty we see in so many places. We are seeing how micro-loans can help to lift people out of the dirt. Wouldn't it be better to spend on something like this than to find themselves having to pay compensation for something it should have strangled a long time ago?

The Church has become worse than the marketplace temple that Christ went berserk in when he proclaimed that they had turned the house of prayer into a den of thieves (Mark 11:15-17). It now appears to also be a den of sexual perverts of all sexual persuasions ... and will probably remain so in the eyes of ordinary people like us if we do not see strong leadership that recognises the dangers in the Church. I could go on in this vein, but we are not here to explore whether the Church regularly commits all of the seven deadly sins."

"Surely it's not just bishops. What about archbishops and cardinals?"

"As I understand it, they are all bishops. I think the different titles just give an indication of how big their ... um, dioceses are and whether they have certain direct roles in the Vatican or not. If it's important to know exactly, it can be checked."

"Not important. What about this statement that is apparently accredited to the Vatican that the priests who commit these crimes are all in English speaking countries?"

Becky laughed. "I thought that was hilarious when I read it. I cannot believe that supposed intelligent, enlightened folk could come out with these statements. These abusers are not thinking linguistically. They think only with one thing and that doesn't speak at all. What about the abuse cases in the largest Catholic country in the world - Brazil? Last I heard, they spoke Portuguese. And in Spanish speaking Latin America from Argentina to Mexico? Most African countries are not native English speaking and the Cafod report and another investigative study by the Boston Globe, this latter also finding many problems worldwide, implicated the Catholic Church in Asia in countries such as the Philippines and China.

But suppose we take the stance and say that these are perhaps exotic countries which the Vatican might find difficult to understand from a cultural point of view, not that I believe that for one minute, European countries were also implicated by Cafod and the Boston Globe study. Our own searches found problems in French speaking

Normandy where Bishop Pican acted in an extraordinarily similar manner to all the other bishops in Ireland, the UK, the U.S. and Canada, Brazil, Columbia, South Africa and so on.

As a former biologist I would have to say that this similarity ... no exactness ... of behaviour could not have originated independently, but rather comes from the same source, Crimen. And what about the German speaking Cardinal Groer of Vienna who was himself an abuser and of abuse by the Polish Catholic Church - Poland of course being the late Pope's own birthplace. I think that just about covers all the major languages. I don't recall having found anything on Greece or Russia. Perhaps other Orthodoxies are more humane ..."

"It says here that the prosecutor in the Pican case said 'This is not a trial of the church, but of a man of the church who failed in his duty'."

"If you look further down you'll also see that his lawyers argued that although the good bishop learned of the priest's activities out-side of the church confessional, he appears to have been motivated by 'what amounts to professional secrets', bringing us right back to Crimen and the wide net it spreads. Perhaps the bishop had the role of psychologist or judge, or mentor or some such thing, and he too was silenced somehow."

"Well he got a conviction against him and a three month sus-pended sentence. Serves him right."

"Kiddo, he will accept this stain on his character in the manner of another priest who way back in 1888, kept secrets to the point where he allowed himself to be imprisoned for a murder that was commit-ted by a man whose confession he'd heard."

"You're kidding!"

"I'm not, you know. Here's his story." Becky pulled out another document which she passed to Lena. "His name was Abbe Doumoulin."

"He was a saint." Lena said after she'd read the article. The priest had only been freed when three years later, the guilt-ridden mur-derer confessed to his crime.

"Yes, and there are many more when we think of people like Mother Theresa of India. Unfortunately the Church is a large and cumbersome organisation which seems to have problems keeping out the criminals. Here is another story about millions that were embezzled from the Church in the U. S. Apparently the religious orders don't keep their books properly, and a couple of priests liked to gamble, so they helped themselves. The Church apparently doesn't help by refusing external annual audits. No other large institution within 'civilised society' is able to avoid this. There are many other stories to show the problems in the Church as an institution, never mind a religious one, but they aren't relevant here."

"The nuns never kept proper books either. They don't want the church goers to stop putting their money on the plates, which would surely happen if they knew that the poor sisters and brothers were not poor at all! But when I think of my own childhood, it's all beginning to come together ... everything. We were their slaves to work and abuse as they would and they were the little gods and goddesses who took, took, took, and fed us the scraps if they bothered to feed us at all."

"And as so much of this seems remarkably similar from religious order to religious order throughout the world, one has to wonder about the other canon laws. Yet when I think of my childhood, I cannot believe that all of these religious orders have to be what they appear to be today. My nuns were also Mercy nuns and amongst the most beautiful and kindly people you could expect to meet anywhere. The priests were Jesuits and they were lovely too. The younger ones ran the youth club and they were just wonderful big brothers to us. The older priests kept mostly to themselves and never bothered us. Whenever we did have contact with them it would be like meeting your granddad. I guess I was just plain lucky. I would certainly have died for any of them if I had to. And in defence of the Church, I would have to argue that my priests and nuns are the norm ... that the majority of religious are caring, nurturing people. However, the blight that is creeping all over the Church is tainting them just as surely as putting poison into the communion wafers taints the entire batch, and that distresses me.

Yet one cannot ignore the fact that too much evil is getting away with too much. I would have no hesitation in letting any young relative of mine associate with the nuns and priests I knew, but there is no way I would allow such associations with those you knew."

Lena sighed and once more found her hand reaching for an article on yet another pile.

"Here is something from the batch of material we collected on the Church. It's a priest on his views about the confessional. He says 'a penitent has the right to go to any parish or priest for the sacrament. Also ... to confess his sins anonymously (behind a screen). If (his) identity is made known for any reason, the confessor has the responsibility to keep secret anything which is confessed. In hearing the sins of parishioners or people I have known, I can honestly say it has not caused me to negatively judge someone. If anything, just the opposite, I have felt a closeness and regard for the penitent because of their courage'.

I cannot believe this. He feels admiration for their 'courage'. Where was that courage when the so-called penitent was brutalising someone weaker than himself? Just where do they get these people from? I cannot believe the numbers of criminals who must surely have gotten away with their crimes because they had the 'courage' to make themselves feel that God would take care of them. A man only has to empty his bile in the confessional. The knowledge that he would not be reported forthwith to the police must surely boost his 'courage' to attack the next person and the next!"

"He or she. We mustn't forget that nuns abused too ... it was not generally sexual abuse, but even that occurred. They were just as evil as the male abusers."

"I don't excuse them. I am simply using the male prerogative of applying the masculine word to all humans. Like he says 'man' when he means 'people'. Anyway, most of them are men."

"Ain't that the truth! Anyway, let's take a break here, maybe prepare a small meal and come back to our discussions refreshed and willing."

"Sounds good to me."

Becky pushed away her bowl that had contained a fish stew of bits of cod, plaice, tiger prawns, Nurnberger sausage and vegetables. She popped the last of her pita bread in her mouth, chewed and swallowed. Then she made a high- pitched sucking noise as she grimaced and hurried her tongue round her mouth looking for any stray bits. Satisfied she took a huge gulp of coffee and said.

"Now that hit the spot!" She declined the offer of afters and stretched her legs out under the table, waiting for Lena to polish off a piece of chocolate gateau. The meal eaten, the two women leisurely cleared away the dishes and as they washed and wiped them, discussed the merits of various ingredients and tastes from different countries.

As they returned to their work table in the lounge Lena said, "It's always women and children ... always."

"No so." Becky returned. "I have heard of men ganging up on others, usually lone men. But I do know what you mean. Abusers are basically cowards. They attack only those they feel sure they can overpower. Women and children are the most vulnerable as they are physically smaller. The men of the cloth who abuse are no less cowards than any other abusers.

There is also a basic disrespect for women and girls, which is why we make up the bulk of the victims. Did you see the reports on attitudes towards women the world over?" "Yes I did. It was weird to realise that there are still men out there who think their wives or even girl friends are their property! I thought that stopped years ago."

"The women's movements did a lot to enlighten some men, and others would always have been fair-minded because of the great respect they have for their mothers, wives and girlfriends, but by and large, yes we are still seen as an adjunct to the male. Just the business of getting married and we show we belong to men by taking their names. Those of us born into a family where there is a male head of household would invariably have his name if he is the father, even if he is not married to the mother." The women sat at the table and began to rifle through the various sheafs even as Becky continued.

"It has a lot to do with that perception of woman belonging to man. If you look at our language, there is a 'he' in every she or her, a 'man' or 'men' in every woman or women, a 'male' in every female, a 'lad' in every lady. Even pronouns for all of us like 'they' and 'them' have got a 'he' in the middle. It is only in a few words like 'girl' and 'feminine' that there is no male inside us. This I think tends to lend the notion, perhaps only on a subconscious level in many cases that 'females' are there simply for males to be in."

"*Did* you go on a course to study all this? Are you some kind of a feminist?" Lena laughed.

"Regarding my observation on language, I never thought deeply about it before I spent a few years in Germany. I was aware of it of course. However in Germany there is 'Mann', 'Frau', 'Junge' for boy and 'Madchen' for girl. However, they go mad when the 'Frau' becomes a worker of any sort, for all the words to describe the profession are male and to speak of a female worker you simply add 'in' to the end of the 'male' word. So a doctor 'Artz' becomes 'Artzin' if it's a woman, a Sekretar becomes a Sekretarin, a Student becomes Studentin and so on. What was astonishing for me too, was although a Junge (boy) got the male article 'der', a Madchen (girl) is used with 'das', the neuter which is generally used for inanimate objects, rather than 'die' which signifies female.

As for feminism, I and you ... we are no less feminist, than a man is masculinist. *Do* you ever hear a man so accused for being concerned about what is best for him. He is free to discuss, mould and alter his role in life and the way he is perceived, as he wishes. He can fight for what he sees as his rights. How often have you heard statements like 'An Englishman's home is his castle', 'it's a man's world', and so on. Is the male ever made to apologise for asserting himself? No! Is he accused of masculinism? No. But a masculinist he is. If he were not, he'd be shunned in every part of the globe. So why shouldn't we be feminist? Why shouldn't we speak of what is right for us? Why are we 'condemned' as being odd, mad feminists? This often comes from those I would describe as 'odd, mad masculinists'.

There are many men who are also feminist for they fight for our rights as much as for their own. Most women are predominantly masculinist, but they are also universally feminist. As long as they want a modicum of a decent life for themselves, they are feminist. People who can fight for the rights of all humans are, I suppose, humanist but right now there is an imbalance in favour of men. So for the sake of rightness, I would be failing my own sex if I were not feminist! When the scales have balanced a bit, I could revert to what would be my norm - that of humanist."

"You are right! It is this imbalance between the sexes that makes us the universal victims. Having said that, it was women who ran our industrial school. Why were they so heartless?"

"That is not easy to answer. There are all sorts of variables that could have caused that environment of abuse to occur. We've read enough to suggest that the nuns were under all sorts of pressure - lack of education, resources and so on. However, in this situation there was also the imbalance of power which is commonly seen between men and women, between the nuns and you children. We hear that women are the gentler sex, and certainly our upbringing seeks to make that so, but we are also human, have the full range of human emotions and behaviours. There is nothing to stop cruel, selfish women from behaving like cruel, selfish men."

"And they were under the control of the bishops ... of the Church." Lena said musingly and lapsed into silence.

Seconds passed and Becky seeming to realise that Lena would add no more to that particular strand in their discussion said, "Here is that article about the Japanese Health Minister I was telling you about. Earlier this year Hakuo Yanagisawa was speaking about the falling birth rate in Japan. He described women as 'birth giving machines' and if I can quote directly, his exact comments were 'because the number of birth giving machines and devices is fixed' ..."

"What?"

"Yes, you're right. I must apologise to the minister. He never mentioned women. But let me continue. '... because the number of birth giving machines and devices is fixed, all we can ask for, is for them to do their *best per* head.' At least the birth giving machines have heads, and can use them to wonder if he was suggesting that women be put back into the situation, where throughout their fertile years they produced baby after baby to the detriment of their own physical and psychological health, and indeed to that of their families as they struggle to feed, clothe and generally provide for so many children."

"And they always just want sons, don't they? Sons have more worth."

"Many of them do want sons and we saw the turmoil they were in when the Japanese Crown Prince and his wife failed to produce one. According to the newspapers, the princess, who previous to her marriage was an independent, well adjusted woman, was all but worn away from all the stress. Fortunately for all concerned, the wife of a younger prince produced the required male heir."

"How very stupid. We've had a queen here in Britain for longer than the law would allow and she's doing a damned good job."

"As did the one she was named for! Anyway, this desire for sons only, led to a massive upsurge in female infanticide in places like China and India. I read a report that stated that in India so many girls were aborted that in two decades the country lost ten million girls! Ten million! So now the government has asked that rather than abort the girls, they should be abandoned after birth. Some are taken to various orphanages, but these babies are being found dumped in toilets, open ground, dark corners. It's a nightmare. One can only hope that babies who are found alive will be well cared for, free from the kind of abuses we see in so many places, but when I read that in places like Calcutta, raped girls are being sold to brothels, I am sceptical of this.

And China as you know has a problem of too many men and not enough women. There are gangs who kidnap this precious resource for sale to whichever man can afford to pay for them. *Discarded* or 'unattractive' women are sold into prostitution. The Chinese government is apparently now trying to promote the value of girls in some places, but ... What's the matter?" This last was said as Becky noticed tears running down Lena's face. The younger woman gave her a piece of paper she had taken from a stack. It was a report on infanticide in China and a photograph showed the tiny corpse of a new-born girl lying in the gutter. A man rode his bicycle by her either not seeing or caring about that small scrap of humanity.

"Would you like us to stop?"

After a few moments, Lena, looking rather subdued insisted on the discussion being continued. "You have helped me so much to make some sense of all this and if we don't continue, I might as well accept failure and stop right here."

"As you wish, but we'll stop anytime it gets to be too much. Okay?" Becky accepted Lena's rueful nod and continued.

"A few months before the Japanese Minister's 'baby making devices' comment, there was a Muslim cleric in Australia who insisted that women who were <u>not</u> covered in a hijab were like 'uncovered meat' thrown outside, for any stray that came along to partake of. His comments were clearly a tacit approval for men who attacked any women who didn't walk around wearing what looks like a bed-sheet, most often black, and presumably three steps behind a man. Men of Islam are of course free to dress comfortably where ever they go.

What was so startling about this, is that this cleric left his own culture where women could dress as he wished, went to another where the norms were different and then tried to impose his views on the population. Can you imagine his reaction if it had happened the other way round? Probably the offending foreigner would in his *pro-scribed culture*, be beheaded for such an absurdity. I must make it clear that I believe that the majority of people who follow the Islamic teachings of their Holy Prophet Muhammad (peace and blessings on him) would not be so intolerant."

"Eh? Why do you say that? Peace and blessings what?" "It is simply a mark of respect that Muslims have for their prophets. I have searched the teachings of many religions to glean what is good and try to use these in my life. I read my Quran as often as I read my Bible. I also use the *Dharma* (or teachings of Buddha) and spend much of my time in contemplation, and I dip into Hinduism which I find similar to Buddhism. I started doing that as a salve for my own childhood abuse and it has been very helpful to me to use all ... rather than one."

"What about the Jewish Bible?"

"Christianity is the child of Judaism. What we call the Old Testament comes direct from the TeNaK, which contains the three main sections of the Jewish Scriptures. They reject our 'Old Testament', presumably because it suggests a 'New' Testament upon which Christianity is based. And of course, they are not Christians. I have Jewish friends who insist that Jesus never died. That he was a good Prophet and man ... not the Son of God. So their version of events about what happened two thousand years ago is also of interest and great worth to the history of the religions. Islamic history and religious beliefs also have the same sources as Judaism and the later Christian faiths."

"Never!"

"Straight up! Go get yourself some holy books. Learn to read!" Becky chuckled at the look on Lena's face. "You ever heard of an old geezer called Abraham?"

"From the Bible? Of course I have!"

"Well, he's the common ancestor. He had two sons of interest to the great religions. Guess which did what."

"Go on." Lena said.

"Isaac, beloved to the Jewish and Christian God, was the father of Judaism and granddad of Christianity. This very same God who we'll now call the Islamic God also looked at Isaac's brother with favour. He told the boy's mother Hagar (who was not Isaac's mother as you'll probably recall) that he would make her son 'into a great nation'. That lad's name was Ishmael, and he became the cornerstone of Islam."

"I thought that was Muhammad!"

"Muhammad was one of their great prophets and just as we revere Jesus, they revere Muhammad. But the sources of the religions are immensely important to both groups."

"You read so much religion ... and yet you say you are an evolutionist?"

"Just as I found that one cannot live by the Church alone and that one cannot live by religions (plural) alone, also in its turn, one cannot live by science alone. All of it adds to me, makes me more substantial in my insubstantiality. All of it makes me more than, less than a speck on a pimple on the bum of a mosquito from a greater galaxy."

Lena laughed.

"Where the church is concerned I like to follow a notion ascribed to the great scientist and one of the oppressed of the Church, Galileo Galilei. He said, 'I do not feel obliged to believe that the same God who has endowed us with sense, reason and intellect has intended for us to forego their use.' Unfortunately too many religious leaders of all stripes, expect us to forego the use of our intellects and depend entirely on theirs. And therein lies loss of independence, loss of adventure, loss of lust for life or just pure madness. We see this every time a religion throws up an extremist, whether that person or persons is Christian, Muslim, Hindu, whatever. Losing independent thought to a fanatical, extremist religious leader is the worse thing that could happen to any of us.

Now let's get back to the point we were making earlier, about our place in this 'man's world'. Every day we read or hear on the news about women and children being kidnapped, raped and murdered by men who clearly believe they are superior to women and that these kinds of behaviours are their unalienable rights. When beliefs of man's superiority are written, by men of course, in the holy texts of so many religions, when even our languages are riven with male in female sub-text, when baby boys are seen as more important than baby girls, it is no wonder we have this burden to carry."

"So until we can have equality on all grounds with men - equal rights in education, health, within the law, indeed equal rights to life, combined with the respect of men in general and in this case churchmen in particular, we, the other half of humanity will always be disadvantaged."

"I wish it were so easy. There are a host of other variables which need to be considered too, such as what makes a bully, what makes domination and power so attractive to some, what makes a sex criminal and so on, but getting the equalities in stature you mentioned would be a start ... You have a lot to think of and it's getting late. You know that there more avenues to explore in order to find and make yourself whole. It will be an uphill battle, but it's one all women must make on some level, and those of us (male and female) who have known abuse must battle more than most. We can get out of the abyss. One step at a time."

Lena saw her friend to the door. "Becky thanks for coming round. It's been great having this discussion with you. It's helped me in a number of areas, not least to do with the book. But how do I get all this down? What should I write?"

Becky laughed as she walked down the path. Her voice drifted back to Lena. "You'll think of something."

Fifteen

Facing the Future

Two days after Becky and I had our 'major' conversation, I finally sat down to put pen to paper, so to speak. It had been a difficult journey for me, running the horror movies of my childhood through again and again, and this time voluntarily and awake.

There were times when I remembered things differently from my dreams ... times when the dreams themselves triggered some memory. A memory might have been adjusted by corrections made by my co-orphans. Other times it might be triggered by a return to some physical place that had been long forgotten.

All of this served to remind me that perhaps not all of my memories as I have written them here are entirely accurate. Perhaps something that would in reality appear trivial is somehow remembered in a manner that should not have been so terrifying. Perhaps some things I gloss over as being of no great importance, because my mind has repressed the true horror so much, that to recall accurately would embrace madness.

Whatever now moulds my mind and my ability to comprehend and compensate for my experiences, I have written about me. This is how it all affected me. I was badly damaged. I know that. Although I try to be a rational, sane, normal human being, I know that the damage exposes itself in times of stress, when often these stresses are so small they can be shrugged off by adults who had healthy childhoods or who simply developed to be more tough than I am. To all my relatives, friends, loved ones past and present, I apologise for the times when I have been unforgivably unreasonable ... for the rages that consumed me - rages that erupted simply because some small or innocent thing you did, triggered the unstable volcano that I was and on occasion still could be. For those of you who stood by me, supported me and loved me despite everything, thank you.

This will be the last chapter in this book, and as you will see, even as I tried to understand everything, I still do not understand. I still ask why? Why did it all happen? Why is it all still happening? On an intellectual level, I can and do understand the underlying processes that permit abuse, slavery, domination in all its forms. However, from an emotional level, it is simply beyond me. Becky made the comment sometime ago about experience and understanding. She said that if you do not experience something in some way, either as a victim or a witness, ... in some way that affects your emotions, you will not understand. When I see the awful pictures of suffering in the media, I find that some involve me emotionally and some I'm hardened against. I understand and empathise with starving people, raped and beaten women and children, sex slaves and so on, and simply dismiss the stupidity, cruelty, and so on, and simply dismiss the stupidity, cruelty, whatever of men and their search for power through national and international wars and mayhem in general.

When I focus on the difficulties of the vulnerable adults who were damaged by the Church, whether in childhood or not, my blood curdles.

The Church argues for the rights of unborn babies, and sometimes in my more cynical moments I wonder whether if some of these children are abandoned and remain unadopted by caring families, are they supposed to provide more fodder for the paedophile devils that exist not just in the Church, but are also 'fine, upstanding' members of the community doing their jobs or volunteering for charitable works? I believe in the sanctity of life and would never terminate the life of any unborn child of mine, but that is probably because I am fulfilled by my pregnancies and the children that come. I therefore do not believe in abortion, but it seems hypocritical to preach against contraception, when they abuse defenceless children and deny them their basic rights to a life free from their filth. This is reprehensible!

The Church's servants almost destroyed my soul and that of countless others. They succeeded in destroying those of many more young people, and as for those who in their despair escaped the demon agents of Rome by killing themselves, well, we all know what the Church does about suicides, don't we? So we must be born and in our vulnerable states we must not complain when their religious orders make our lives hell, and above all we must not take our own lives when that hell becomes too much to bear! What a Church! What a laugh ... for those who control us!

They called the Industrial Schools *cum* orphanages, institutions of charity - is that what their agents showed us children? Charity? I'd give it a different name - a more fitting name, but one which will do the Church no favours.

They said later that the nuns were overworked, not well enough trained in child care and so forth, but had they not set themselves up as capable of caring for hundreds of children for whatever cash they could glean from the Government - all the while insisting how poor they were and how little they earned? They set themselves up as God's servants - the Sisters of Mercy or the 'Mercy Sisters' as they called themselves. We called the merciless Sisters for they seemed not to have one ounce of pity for those they abused.

The nuns themselves said that they should have had some more training, but were they not trained to do God's work? To be merciful? To care? To nurture God's creatures? What training do you need to know it is wrong to abuse anyone, and especially small, defenceless children? What training do you need to know that it is a sin to allow sexual abuse of anyone but especially someone in your care, to occur unabated and unpunished? What training do you need to know what is right and what's wrong? What training do you need to be a human being? And they were right! They needed some training for either they were great, conscienceless fools or they were no human beings.

They also said that they were not allowed to show affection for the children in their care. Fair enough, but did they have to go to the opposite extreme? Was that the order they received? I think not. And if they were not allowed to show affection, why did so many appear to have favourites?

This is supposed to be the Church - the House of God I was expected to believe in. Yet all I can see are the hooves and horns that reside throughout, from the Vatican to the parishes all over the world. After all the abuse and the horrors, do they really expect people to believe in what they preach? To allow them to be the protectors of their souls? And I don't just mean people like us - the abused. No parent worth his or her salt would willingly allow his/her children to be in the company of a possible paedophile, priest or not. I certainly wouldn't let my own little daughter near them. No parent would wish these men to have access to their children's souls, and if we cannot trust our priests, how can we trust our Church?

They speak out against 'fornication', and pontificate about having children out of wedlock, and guess who happily fornicate, producing children who would have to bear the stigma of illegiti-macy - none other than the priests and bishops. If as it seems they raise themselves to the level of 'gods' here on Earth, do they think that because it's a 'Holy William', the children are virgin births ... divine providence perhaps? If so, why do they not show them the utmost respect as worthy of a virgin birth? Why do they hide their children away if they can? Possibly not shame - more like arrogance, deceit and a belief that they can do whatever they like and they will go unpunished, protected by their leaders. How can they demand abortion for women they impregnate when they condemn contraception? And how many have presided over the funerals of victims whose deaths they caused either directly by their actions or indirectly by their inaction? How many more of the seven deadly sins have we covered so far?

They fuss and bother about gays and lesbians but at least they do not generally produce children and especially not children they will throw to the lions of a Church that rejects them. When I learned that we in Ireland were not alone, I searched far and wide for other information. I read about an American Bishop of the Church who said about adoptions by same-sex families, "*Our* teaching on marriage and family life precludes these kinds of adoptions. We need to find another way to help this vulnerable population. How, remains to be worked out." Well it's already been worked out, old son. Rather than place orphans in a same-sex family, the vast majority of whom would not abuse them, gift them to one of your priests for his pleasure and the children's pain and terror, as he is moved to parishes round the country. Then when he's done in one land and it looks like everyone will learn about what he is up to, ship him off to another country, and move him round that one, with or without the child given up for his pleasure.

Of course children must not knowingly be placed in families which will abuse them, but same-sex couples are greatly in the minority and the majority of them will not be paedophiles. All 'non-paedophile' homosexual families need is the kind of instruction that 'non-paedophile' heterosexual families get with the additional requirement that the child has reasonable exposure to a 'mother' or 'father' figure as needed for the child's completeness.

So why does the Church give protection to so many demons who run to their protective Father in Rome when civil law starts to hunt for them? The Church must get rid of ALL its known offenders not just 'a tiny minority' of them. They must inform the civil authorities so these monsters could be kept away from their target victims. They owe it to the women and children - boys and girls, whose souls they are supposed to be nurturing.

In 2006, Panorama, that well-respected BBC programme which has been uncovering truths for as long as I can remember, aired the disclosure of its investigation into the abuse of children by ordained Roman Catholic paedophiles, Sex Crimes and the Vatican at just the right time for me. The programme included testimonies given by upholders and interpreters of canon and civil law, victims and their families. The most remarkable testaments for me were given by two priests, one a canon lawyer and the other an ex-monk. They explained how according to canon law, Crimen Sollicitationis (1962) and its 2001 successor, the Church was able to act as judge, jury and controller of the fates of every-one concerned.

The 2001 amendment (or guidelines), which was made after the scandals and details of Crimen were made public, was meant to be applied until the Vatican itself investigated the crimes of the paedophiles, and as all parties were under the seal of confession, this meant that only they and the Vatican knew what was going on. Cardinal Joseph Ratzinger, as leader of the Congregation for the Doctrine of the Faith dealing with faith and morals, sent out a letter with the guidelines, the contents of which I acquired from the BBC's website. It stated:

> With this letter, we hope that not only will these serious crimes be avoided, but, above all, that the holiness of the clergy and the faithful be protected ...

Clergymen whose sexual abuse activities were brought to the bishop's attention would then go either before a local ecclesiastical court or the Vatican Congregation which would be the appeal court in either case. All hearings would be held in secret.

The words underlined above particularly told me that nothing would be done differently. The Church was still hiding the light of honesty under a bushel. I didn't underline the faithful above for were we the abused, also not the faithful? What protection did the Church offer us?

In any event, when the Panorama programme aired, there were still paedophile priests abusing women and children, being protected by the Church, being moved from one parish to the next, five years after the 2001 amendment. Presumably this time it was with the direct blessing of the Vatican and the Pope, who most certainly would have had the details of the offenders' activities.

The police were not allowed to be informed as that would break confessional seal, but even so, in strongly Catholic countries, if the police got wind of what was happening, presumably the seal of confession would be applied to them too and their hands would effectively be tied. Certainly in Ireland, the Garda seemed unwilling or unable to do anything with the reports they did get. It is only in comparatively recent years that they have pushed for the prosecution of the Sean Fortunes and Brendan Smiths in the Church. Fortune escaped his fate through suicide. Smith did not serve long in prison. He apparently had a heart attack!

The threat of ex-communication was a strong weapon used by the Church to coerce individuals into committing the civil crime of failing to report a crime, in order that its secrets be kept. So in a way, the Church was further guilty of forcing people to aid and abet it in criminal actions. In strong Catholic communities, ex-communication would in all likelihood mean loss of prestige, work, friends and even family, perhaps forcing individuals who speak out to seek homes in lands where State and Church were entirely separate and/or where Catholicism was not the dominant religion. Such a life would be unimaginable to some, and so the Church for decades at least, had total control over the lives of its adherents.

So who knew what and when? The priests and nuns who abused knew they were doing wrong as they were doing it or they would have been open about their activities, and not have had the ingenious explanations I've heard about why a child needs hospitalisation or even a grave.

The Bishops knew they were doing wrong when the abuse was happening as they moved priests around the land. Occasionally a Bishop was also guilty of abuse and one wonders how many more of those in the upper echelons are or were abusers (do they ever stop)?

The Church clearly knew it was doing wrong or we would have not had all this messing around with Crimen and it's successor. Church leaders insisted on the seal of the confessional being placed both on the one confessing (often the abuser) and their young, helpless victims, so their dirty secrets and their vast fortune would be kept safe. Didn't the Christ say it would be easier for a rich man to go through the eye of a needle than to enter the kingdom of Heaven? I wonder what He would think of a fabulously rich Church and those who directly enjoy its wealth.

This entire business of the seal of the confessional is dicey. Every Roman Catholic rapist, murderer or whatever is protected by the

Church, and every victim is abandoned or even punished if they seek redress. So whose Church is this, that protects the evil and sends the innocent to hell in a handbasket, or to some horrible place called Purgatory should they try to escape by taking the only option left to them - their own lives?

By protecting the devil, it becomes the devil's church, and they cannot claim that their canon laws do not protect and mollycoddle evil and deny the abused would-be righteous. There have been too many cases, too many confessions, too many pay-offs.

In terms of my religious background, I can no longer listen to those people of the cloth and Catholic society, who preach so much about their faith, righteousness and morality and try to hand it down to people like myself. One commandment for example, says "thou shall not lie" (in the vernacular). They lied. Why should I hear their words?

They preach that faith, love, hope are what we are to live by. How very hypocritical. They destroyed my faith, my hope and my ability to love for years. It was decades before I was able to recover but a part of that was taken from me. I'm glad God talks directly to my heart, otherwise these people would have wiped out my spirituality all together.

Those nuns and others I had the misfortune to have become involved with during my childhood, either directly or indirectly stole my innocence and debased my body (surely a precious, holy object to them if they believe their own teachings that 'God lives within us' and that we are made in the Creator's 'image and likeness'). They destroyed my self- esteem, my sense of purity and stole so much of my ability to function normally without a feeling of deep-seated guilt and angst, that it took many years to recover but a part of that. Christ was appalled by the way the temples were being used. I wonder what He would make of this lot who steal so much that is irreplaceable, no matter how well we seem to cope, and the leaders who protect them!

They say that they come to be our moral leaders ... to guide us to the miracles of God, but I don't see it. I've been dipping into a new Bible I bought after Becky left the other day, and this quote speaks to me when I think of our moral leaders. Beware of false prophets, who come to you in the clothing of sheep, *but* inwardly they are ravening wolves. By their fruits you shall know them. Do men gather grapes of thorns, or figs of thistles? Even so every good tree bringeth forth good fruit, and the evil tree bringeth forth evil fruit. A good tree cannot bring forth evil fruit, neither can an evil tree bring forth good fruit. Every tree that bringeth not forth good fruit, shall be cut down, and shall be cast into the fire. Wherefore by their fruits you shall know them. Matthew 7:15-20

The Panorama programme which so impressed me and all of my co-orphans (we all finally saw it) mentioned a Catholic American Governor who having sat on a committee to listen to cases of abuse by priests on American children, resigned in disgust. I was so intrigued that I looked him up on the Internet. Governor Frank Keating is described as a staunch Catholic. Presumably he hoped to find some way to clear the Church's name from the morass of filth it was wallowing in. What he learned disturbed him so much that he could no longer participate in the proceedings. He compared the Church with the Mafia saying, "To resist Grand Jury Subpoenas, to suppress the names of offending clerics ... that is the model of a criminal organisation, not my Church." If a powerful but honest, God-fearing person, who having heard the evidence could react this way, how can the Church continue to play ostrich, keeping its head firmly buried in the sand and its ass in the air. Of course if all of it's so called 'cured' and much protected paedophiles are homosexual, perhaps it likes this position. I know that I have said this before but I do not for one moment believe that homosexuals are the majority in the Church. Yet, even with my experiences and subsequent knowledge of the scale of the abuse and the sex of the abused, the Church's focus on this one small group makes it difficult to have any other mental image!

It appears that in accordance with the 2001 amendment to Crimen Sollicitationis, even the stewards of the Vatican are unable to co-operate with upholders of civil law, and documents sent to the Vatican regarding the case of a priest (one of several wanted for sex crimes in the U.S.), who had been given refuge in Vatican City, were returned unopened. As the Vatican is a sovereign state, this was an effective gambit.

According to a Vatican spokesman Father Federico Lombardi, the execution of Saddam Hussein on January 30th, 2006 was tragic news which risked fomenting a vendetta and sowing new violence in Iraq. He added that "one can only hope that all responsible parties truly make every effort so that glimmers of reconciliation and peace can be found in such a dramatic situation." An admirable sentiment but it cuts both ways. The Church's role in all the abuse and violence perpetrated on the Catholic children in its care is a far cry away from what it pontificates for the Islamic people of Iraq.

Does the Church really expect those of us who still live with the terror of what happened to reconcile with it even as it continues to absolve itself from any of its responsibilities? Can it really sound so impressive when advising other groups and so inept when dealing with its own dirt? Perhaps the Church needs a lesson about 'pissing in the wind'? It believes in its own righteousness but ignores biblical quotes like this one. Again the kingdom of heaven is like to a net cast into the sea, and gathering together of all kind of fishes. Which, when it was filled, they drew out, and sitting by the shore, they chose out the good into vessels, but the bad they cast forth. So shall it be at the end of the world. The angels shall go out, and shall separate the wicked from among the just. And shall cast them into the furnace of fire: there shall be weeping and gnashing of teeth. Matthew 13:47-50

Supporters of the Church defend it against the Panorama pro-gramme with the fervour of those who have not suffered what thousands of children all over the world have had to endure. Have they felt the fire of a child's body being invaded by objects designed for adult sexual intercourse? Have they been starved to the point where eating the dirt on the ground and drinking their own urine seemed like a feast? Have they been beaten sometimes till close to death, and we suspect that some did succumb but were quickly disposed of to avoid investigation? Have they been threatened with being cast out and likely down, if they spoke of the appalling injustices that were being perpetrated against them? The Church itself basks in their approval and does too little to remove the evil within.

Woe to you scribes and Pharisees, hypocrites; because you tithe mint, and anise, and cummin, and have left the weightier things of the law; judgment, and mercy, and faith. These things you ought to have done, and not to leave those undone. Blind guides, who strain out a gnat, and swallow a camel. Woe to you scribes and Pharisees, hypocrites; because you make clean the outside of the cup and of the dish, but within you are full of rapine and uncleanness. Thou blind Pharisee, first make clean the inside of the cup and of the dish, that the outside may become clean. Woe to you scribes and Pharisees, hypocrites; because you are like to whited sepulchres, which outwardly appear to men beautiful, but within are full of dead men's bones, and of all filthiness. So you also outwardly indeed appear to men just; but inwardly you are full of hypocrisy and iniquity. Matthew 23:23-28

Until all of them, those bishops and their supporters, have walked that 'mile in our shoes', what they say will cut no ice with us, for we know! And now that the cat is out of this bag, unless the Church does something Christ-like about it, it and all heinous acts in the future will stay out of the bag. Does the Church and its supporters really want to see the crisis they have caused and tried to cover up get even worse? And it will, unless they can learn the humility Christ sought to teach us, accept that there be demons amongst them, cast them all out to the fires where they belong, provide whatever help victims need to renew that which they can and set about trying to rebuild the faith in the would-be faithful. That is the only option the Son of God would offer them. It's the only option the victims of the Church can accept.

The Catechism of the Catholic Church advises us from childhood on what is sinful. The numbers in brackets following the description of sin refer to related paragraphs in the Catechism. I look at these and wonder about the Church's stance.

Sin is disobedience to God, an offense against him. It is also, as stated in the Catechism of the Catholic Church, "an offense against reason, truth, and right conscience; it is failure in genuine love for God and neighbour caused by a perverse attachment to certain goods." (1849-1850)

Here I would ask, <u>has the Church sinned</u>?

Responsibility for mortal sin can be lessened by "unintentional ignorance," passions, external pressures and pathologies. *Greater responsibility is imputed to anyone sinning through malice or hardness of heart, or to <u>one who pretends not to know the seriousness of the sin</u>.* (1859-1860)

The evidence shows that the Bishops and the Vatican who claimed they didn't know, in fact did know what was going on for many years! Years in which they sent priests for therapy before throwing the wolves back to the sheep. <u>Did the Church sin</u>?

By mortal sin a person turns away from God and so loses the gift of charity and sanctifying grace. Mortal sin takes away the merit of the person's previous good actions and deprives one of the right to eternal happiness in heaven. Sincere repentance can reverse these effects. (1861)

I, for one, don't think that God is stupid. He must be fed- up though, of those who sin their entire lives while purporting to be good, hoping that repentance in their feeble years or even a death-bed repentance will reverse the effects of their mortal sins. Yet, so many men and women of the cloth committed these sins, even to the point of killing themselves before they could be punished by civil laws, that the only message I can hear from all this is 'we'll do what we like even whilst holding all of you to ransom, because the fact is there really is no God, so we might as well have our fun before we die'. I don't want to hear this message, but by supporting these offenders the Church is also supporting their message. Now tell me, <u>does the Church sin</u>?

Sins of omission are the failure to do something one should have done.

Do I even need to get into this one? <u>The Church sinned!</u> And as it teaches that sins of omission can be mortal sins, I leave them to judge themselves.

Of the seven capital (or deadly) sins, listed under paragraph 1866 of the Catechism, the only one I am concerned with is that of the lust that we children were subjected to by persons (clerical and otherwise) protected by the Church under *Crimen* and the confessional seal. From the number of public apologies made by various orders, and the 'regret' shown by the Vatican, there is no doubt that the Church sinned grievously here. And before detractors start jumping up and down, we all know about the phenomena of being 'tarred with the same brush'. *Crimen* simply changed what was possibly a small paintbrush into an enormously gigantic one.

> The sins that cry to heaven are ... voluntary murder (and some of us did die at the hands of our abusers), ... sodomy ... taking advantage of the *poor* ... *oppression* of foreigners, *widows* and orphans ... injustice toward a *worker (1867)*.

My life and those of my co-orphans were filled with these sins that cry to heaven, all of which were perpetrated by the servants of the institution which tells us we reap our rewards in heaven. Why then did we have to spend our childhoods in hell? <u>Did the Church sin?</u>

And what do they tell us about the wages of sin?

> The sins against the *Holy* Spirit are <u>despair of one's salvation</u>, presumption of saving oneself without merit or repentance, *resisting the known truth*, envy of the graces received *by* others, *obstinacy in one's sins*, and final impenitence. *(1864)*

In this the Church was guilty twice for did they not create the despair that we orphans and no doubt all the other abused women and children all over the world felt? Are they not guilty of resisting the known truth? Of being obstinate in their own sinning, compounding one with another even worse? <u>Did the Church sin?</u> You tell me.

And here is a nice clincher.

> Although sin is a personal act, we share in the responsibility for another person's sin if we cooperate with them in any of the following ways: by directly and freely taking part in the sin; by our advice, encouragement or approval; by not reporting them or trying to stop them when we are obliged to; by protecting or hiding them. (1868)

The Church has no place to hide on this one. Their hands are upon what is evil, to do it diligently; the prince and the judge ask for a bribe, and the great man utters the evil desire of his soul; thus they weave it together (Micah 7:3).

And here is another. Even as the Church pontificates on world matters touching on this or that subject, its Industrial Schools in Ireland and other such institutions in other countries had and have a clear history of the sin described below.

> Social sin arises when people copy or cooperate with one another in allowing and promoting sin. This is often evident in what becomes socially acceptable or what is institutionalized in the social structure or laws.
>
> ... (examples) would be slavery, child labour, neglect of the poor or marginalised. (1869)

I ask you, <u>did the Church sin</u>?

From my understanding, it seems that the Church disapproves of what is described as 'the false theory' of situation ethics.

> Situation ethics teaches that there is no fixed moral code given to human beings by the Creator. It holds that individuals must make moral choices according to a particular situation-that is, what is right or best in this moment for me.

On this, The Church argues that these choices could be made on what suited the individual best, rather than on what it saw as right. Would situation ethics not have allowed moral Churchmen and women do the right thing by the victims, by reporting their abusing colleagues to the civil authorities, who in the case of civil crime must take precedence over canon law? By denying their servants this option, <u>did the Church sin</u>?

It seems to me too, that whilst the Church rejects the "fundamental option" theory, this is precisely what they practised.

> The "fundamental option" theory teaches that a good person can do something considered gravely sinful, and yet that particular action is not gravely sinful for him or her. This is because the person's basic choice, or fundamental option is for God and the good. The theory holds that one gravely sinful act (a mortal sin) is not enough to separate one from God; a series of gravely forbidden acts would be required to prove that one's option has changed. This teaching is false. It is not what the Church teaches regarding sin, free will and personal responsibility for each of one's actions.

So why it is that they sent abusers off for 'therapy', whilst denying the same to the victims? Why did they then return the presumably 'cleansed' perpetrator back into the community to carry out their 'series of gravely forbidden acts'? Would you say the Church sinned?

As I worried and gnawed at the sharp bone that was buried deep within my psyche, I tried to be as fair as I could to all concerned. I really did. I even re-visited the nuns, most now feeble old women, and deep in my heart I could not find myself to hate them. Pity? Yes, but then I am flawed. I would never have been perfect. Who is? But I am more flawed than I should have been.

I tried to be fair to the Church too, not just for myself, but for those of my co-orphans who needed to believe in the deep-rooted goodness and sanctity of the Church. My researches threw me headlong into all sorts of matters and injustices perpetrated by the Church over the ages. The most interesting of these was the role of the Church in Germany and France regarding the Holocaust. Recently, Pope Benedict XVI made overtures to the Jewish communities that many have welcomed and praised. However, the Church has yet to accept responsibility for its actions during this horrendous period in history, according to Jewish sources. Then, the Church blamed individual priests for turning their eyes away from the plight of the Jewish people. *Now*, it blames individual priests for the sexual abuse and bringing shame onto the Church.

Then, it claimed that it was not empowered to act to help the hapless victims. *Now*, it simply ignores us unless we have ferocious lawyers in our back pockets. What other empowerment does the Church need? Is God not all powerful? And had He not transferred his power to the Church of Rome? Is that not what we're taught? What more do they need? Certainly the Bishops of all stripes (ie. from the Pope across the various types of bishops) are acting as though they are not empowered to help us hapless victims. Whenever they have had to pay compensation or take some form of supporting action for victims, it's because they've been forced to, either by circumstance or by civil law. They are all powerful*!* Didn't the First Vatican Council declare in 1870, that the Church is free of error on matters of doctrine and morality? *Do* they then think that what they did to us was right? Are they so arrogant? Prideful? <u>Did the Church sin?</u> <u>Is it sinning still?</u>

In a turbulent 1930s and 1940s Europe, the Roman Catholic Church was the most important institution that had the moral stature and strength to denounce the Nazis and stop their crazy slaughter. *Did* it do so? It did not*!* What would Christ say? <u>Did the Church sin</u>?

In the fifty or so years we appear to have recognised the Church's role in abusing women and children (though only God knows how long this had been going on for), the Roman Catholic Church is the institution responsible and it has the moral stature and strength to stop their religious orders from behaving like common criminals. Has it done so? Other than failing to protect a handful of priests from civil court, and throwing out another handful, it has not*!* Not so far. It has not relinquished its dark secrets about these serious crimes. Will it ever? You tell me*!* <u>Has the Church sinned</u>?

As it did with the Holocaust, the Church does not acknowledge that it failed miserably. Instead, it hides behind a few disgraced churchmen showing the world its craven cowardice. I was heartened to see that German bishops in 1995 admitted that the church community was only concerned with saving itself, leaving the millions of

Jews to their fate. Two years later, French bishops acknowledged that by turning their faces away from the plight of these unfortunate people, a sin had been committed. Their spokesman said, 'We confess this sin. We beg God's pardon, and we call upon the Jewish people to hear our words of repentance.' The Church's response via Pope John Paul II and Cardinal Edward Cassidy, in charge of Jewish-Catholic relations, was to try to minimise the statements of the French and German bishops.

They appear to be showing the same contemptuous attitude to the abused among 'the Faithful', many of whom have lost their faith because of all the Church never did!

All my life I have had to struggle against what I still see as the demons of and in the Church, and the Irish State, acknowledging their own responsibility paid us compensation according to what we endured and how we coped. It was not the fairest of methods, as people who were devastated by a small amount of abuse received more that those who suffered rather more abuse but managed to make a bit of a life for themselves. I know now that if I had not struggled to educate myself and stay sane, I would have been more generously treated. I am not complaining mind, because I believe that the State had its collective hands tied by the threat of ex-communication. The State too was a victim of sorts, and I have deliberately kept away from an analysis of the State's role in all this, because considering their collaboration with the Church would require another book. For those of you who wish to read more on the State's role, I would recommend Rafferty and O'Sullivan's rather excellent book, Suffer the little children which covers some of these issues.

The laws surrounding child care in Ireland have now been amended, so hopefully the State will prove a more successful guardian for successive generations of 'at risk' children. I wish the powers that be every success, for I believe that the State is genuine in its attempt to redeem itself and protect those who will after all be the future of the country.

For us abused however and for me in particular ... well, we have crosses to bear. I find especially hard, the 'post traumatic stress' that lives with me and may stay with me forever. There are good days and bad days. Times when I just wish I could lift my self-esteem and stop being over impulsive or aggressive. It debilitates me even when I am reasonably happy because I just don't know when it's going to come out and hit me with the power of a runaway train and I'm aware of always having to keep myself on a tight rein. I sometimes think I will ever trust anyone ever, which is a sad thing to say, but I can't help it. Then *Scott*, my family and friends show me how much loved I am and I feel a heavy guilt for having ever doubted them. And so it goes on always hanging on the edge, one way or another. This is the life I've been condemned to by the *Servants of God* ... the employees of a Church that I struggle still to continue to accept as my Church, my Sanctuary.

Today *Scott* and I have a beautiful three-year-old. It seems that God wanted me to have a child after all. *Maisy* is my life and I must try to stay strong for her. *Scott* has a lot to deal with in terms of my past baggage but he has taught me how love should be. Even so, the old devil called '*Don't Trust*', my own personal '*delirium tremens*', remains with me. And all I can do, every time he's not with me, is try*!*

I remember the day, it seems so long ago but is in fact less than a year, when I looked at the face of my new found friend sitting across from me at my kitchen table and I said, "Becky, you have listened to all I've had to say and not once have you given me any advice. Is there anything you would say?"

"Have you thought of writing all this down? Not necessarily for publication, but for your daughter. One day she might need to understand all this."

"I have thought about it, but some of my friends from the Industrial *School* think I should let things lie."

"They must do what they need to do. You must do what you need to do."

Now so many months later and after much discussion with my co-orphans, my family and Becky, I have ... and I reserve my last words for the Church that I still, despite everything believe in, and its supporters.

As I struggled with my own feelings, listened to others who suffered dreadfully at the hands of your religious orders, observed the response from those who had the power to do something to save us from the hell we were in, I think of the Christ and the Church he wanted built in his name. His teachings were of love and light, of what is right, honest and just, not abuse, darkness, sin, secrecy and injustice. And yes he preached of forgiveness and turning the other cheek, and many of the abused would forgive the Church its lapses in its duty to protect them, and even turn the other cheek.

But realistically, if you continue to allow these monsters, these children of Satan to abuse the innocent and be protected by the Church, do you really believe that the people, the families affected would forgive you? That ordinary people, learning of what happened would truly ever trust the Church again? Do you think that God would forgive you? Or would He, like Jesus in the synagogue, tear everything down and start afresh. After all, what the Jewish- born Jesus of Nazareth did, was to start a new religion which St Peter and the other disciples are recorded as having promoted. So tell me Pope Benedict, you who amended canon law in such a way that it made it possible for these demons to move from parish to parish abusing, raping, sodomising and generally fornicating whilst evading prosecution by civil law, what would God do? Rain fire and brimstone on the Vatican as you looked at all those cases you ordered specifically to be sent there and did nothing constructive about them? Throw you off your papal throne? Or do you fear that if you look too deeply into the darkness that infests the Church, that you would be turned into a pillar of something unhealthy? I mean no disrespect, but I am one of the betrayed. I can't say 'was' because even now, I feel that betrayal very keenly.

All those young people who came from all over the world to salute you Pope Benedict, when you visited Cologne and Bonn in your homeland - would they have been so keen to greet you as their Pope if they'd had the bad luck to have to depend on the Church you helped lead as Cardinal Ratzinger, for all their needs? Or indeed if they had realised exactly how these abuses were able to be perpetrated for so long? Crimen came about in 1962, and as these things occur slowly, the Vatican must have been aware of the problems long before then to even think of such a law! So how long has this been going on?

I beg you, do something now before you become known as the man who caused the dissolution, figuratively speaking, of the rock upon which the Church was built and turned it into the sandy slope upon which so many children were allowed to slide into the abyss. Throw the demons out so they can be dealt with by civil law. Do your duty, whatever it takes, to wash the Church clean of the devils within it and of the stain of these suppurating sins. Be known as the Pope who followed the Christ and did what was needed so that the Church could live. That, Pope Benedict, would only be doing your job.

In your new year message for 2006/2007 you prayed for peace and justice in the world. We, the abused children of the Catholic Church applaud you even as we say that for us, there can be no peace without justice.

For those of you who would say that I am looking for some kind of witch hunt, I ask you to stop right there. First, I am not the Church which participated in the original witch hunts of the middle ages (see Malleus Maleficarum ie. the Witches' Hammer) destroying possibly millions of enlightened women and trapping all others under the heels of men. If anything, I am probably now to be considered a witch for speaking out in the way I have. Second, the very existence of Crimen tells us that priests were abusing women and children of either sex, long before the law on how to deal with them came into being. In any event, young priests abusing women and children during the sixties, would now be in their late sixties and older. They might well be amongst the ranks of the various types of bishop as we saw in the case of the Viennese Cardinal.

These people not only shape the ideas and moralistic behaviour of young priests and nuns, they also have a powerful control over the millions who adhere to the Catholic faith, prince and pauper, politician, doctor and artisan ... every profession you can think of. A slap on the hand for a serious crime, and a 'holiday' with a psychologist is no way for the Church to deal with its problems. The rot has to be cut out! ... the limb amputated if that is what it takes to save the life of the Church.

No-one is making unreasonable demands. A single priest truly sorry for his single transgression could be forgiven I suspect, as long as he is removed from whatever his temptation is. But here we are speaking of sustained, widespread criminal activity, spread over incredibly long periods of time and all with the knowledge of the Church.

Are the souls of so many worth so little, then? What we abused ask for is only just and right. For many of us, there can really be no forgiveness without justice. We need to have closure like any other people in any other seriously disturbing event. To deny this would be to side with evil and if the Church cannot see this, we cannot easily forgive it either.

And we want to! Many of us desperately want to! To all of you I beg ... fight! Make it safe for our children. Fight to get justice for us all ... to make us strong in faith again. Fight to cleanse the Church and make it strong in faith again. Remind it of its role as handed down by the teachings of the Holy Book that promotes strong moral fibre ... this Holy Book that was created through the consensus of both 'holy' and 'unholy' groups and with various concessions garnered or lost. But as Becky said, it's a book worth having. Now the Church too must look to itself if it wishes to remain as 'worth having'.

Often we ignore ancient rulings in the Holy Book because the ruling seems too extreme - like an eye for an eye. So why can't we remove more modern, stupid laws that are written by man (rather than 'sent' to one of the prophets of old) and that help to promote evil in our Church.

We need faith! We need to have faith in our Church, and the men who run it have to take lessons from the Christ's own demeanour. He acted with humility as he cared for his flock with wisdom and love.

Remember Christ was not simply concerned about his disciples but with the souls of all his flock. He was certainly not concerned about the Judas who betrayed him, even though for the betrayal to have happened, Judas must have been programmed to behave as he did and was therefore only doing God's will. For without his betrayal, there would be no crucifixion at that time and place, the implications of which could have been enormous. Someone had to betray Jesus! Yet Judas was allowed to collect his reward by descending to that very hot place we are told about. So why do the disciples today, the Bishops of the Catholic Church bend over backwards to protect those who are clearly acting against Gods laws, in other words not even as good as Judas was, in acting as God wanted him to?

Do not destroy our faith by protecting the children of Satan. People need faith, even many of those of a scientific bent have to have some kind of faith. Like Becky.

Pope Benedict! All we ask is that you get the wolves out of the flock. It is your duty as the Shepherd of Christ. You are here to nurture our faith. Don't forsake the children of the Church. I ask you from my heart!

(out of that hell ©)

CHORUS

You have to let it go   Then the final day had come
drive the pain from your heart
You have to let it go   stumble, bumble your way through
or it will tear you apart   a life that wasn't clean

                                   As you search through all
They took you in   the dark, the bitterness
with polished grins   and pain
promised you'd be fine   in all your nightmares
They took the money   was the dream
as they sat over glasses   you'd find yourself again
of wine
                                   Then came the day
And when the gov'ment   you found your heart
boys were gone   a faTmily again
they smashed you   all fought for through a
in the face   busy life full of
They said forget   endless pain ... in the main
your childish dreams   You have to let it go
for this is not the place
for such things   from your life
CHORUS
                                   You have to let it go
                                            don't let it
They took away your   tear you apart
innocence   You have to let it go
gave you only pain   drive the pain
They took away your   from your heart

joy in life
made you take the
blame
They deafened you with songs of praise
tossed you in the well from which you found
you couldn't climb out of that holy hell

And this is
Lena's song

Printed in Great Britain
by Amazon